Covenants Prophecies and Hymns of the Old Testament

Sidney B. Sperry

Other volumes in the Sperry Symposium Series
from Deseret Book Company

Out of Obscurity: The LDS Church in the Twentieth Century
The Book of Mormon: The Foundation of Our Faith
The Testimony of John the Beloved
Voices of Old Testament Prophets
The Doctrine and Covenants, a Book of Answers
Nurturing Faith through the Book of Mormon
The Apostle Paul: His Life and His Testimony
Thy People Shall Be My People
The Heavens Are Open
Doctrines of the Book of Mormon
The Lord of the Gospels
A Witness of Jesus Christ
Doctrines for Exaltation

Covenants, Prophecies, and Hymns of the Old Testament

The 30th Annual
Sidney B. Sperry Symposium

Deseret Book
Salt Lake City, Utah

Visit us at www.deseretbook.com

Library of Congress Cataloging-in-Publication Data

Covenants, prophecies, and hymns of the Old Testament.
p. cm.
Includes bibliographical references and index.
ISBN 1-57008-733-4 (hardcover : alk. paper)
1. Bible. O. T.—Criticism, interpretation, etc. 2. Church of Jesus Christ of Latter-day Saints—Doctrines. 3. Mormon Church—Doctrines. I. Deseret Book Company.

BS1171.2 .C68 2001
221.6'088'283—dc21

2001003979

Printed in the United States of America 72876-6864
Quebecor World Book Services, Fairfield, PA

10 9 8 7 6 5 4 3 2 1

Contents

Preface

The subject of the 2001 Sidney B. Sperry Symposium at Brigham Young University is the Old Testament. Because the Old Testament contains half the volume and half the number of chapters in the standard works of The Church of Jesus Christ of Latter-day Saints, the potential material available for this symposium seemed almost overwhelming. Yet the Old Testament is a tremendous resource that Church members may not fully appreciate or use. For example, surveys indicate that approximately three-quarters of the members of the First Presidency and the Quorum of the Twelve Apostles use passages or stories from the Old Testament in their general conference talks. In contrast, less than one-fifth of sacrament meeting speakers typically use the Old Testament. As the symposium committee, we decided to assist both students and teachers of the scriptures to gain key insights into this large work of scripture by concentrating on just three books: Deuteronomy, Isaiah, and Psalms.

Why these three Old Testament books? The qualities that make Deuteronomy, Isaiah, and Psalms unique and especially valuable have been demonstrated through the ages. We can recognize their significance in ancient, modern, and future contexts. In ancient times, these three books were quoted by Jesus, Paul, and others in the New Testament more often than the other thirty-six books of the Old Testament (Bible Dictionary, s.v. "Quotations," 756–59). These same three books were also of primary significance among the Essenes of the Jewish community, and more fragments of these books have been found among the Dead Sea Scrolls than the other Old Testament books.

Deuteronomy, Isaiah, and Psalms also have great contemporary value for modern readers because they provide important teachings, prophecies, and inspiration. Although together they constitute only 7.7 percent of the volume of the Old Testament, at least one of them is referenced in 77 percent of all the entries in the Topical Guide of the Latter-day Saint edition of the King James Version of the Bible in which there are at least six references from three or more Old Testament books. These three books are a major resource for many important doctrines and topics of the gospel.

And they will continue to have future value for members of the Church, not only providing key prophecies about events of the last days but also preparing Latter-day Saints for their own eternal destiny. In Deuteronomy we find gospel insights and temple covenants for all dispensations. In Isaiah we find prophecies and poetry of the Old Testament's most profound prophet. And in Psalms we find gems of wisdom and inspiration from an Old Testament book Jesus quoted from so often.

In attempting to understand the prophetic and poetic nature of the Old Testament writings, we find that Deuteronomy, Isaiah, and Psalms provide the scriptural foundation for the Old Testament, which in turn provides the historical and prophetic context for the rest of the standard works. It is interesting to note how Jesus used these three books in his teachings that are recorded in the New Testament. He used Deuteronomy to handle the hard questions and entrapment situations posed by the scribes and Pharisees. He used Isaiah to teach important gospel concepts to his apostles and disciples. And Psalms were frequently a resource as he taught the people in general.

Likewise, we who read and study and ponder the Old Testament today will find a rich resource and a wide variety of gospel insights in Deuteronomy, Isaiah, and Psalms to help us in the many contemporary challenges we face. The covenants, prophecies, and hymns of the Old Testament are a valuable inspiration for us all.

The 2001 Sydney B. Sperry Symposium Committee

Victor L. Ludlow, Chair
Dee Darling
Jerome M. Perkins
Patty A. Smith
Vern D. Sommerfeldt

1

A Precious and Powerful Witness of Jesus Christ

John M. Madsen

The Old Testament is a precious and powerful witness of Jesus Christ, even though the sacred name and title *Jesus Christ* is not to be found within its pages today. "Many plain and precious things" were indeed "taken away from the book" (1 Nephi 13:28), but the central and fundamental message of the Old Testament, and indeed of all scripture, is that salvation may be found only in and through his holy name.

All Scripture and All Prophets Testify of Christ

Jacob, the brother of Nephi and an Old Testament period prophet, testified: "We knew of Christ, and we had a hope of his glory many hundred years before his coming; and not only we ourselves had a hope of his glory, but also all the holy prophets which were before us. Behold, they believed in Christ and worshiped the

Elder John M. Madsen serves as a member of the Seventy of The Church of Jesus Christ of Latter-day Saints.

Father in his name, and also we worship the Father in his name" (Jacob 4:4–5; see also 2 Nephi 11:2–4).

President Joseph Fielding Smith taught that "all revelation since the fall has come through Jesus Christ, who is the Jehovah of the Old Testament. In all of the scriptures, where God is mentioned and where he has appeared, it was Jehovah who talked with Abraham, with Noah, Enoch, Moses and all the prophets. He is the God of Israel, the Holy One of Israel; the one who led that nation out of Egyptian bondage, and who gave and fulfilled the Law of Moses. The Father has never dealt with man directly and personally since the fall, and he has never appeared except to introduce and bear record of the Son."[1]

President Spencer W. Kimball declared that "the Old Testament prophets from Adam to Malachi are testifying of the divinity of the Lord Jesus Christ and our Heavenly Father. Jesus Christ was the God of the Old Testament, and it was He who conversed with Abraham and Moses. It was He who inspired Isaiah and Jeremiah; it was He who foretold through those chosen men the happenings of the future, even to the latest day and hour."[2]

I know of no more powerful and wonderful summary of the identity and role of the Lord Jesus Christ than the statement published to the world 1 January 2000 by the First Presidency and the Quorum of the Twelve Apostles entitled "The Living Christ," from which I quote some key phrases:

"[Jesus Christ] was the Great Jehovah of the Old Testament, the Messiah of the New. Under the direction of His Father, He was the creator of the earth. . . .

"He gave His life to atone for the sins of all mankind. . . .

"He was the Firstborn of the Father, the Only Begotten Son in the flesh, the Redeemer of the world.

"He rose from the grave to 'become the firstfruits of them that slept' (1 Corinthians 15:20). . . .

"He will someday return to earth. . . . He will rule as King of Kings and reign as Lord of Lords, and every knee shall bend and every tongue shall speak in worship before Him. Each of us will stand to be judged of Him. . . .

"His duly ordained Apostles [bear testimony] that Jesus is the Living Christ, the immortal Son of God. He is the great King Immanuel, who stands today on the right hand of His Father. He is the light, the life, and the hope of the world."[3]

Jehovah Was Jesus Christ

Jesus Christ was the Great Jehovah of the Old Testament. How can we show this truth from the scripture? We begin with Father Adam, who was commanded: "Wherefore teach it unto your children, that all men, everywhere, must repent, or they can in nowise inherit the kingdom of God, for no unclean thing can dwell there, or dwell in his presence; for, in the language of Adam, Man of Holiness is his name, and the name of his Only Begotten is the Son of Man, even Jesus Christ, a righteous Judge, who shall come in the meridian of time" (Moses 6:57).

Enoch was shown the crucifixion of the Lord Jesus Christ: "And the Lord said unto Enoch: Look, and he looked and beheld the Son of Man lifted up on the cross, after the manner of men; and he heard a loud voice; and the heavens were veiled; and all the creations of God mourned; and the earth groaned; and the rocks were rent; and the saints arose, and were crowned at the right hand of the Son of Man, with crowns of glory" (Moses 7:55–56).

When the priests of Elkanah were about to "offer up" Abraham as a "sacrifice" to their "dumb idols" (Abraham 1:8, 7; see also 1:9–15), he lifted up his voice to God. And to Abraham the Lord Jesus Christ declared: "Abraham, Abraham, behold, my name is Jehovah, and I have heard thee, and have come down to deliver thee" (Abraham 1:16; see also 2:7–8).

Abraham could forever afterward testify that his Savior and Redeemer and Deliverer was the Great Jehovah. Abraham understood that Jehovah would come to earth and minister among men as their Savior and Redeemer, as we learn from the following:

"And it came to pass, that Abram looked forth and saw the days of the Son of Man, and was glad, and his soul found rest, and he believed in the Lord; and the Lord counted it unto him for righteousness" (JST Genesis 15:12; see also Genesis 22:14; Helaman 8:13–23).

To Moses the Lord declared: "I am the God of thy father, the God of Abraham, the God of Isaac, and the God of Jacob. And Moses hid his face; for he was afraid to look upon God" (Exodus 3:6).

To Moses, the Lord also revealed: "I AM THAT I AM: and he said, Thus shalt thou say unto the children of Israel, I AM hath sent me unto you. . . . Thus shalt thou say unto the children of Israel, The Lord God of your fathers, the God of Abraham, the God of Isaac, and the God of Jacob, hath sent me unto you" (Exodus 3:14–15).

Then, according to the King James Version, the Lord declared to Moses: "I am the Lord: And I appeared unto Abraham, unto Isaac, and unto Jacob, by the name of God Almighty, but by my name JEHOVAH was I not known to them" (Exodus 6:2–3).

The Joseph Smith Translation of this same verse reads differently: "And I appeared unto Abraham, unto Isaac, and unto Jacob. I am the Lord God Almighty; the Lord JEHOVAH. And was not my name known unto them?" (JST Exodus 6:3).

Also in the Joseph Smith Translation, Exodus 34, we read: "For thou shalt worship no other god; for the Lord, whose name is Jehovah, is a jealous God" (JST Exodus 34:14).

And in Psalms we read: "Let them be confounded and troubled for ever; [speaking of the enemies of God] yea, let them be put to shame, and perish: That men may know that thou, whose name alone is JEHOVAH, art the most high over all the earth" (Psalm 83:17–18; see also 3 Nephi 11:14).

In the New Testament, John records the words of the Savior, which confirm his identity as the Great Jehovah, or I AM. His testimony so offended the Jews that they took up stones to kill him (John 8:59). Jesus said, "Your father Abraham rejoiced to see my day: and he saw it, and was glad. Then said the Jews unto him, Thou art not yet fifty years old, and hast thou seen Abraham? Jesus said unto them, Verily, verily, I say unto you, Before Abraham was, I am" (John 8:56–58).

In these latter days, the Lord Jesus Christ also has confirmed his identity as the Great Jehovah, or I AM, who spoke to Abraham and Moses (Exodus 3:6, 14–16). To the Prophet Joseph Smith in September 1830, the Lord declared: "Listen to the voice of Jesus Christ, your Redeemer, the Great I AM, whose arm of mercy hath atoned for your sins" (D&C 29:1).

And in a subsequent revelation through the Prophet Joseph, the Lord again declared: "Hearken and listen to the voice of him who is from all eternity to all eternity, the Great I AM, even Jesus Christ—The light and the life of the world; a light which shineth in darkness and the darkness comprehendeth it not; the same which came in the meridian of time unto mine own, and mine own received me not" (D&C 39:1–3; see also 38:1).

Then, when the Lord appeared in majesty and glory to the Prophet Joseph Smith and Oliver Cowdery in the Kirtland Temple, Joseph testified: "We saw the Lord standing upon the breastwork of the pulpit, before us; and under his feet was a paved work of pure gold, in color like amber. His eyes were as a flame of fire; the hair of his head was white like the pure snow; his countenance shone above the brightness of the sun; and his voice was as the sound of the rushing of great waters, even the voice of Jehovah, saying: I am the first and the last; I am he who liveth, I am he who was slain; I am your advocate with the Father" (D&C 110:2–4; see also Revelation 1:13–18).

The Lord Jesus Christ was indeed the Great Jehovah of the Old Testament and the Messiah of the New. He is the "Living Christ, the immortal Son" of the Living God, the Savior and Redeemer of the world.[4]

Salvation Comes Only through Jesus Christ

Let us consider how the scriptures show the central and fundamental message of the Old Testament is that salvation is obtained only in and through the name of Jesus Christ.

The book of Moses, which is Joseph Smith's translation of Genesis, reveals that all of the prophets from Adam to Noah understood the plan of salvation, or "the Gospel" (Moses 5:58–59). They understood that salvation is "only in and through the name of Christ" (Mosiah 3:17). For example, the Lord said to Adam:

"If thou wilt turn unto me, and hearken unto my voice, and believe, and repent of all thy transgressions, and be baptized, even in water, in the name of mine Only Begotten Son, who is full of grace and truth, which is Jesus Christ, the only name which shall be given under heaven, whereby salvation shall come unto the children of men, ye shall receive the gift of the Holy Ghost, asking all things in his name, and whatsoever ye shall ask, it shall be given you" (Moses 6:52; see also vv. 57–62; 7:45–47; 8:19–24).

It should be noted that in Moses 6:52, 54, 57, and 59 (as also in D&C 29:1, 41–46) the Lord Jesus Christ speaks as if he were God the Father. By the law of divine investiture, the Son represents the Father in all matters here upon the earth, so he may speak as if he were God the Father.[5]

The Book of Mormon, which is essentially an Old Testament record, confirms that prophets in Old Testament times knew the plan of redemption and knew that salvation is only in and through the name of Jesus Christ. Nephi, son of Lehi, said:

"According to the words of the prophets, the Messiah cometh in six hundred years from the time that my father left Jerusalem; and according to the words of the prophets, and also the word of the angel of God, his name shall be Jesus Christ, the Son of God.

"And now, my brethren, I have spoken plainly that ye cannot err. And as the Lord God liveth that brought Israel up out of the land of Egypt, . . . there is none other name given under heaven save it be this Jesus Christ, of which I have spoken, whereby man can be saved" (2 Nephi 25:19–20; see also 10:3; 31:2–21).

King Benjamin testified: "Salvation cometh to none such except it be through repentance and faith on the Lord Jesus Christ.

"And the Lord God hath sent his holy prophets among all the children of men, to declare these things to every kindred, nation, and tongue, that thereby whosoever should believe that Christ should come, the same might receive remission of their sins, and rejoice with exceedingly great joy, even as though he had already come among them. . . .

"And moreover, I say unto you, that there shall be no other name given nor any other way nor means whereby salvation can come unto the children of men, only in and through the name of Christ, the Lord Omnipotent" (Mosiah 3:12–13, 17; see also 5:7–8; 13:32–35; 1 Nephi 6:4; Alma 38:9; Helaman 5:9–11).

Before turning again to the Old Testament, we should note that ancient prophets referred to Jesus Christ by various names or titles, including God, Jehovah, Messiah, Savior, Redeemer, Deliverer, the God of Israel, the Holy One of Israel, and many others. We should also note that the Hebrew word for the name Jehovah was almost always translated in the King James Version of the Old Testament as "Lord," or "the Lord." It appears thousands of times in the Old Testament.[6]

A few representative passages from the Old Testament indicate that salvation is to be found only in and through the Lord Jesus Christ, whom we have shown to be the Great Jehovah. In most of the passages that follow, we may appropriately add the sacred name and title *Jesus Christ* after each use of the title *Lord* or *the Lord.*

From Psalms we read:

"The Lord [Jesus Christ] is my rock, and my fortress, and my deliverer; my God, my strength, in whom I will trust; my buckler, and the horn of my salvation, and my high tower" (Psalm 18:2; see also 27:1).

"O come, let us sing unto the Lord [Jesus Christ]: let us make a joyful noise to the rock of our salvation" (Psalm 95:1).

"I will take the cup of salvation, and call upon the name of the Lord [Jesus Christ]" (Psalm 116:13).

"I have longed for thy salvation, O Lord [Jesus Christ]; and thy law is my delight" (Psalm 119:174).

"For the Lord [Jesus Christ] taketh pleasure in his people: he will beautify the meek with salvation" (Psalm 149:4).

From the prophet Isaiah we read:

"Behold, God is my salvation; I will trust, and not be afraid: for the Lord JEHOVAH is my strength and my song; he also is become my salvation. Therefore with joy shall ye draw water out of the wells of salvation" (Isaiah 12:2–3).

"The Lord [Jesus Christ] is our judge, the Lord [Jesus Christ] is our lawgiver, the Lord [Jesus Christ] is our king; he will save us" (Isaiah 33:22).

"I, even I, am the Lord [Jesus Christ]; and beside me there is no saviour" (Isaiah 43:11; see also vv. 3, 15).

"For thy Maker is thine husband; the Lord of hosts is his name; and thy Redeemer the Holy One of Israel; the God of the whole earth shall he be called" (Isaiah 54:5; see also 41:14; 44:24; 48:17; 60:16; and compare 3 Nephi 11:14).

Other Old Testament prophets bore similar testimony (such as we find in Job 19:25; Jeremiah 50:34; Hosea 13:4; Jonah 2:9; Micah 7:7; Habakkuk 3:8; and Zechariah 9:9), for they knew, as did all the prophets from the beginning, to whom they should look for salvation.

In the New Testament, we read these powerful words of testimony spoken by the apostle Peter:

"Be it known unto you all, and to all the people of Israel, that by the name of Jesus Christ of Nazareth, whom ye crucified, whom God raised from the dead, even by him doth this man stand here before you whole.

"This is the stone which was set at nought of you builders, which is become the head of the corner.

"Neither is there salvation in any other: for there is none other name under heaven given among men, whereby we must be saved" (Acts 4:10–12; see also 10:43; Psalm 118:22; Matthew 16:13–16).

John the Beloved, our Savior's disciple, summarizes the purpose of his own writings and of all scripture when he testified: "But these are written, that ye might believe that Jesus is the Christ, the Son of God; and that believing ye might have life through his name" (John 20:31; see also 2 Nephi 11:2–4; Jacob 7:10–11; Alma 33:14; Moses 6:63).

In Doctrine and Covenants 18, the Lord declares: "Take upon you the name of Christ, and speak the truth in soberness. And as many as repent and are baptized in my name, which is Jesus Christ, and endure to the end, the same shall be saved. Behold, Jesus Christ is the name which is given of the Father, and there is none other name given whereby man can be saved" (D&C 18:21–23).

And from section 20 of the Doctrine and Covenants, we read: "As many as would believe and be baptized in his holy name, and endure in faith to the end, should be saved—

"Not only those who believed after he came in the meridian of time, in the flesh, but all those from the beginning, even as many as were before he came, who believed in the words of the holy prophets, who spake as they were inspired by the gift of the Holy Ghost, who truly testified of him in all things, should have eternal life,

"As well as those who should come after, who should believe in the gifts and callings of God by the Holy Ghost, which beareth record of the Father and of the Son; . . .

"And we know that all men must repent and believe on the name of Jesus Christ, and worship the Father in his name, and endure in faith on his name to the end, or they cannot be saved in the kingdom of God" (D&C 20:25–27, 29; see also 76:1; 109:4).

From the foregoing passages (as well as others that could be cited), we see that the central and fundamental message of the Old Testament, and indeed of all scriptures, is that salvation is only in and through the name of Jesus Christ.

The Old Testament Bears Witness of Jesus Christ

Let us consider how the Old Testament bears further witness of Jesus Christ. Perhaps the following account of the resurrected Lord in speaking with two of his disciples as they journeyed to Emmaus (Luke 24:13–27) will illustrate:

"Then [Jesus] said unto them, O fools, and slow of heart to believe all that the prophets have spoken: Ought not Christ to have suffered these things, and to enter into his glory? And beginning at Moses and all the prophets, he expounded unto them in all the scriptures the things concerning himself" (Luke 24:25–27).

That the Old Testament bears witness of the Lord Jesus Christ and his great mission of redemption is further illustrated in the account of what occurred when the risen Lord appeared to his disciples later that same evening. Luke records:

"And [Jesus] said unto them, These are the words which I spake unto you, while I was yet with you, that all things must be fulfilled, which were written in the law of Moses, and in the prophets, and in the psalms, concerning me.

"Then opened he their understanding, that they might understand the scriptures,

"And said unto them, Thus it is written, and thus it behoved Christ to suffer, and to rise from the dead the third day" (Luke 24:44–46; see also vv. 33–43).

These words spoken by Peter on the day of Pentecost indicate that he understood that the Old Testament bears clear and powerful witness of Jesus Christ: "But those things, which God before had shewed by the mouth of all his prophets, that Christ should suffer, he hath so fulfilled" (Acts 3:18).

The apostle Paul confirms that the Old Testament bears clear and certain witness of Jesus Christ. He wrote to the Corinthian Saints, saying, "For I delivered unto you first of all that which I also received, how that Christ died for our sins *according to the scriptures;* and that he was buried, and that he rose again the third day *according to the scriptures*" (1 Corinthians 15:3–4; italics added).

Paul further testified that "in the reading of the Old Testament," the "vail" that blinded the minds of ancient Israel, and "the same vail" that continued to blind the minds of the Jews even in his own day, "is done away in Christ" (2 Corinthians 3:13–14).

The Law of Moses, the Prophets, and the Psalms

We can only imagine what it would have been like to be among his disciples when the resurrected Lord appeared and "opened . . . their understanding that they might understand the scriptures" (Luke 24:45). The Lord reminded his disciples that all things had to be fulfilled that were written "in the law of Moses, and in the prophets, and in the psalms" (Luke 24:44). Let us briefly consider the law of Moses, the prophets, and the psalms.

What was the spirit and intent of the "law of Moses" (Luke 24:44), as recorded in the Old Testament? Nephi, son of Lehi explains:

"Notwithstanding we believe in Christ, we keep the law of Moses, and look forward with steadfastness unto Christ, until the law shall be fulfilled.

"For, for this end was the law given; wherefore the law hath become dead unto us, and we are made alive in Christ because of our faith; yet we keep the law because of the commandments.

"And we talk of Christ, we rejoice in Christ, we preach of Christ, we prophesy of Christ, and we write according to our prophecies, that our children may know to what source they may look for a remission of their sins.

"Wherefore, we speak concerning the law that our children may know the deadness of the law; and they, by knowing the deadness of the law, may look forward unto that life which is in Christ, and know for what end the law was given. And after the law is fulfilled in Christ, that they need not harden their hearts against him when the law ought to be done away" (2 Nephi 25:24–27).

King Benjamin testified: "The Lord God saw that his people were a stiffnecked people, and he appointed unto them a law, even the law of Moses.

"And many signs, and wonders, and types, and shadows showed he unto them, concerning his coming; and also holy prophets spake unto them concerning his coming; and yet they hardened their hearts, and understood not that the law of Moses availeth nothing except it were through the atonement of his blood" (Mosiah 3:14–15; see also 2 Nephi 11:4; Jacob 4:5).

Abinadi declared: "And now I say unto you that it was expedient that there should be a law given to the children of Israel, yea, even a very strict law; for they were a stiffnecked people, quick to do iniquity, and slow to remember the Lord their God;

"Therefore there was a law given them, yea, a law of performances and of ordinances, a law which they were to observe strictly from day to day, to keep them in remembrance of God and their duty towards him.

"But behold, I say unto you, that all these things were types of things to come.

"And now, did they understand the law? I say unto you, Nay, they did not all understand the law; and this because of the hardness of their hearts; for they understood not that there could not any man be saved except it were through the redemption of God" (Mosiah 13:29–32).

In Alma 25 we read: "Yea, and they did keep the law of Moses; for it was expedient that they should keep the law of Moses as yet, for it was not all fulfilled. But notwithstanding the law of Moses, they did look forward to the coming of Christ, considering that the law of Moses was a type of his coming, and believing that they must keep those outward performances until the time that he should be revealed unto them.

"Now they did not suppose that salvation came by the law of Moses; but the law of Moses did serve to strengthen their faith in Christ; and thus they did retain a hope through faith, unto eternal salvation, relying upon the spirit of prophecy, which spake of those things to come" (Alma 25:15–16; see also 34:10–14).

We learn more about the law of Moses from the risen Lord, who declared to the Nephites: "Behold, I say unto you that the law is fulfilled that was given unto Moses. Behold, I am he that gave the law, and I am he who covenanted with my people Israel; therefore, the law in me is fulfilled, for I have come to fulfil the law; therefore it hath an end" (3 Nephi 15:4–5).

The apostle Paul summarized the purpose of the law of Moses when he declared: "Wherefore the law [of Moses] was our schoolmaster to bring us unto Christ" (Galatians 3:24; see also JST Galatians 3:24; Hebrews 10:1–31).

Representative of all "the prophets" (Luke 24:44) are passages from Isaiah that testify of Jesus Christ. Let us consider a few of them. For example,

"Therefore the Lord himself shall give you a sign; Behold, a virgin shall conceive, and bear a son, and shall call his name Immanuel" (Isaiah 7:14). Matthew testifies that the birth of Jesus to the Virgin Mary is in fulfillment of Isaiah's prophecy regarding

Emmanuel: "And she shall bring forth a son, and thou shalt call his name JESUS: for he shall save his people from their sins. Now all this was done, that it might be fulfilled which was spoken of the Lord by the prophet, saying, Behold, a virgin shall be with child, and shall bring forth a son, and they shall call his name Emmanuel, which being interpreted is, God with us" (Matthew 1:21–23; see also D&C 128:22–24).

Now we turn to the immortal words of Isaiah that are familiar to unnumbered millions through the music of Handel's *Messiah:* "For unto us a child is born, unto us a son is given: and the government shall be upon his shoulder: and his name shall be called Wonderful, Counsellor, The mighty God, The everlasting Father, The Prince of Peace" (Isaiah 9:6).

Who is this "child"? "Whose son is he?" (Matthew 22:42). Who is this "mighty God, The everlasting Father, The Prince of Peace" spoken of by Isaiah? The scriptures reveal clearly who he is.

He is Jesus Christ, born into this world as the "Only Begotten Son" (Jacob 4:5, 11; see also 2 Nephi 25:12; D&C 49:5; 76:13; 93:11; Moses 5:57; John 1:14, 18) of God, "the Eternal Father," and of Mary, "after the manner of the flesh" (1 Nephi 11:21, 18; see also 2 Nephi 32:6; Mosiah 3:8; Galatians 4:4; 1 John 4:9).

He is Jesus Christ, the long-awaited "Messiah," the "Savior" and "Redeemer of the world" (1 Nephi 1:19; 10:4–5; see also 10:6–17; 2 Nephi 2:6–10; D&C 13; 18:47; 43:34; 93:7–9; John 1:41; 4:42; Revelation 5:9), of whom all "the prophets testified" (3 Nephi 11:10; see also Mosiah 3:13; Helaman 8:13–23).

He is Jesus Christ, the "Lamb of God," who was "judged of the world; . . . lifted up upon the cross" (1 Nephi 11:32–33; see also Moses 7:47; John 1:29) and "crucified" (1 Nephi 19:10; see also 19:9, 13–15; 2 Nephi 6:9; Mosiah 3:9; 15:7–9; D&C 20:23; 45:52; Matthew 28:5; Acts 2:36) to "atone for the sins of the world" (Alma 34:8; see also 22:14; 33:22–23; Mosiah 3:11–18; D&C 35:2; 46:13; 53:2; 1 Peter 3:18).

He is Jesus Christ, who, before condescending to "come down from heaven" to dwell "among the children of men" (Mosiah 3:5; see also 3:6–8; D&C 88:6; John 1:14; 6:38; Hebrews 2:9), was none other than the "Great Jehovah," who gave "the law" unto Moses on the mount (3 Nephi 15:5).

He is Jesus Christ, "the Father of heaven and earth, the Creator of all things from the beginning" (Mosiah 3:8; see also 2 Nephi 9:6; Alma 11:39; Helaman 14:12; 3 Nephi 9:15; D&C 38:1–3; 76:24; Moses 1:33; John 1:3; Hebrews 1:2), whose "infinite atonement" (2 Nephi 9:7; see also 2:6–10; Alma 34:8–16; 36:17–18; D&C 76:40–42, 69) brings "the resurrection of the dead" (Helaman 14:15; see also 14:16–19; 2 Nephi 9:9–13, 21–22; Jacob 4:11–12; Alma 11:42–45; 40:23; D&C 88:16–17; Philippians 3:21; 1 John 3:2).

He is Jesus Christ, "the Eternal Judge of both [the] quick and [the] dead" (Moroni 10:34; see also 2 Nephi 9:13–17, 41: Mosiah 3:10, 18; 3 Nephi 27:13–15; Mormon 3:20–22; Moses 6:57; John 5:22; Acts 10:34–42; Romans 2:16; 14:10).

He is Jesus Christ, "the Lord Omnipotent who reigneth, who was, and is from all eternity to all eternity" (Mosiah 3:5; see also 3:6–8, 18; 5:15; Matthew 28:18; Ephesians 1:22; Revelation 19:6).

Next we turn to Isaiah 53. This glorious prophecy fulfills the very purpose and spirit of prophecy as explained by the apostle Peter when he declared, "The testimony of Jesus is the spirit of prophecy" (Revelation 19:10). Isaiah eloquently describes and bears testimony of the life and mortal ministry and of the infinite atonement wrought by the Lord Jesus Christ. Latter-day prophets and New Testament writers alike testify that Isaiah's prophecy refers to the mission and death of Christ.[7]

Perhaps the most compelling evidence confirming that Isaiah 53 is a prophecy of the Lord Jesus Christ is the testimony of Abinadi, which, like the Book of Mormon itself, cries from the dust to all the world (2 Nephi 26:12–17; 33:4–13; Mormon 8:14–24; Moroni 10:27).

Abinadi, facing a martyr's death at the hands of King Noah and his priests, quoted the whole of Isaiah 53 (Mosiah 14) and explained its meaning (Mosiah 15), thus confirming his witness that the Messiah who would come and atone for the sins of mankind was the very same Lord of whom Isaiah bore such powerful and prophetic witness!

It is noteworthy that Abinadi, in the face of death, testified of Christ, who would come to break the bands of death, as if he had already come. Abinadi declared:

"And now if Christ had not come into the world, speaking of things to come as though they had already come, there could have been no redemption.

"And if Christ had not risen from the dead, or have broken the bands of death that the grave should have no victory, and that death should have no sting, there could have been no resurrection.

"But there is a resurrection, therefore the grave hath no victory, and the sting of death is swallowed up in Christ.

"He is the light and the life of the world; yea, a light that is endless, that can never be darkened; yea, and also a life which is endless, that there can be no more death" (Mosiah 16:6–9; see also vv. 10–15).

We would all do well to examine our own testimony of the Lord Jesus Christ in light of the testimony of Abinadi.

Finally, from Isaiah 61 we read: "The Spirit of the Lord God is upon me; because the Lord hath anointed me to preach good tidings unto the meek; he hath sent me to bind up the brokenhearted, to proclaim liberty to the captives, and the opening of the prison to them that are bound; to proclaim the acceptable year of the Lord, and the day of vengeance of our God; to comfort all that mourn" (Isaiah 61:1–2).

Jesus leaves absolutely no doubt about the meaning of these prophetic words. Having commenced his mortal ministry, he returned to Nazareth and "went into the synagogue on the Sabbath day, and stood up for to read" (Luke 4:16–17). He then read Isaiah 61:1 and 2. Then, having closed the book, he sat down and said, "This day is this scripture fulfilled in your ears" (Luke 4:18–21).

Now we shall consider a few selected passages from "the Psalms" (Luke 24:44). It is significant to note that the Savior and other New Testament writers quoted more frequently from the Psalms than from any other book in the Old Testament.

We begin with the psalm containing some of the very words spoken by the Savior from the cross, as he hung in unspeakable agony: "My God, my God, why hast thou forsaken me? why art thou so far from helping me, and from the words of my roaring?" (Psalm 22:1; see also Matthew 27:46).

Now consider these prophetic words which so graphically describe the feelings, the humiliation, the suffering, and the agony endured by the Savior during his crucifixion:

"All they that see me laugh me to scorn: they shoot out the lip, they shake the head, saying, He trusted on the Lord that he would deliver him: let him deliver him, seeing he delighted in him" (Psalm 22:7–8; see also Matthew 27:39–43).

"I am poured out like water, and all my bones are out of joint: my heart is like wax; it is melted in the midst of my bowels. My strength is dried up like a potsherd; and my tongue cleaveth to my jaws; and thou hast brought me into the dust of death. For dogs have compassed me: the assembly of the wicked have inclosed me: they pierced my hands and my feet. I may tell all my bones: they look and stare upon me. They part my garments among them, and cast lots upon my vesture" (Psalm 22:14–18; see also Zechariah 12:10; 13:6; Matthew 27:35; Mark 15:24–25; John 19:37).

"Reproach hath broken my heart; and I am full of heaviness: and I looked for some to take pity, but there was none; and for comforters, but I found none. They gave me also gall for my meat; and in my thirst they gave me vinegar to drink" (Psalm 69:20–21; see also John 19:28–30).

In the following psalm, we see clear reference to the betrayal of Jesus by Judas: "Yea, mine own familiar friend, in whom I trusted, which did eat of my bread, hath lifted up his heel against me" (Psalm 41:9; see also 55:12–13; Matthew 26:20–23; John 13:18–19).

Verses from the Psalms also give us references to scenes from the ministry and teachings and resurrection of Jesus Christ:

"For he shall give his angels charge over thee, to keep thee in all thy ways. They shall bear thee up in their hands, lest thou dash thy foot against a stone" (Psalm 91:11–12; see also Matthew 4:5–6; Luke 4:10–11).

"Then they cry unto the Lord in their trouble, and he bringeth them out of their distresses. He maketh the storm a calm, so that the waves thereof are still" (Psalm 107:28–29; see also 89:8–9; Matthew 8:24–27).

"The stone which the builders refused is become the head stone of the corner" (Psalm 118:22; see also Matthew 21:42; Acts 4:10–12).

"And had rained down manna upon them to eat, and had given them of the corn of heaven" (Psalm 78:24; see also 78:25–27; John 6:31–35).

"I have said, Ye are gods; and all of you are children of the most High" (Psalm 82:6; see also Matthew 5:48; John 10:34–36).

"Therefore my heart is glad, and my glory rejoiceth: my flesh also shall rest in hope. For thou wilt not leave my soul in hell; neither wilt thou suffer thine Holy One to see corruption" (Psalm 16:9–10; see also Acts 2:22–32).

"The Lord said unto my Lord, Sit thou at my right hand, until I make thine enemies thy footstool" (Psalm 110:1; see also Matthew 22:41–45).

Conclusion

From the passages cited, and a host of others that could be, we can see that the Old Testament is a precious and powerful witness of Jesus Christ. Prophets ancient and modern bear solemn witness that salvation is possible only in and through his holy name.

Notes

1. Joseph Fielding Smith, *Doctrines of Salvation,* comp. Bruce R. McConkie, 3 vols. (Salt Lake City: Bookcraft, 1954–56), 1:27.

2. Spencer W. Kimball, "Revelation: The Word of the Lord to His Prophets," *Ensign,* May 1977, 76.

3. "The Living Christ," *Ensign,* April 2000, 2–3.

4. Ibid., 3.

5. For a better understanding of this principle, see "The Father and the Son: A Doctrinal Exposition by the First Presidency and the Twelve," in James R. Clark, *Messages of the First Presidency of The Church of Jesus Christ of Latter-day Saints,* 6 vols. (Salt Lake City: Bookcraft, 1965–75),

5:26–34; James E. Talmage, *The Articles of Faith,* 12th ed. (Salt Lake City: The Church of Jesus Christ of Latter-day Saints, 1924), 465–73.

6. See Talmage, *Jesus the Christ,* 3d ed. (Salt Lake City: The Church of Jesus Christ of Latter-day Saints, 1916), 36–37.

7. Smith, *Doctrines of Salvation,* 1:23–25; Talmage, *Jesus the Christ,* 47, 612–14, 655; Matthew 8:17; John 12:38; Acts 8:27–35; 1 Peter 2:24–25.

2

Being a Covenant People

Amy Blake Hardison

As Latter-day Saints, we are a covenant people. Too often, however, we fail to grasp the profound implications of this sacred privilege and obligation. The books of Deuteronomy and Isaiah provide powerful insights into the nature and history of covenant making, the language of covenants, and the blessings and cursings that flow from keeping or breaking covenants. Perhaps most important, a study of the covenants in Deuteronomy and Isaiah enables us to grasp the unparalleled blessings available to us as a covenant people, inspires us to live up to our privileges and responsibilities, and deepens our love and gratitude to a God who has covenanted to strengthen us, uphold us, and redeem us.

Covenants and Suzerain-Vassal Treaties

In the ancient Near East, two groups of people did not coexist without defining their mutual rights. This could be done by war and subjugation or by a formal treaty. Occasionally these treaties were

Amy Blake Hardison teaches at the Tempe Arizona Institute of Religion.

made between equal nations, in which case both negotiated the terms. All extant treaties, however, were made between a major power (the suzerain) and a weaker, subordinate kingdom (the vassal). In such treaties, the suzerain set the terms and the vassal's only say was whether to accept or reject the treaty. These suzerain-vassal treaties are significant because they are patterns for God's covenants with his people. But why would spiritual covenants be patterned on earthly, temporal treaties?

One reason for the resemblance between covenants and treaties is that "when God speaks to the people, he does it in a manner to suit their circumstances and capacities."[1] Ancient Israel was familiar with suzerains and vassals and their treaties, just as we are familiar with our current political systems. In fact, the suzerain and his empire are the "ancient world's highest achievement in government."[2] Thus, suzerain-vassal treaties were a natural metaphor, a metaphor that suited the circumstances of the Israelites.

Another reason these treaties were an appropriate pattern for God's covenants with his people is that Israel was to be "a kingdom of priests, and an holy nation" (Exodus 19:6). *Priests* and *holy* are words that belong in a religious domain, but *kingdom* and *nation* are political words. Israel was to be not only God's Church but his kingdom. Jehovah is not only the great High Priest but the King of kings—the ultimate Suzerain. Israel is his vassal.

Ancient Near Eastern treaties and covenants typically included six elements: (1) a preamble, (2) a historical prologue, (3) the terms of the covenant, (4) the blessings and cursings for keeping or breaking the covenant, (5) a list of witnesses to the covenant, and (6) instructions on depositing the covenant in a safe place and reading it publicly at specified times.[3] Of course, not all of these elements existed in every treaty, and their order within the treaty could vary.

The preamble identified the parties making the covenant, placed the establishment of the covenant in a time and place, and contained a token of the superior authority of the suzerain.[4] In the Sinai covenant, the token of God's superior authority was his coming down in a cloud, a sign of divine glory, power, and authority. In the preamble in Deuteronomy, the token of God's superior authority was the defeat of the Amorite kings Og and Sihon (Deuteronomy 1:4).

Following the preamble was the historical prologue, a review of the relationship between the suzerain and vassal with special emphasis on the benevolent actions of the suzerain. Any rebellious actions on the part of the vassal would surely be noted. In Deuteronomy this historical review covers several chapters and includes a detailed account of the victory over Og and Sihon, references to Israel's miraculous deliverance from Egypt, and reminders of God's constant support throughout the wilderness experience.

The next section of the covenant, the defining of the terms, evolved out of the first two sections. Based on who the suzerain was and what he had done for the vassal in the past, the suzerain set the terms of the covenant.[5] The basic covenant stipulations for Israel were the Ten Commandments, but God also established a code of laws that governed the implementation of these commandments in daily life. This code constitutes the bulk of Deuteronomy and covers a variety of rules, from how to conduct religious rituals to how to treat one another.

The treatment of one's fellowman was regulated by covenant because traditionally kings were to administer justice and make sure the poor and weak of society were cared for and not oppressed. As Suzerain and King of Israel, God commanded his people to "open thine hand wide unto thy brother, to thy poor, and to thy needy, in thy land" (Deuteronomy 15:11) and to "not pervert the judgment of the stranger, nor of the fatherless; nor take a widow's raiment to pledge" (Deuteronomy 24:17). Perverting judgment referred to giving special treatment to the wealthy and influential in the courts of law and abusing the rights of the destitute and inconsequential because of their mean status. A widow's raiment was not to be taken "to pledge" (as a deposit or security for a debt) because neither her necessities nor her dignity were to be taken. The oppression of the poor and the weak often got Israel into trouble with God's justice during the time of Isaiah.

Other covenant stipulations required Israel to marry inside the covenant and to teach the children about their covenant relationship (Deuteronomy 7:3; 6:7).

As an incentive to keep the terms of the covenant/treaty, most treaties contained blessings and cursings. This aspect of ancient treaties should be quite familiar to Latter-day Saints. Temple covenants are accompanied by transcendent promises and blessings. In addition, both ancient and latter-day scriptures contain incredible covenant promises: to have a posterity as numerous as the stars in the heavens and the sand upon the seashore, to walk and not be weary, and to have the windows of heaven opened through which the Lord pours out blessings. Covenant curses are equally impressive but far more terrifying: pestilence, disease, being swept off the face of the land, and being cut off from the presence of the Lord. Deuteronomy 28 through 30 is the most extensive catalogue of curses and blessings contained in scripture.

The witnesses for ancient Near Eastern treaties included objects, men, and gods. Both Deuteronomy and Joshua speak of stones inscribed with covenant stipulations being set up as witnesses to Israel's covenant renewal (Deuteronomy 27:2–3; Joshua 24:27).[6] Later, the pillars of the temple became witnesses to covenant ceremonies.[7] A particularly interesting witness from the Latter-day Saint perspective is the heavens and the earth (Deuteronomy 4:26; 32:1; Isaiah 1:2; Alma 1:15). Many scholars recognize this unique pair of witnesses but aren't quite sure what "the biblical writers meant by it."[8] As Latter-day Saints we understand that the most sacred covenants we make are sworn before heavenly and earthly witnesses.

Mortal witnesses included the people making the covenant—as in Exodus 19:8 when "all the people answered together, and said, All that the Lord hath spoken we will do" (see also Mosiah 5:2)—and the prophets. Isaiah personally witnessed the Northern Kingdom being destroyed by the Assyrians. Jeremiah, Ether, and Moroni survived annihilating wars in order to add their witnesses that great destruction came upon the people because they had broken their covenants. As readers of these records, we too become witnesses.[9]

The divine witnesses included the gods of both suzerain and vassal nations. Thus, when Israel made a covenant with Assyria, Israel swore fidelity to the terms of the treaty before YHWH. When Israel violated that treaty, the Assyrian ruler, Sennacherib, sent his official, Rabshakeh, to Israel to call for the surrender of Jerusalem. Rabshakeh shouted so all could hear, "Am I now come up *without the Lord* against this land to destroy it? *the Lord said unto me,* Go up against this land, and destroy it" (Isaiah 36:10; italics added). Though the Assyrians did not worship YHWH, Israel did, and because YHWH was a witness to the now-broken treaty, the unbelieving Assyrians came against Israel in the name of Israel's God and with his sanction.

Finally, the last element of the covenant gave instructions that it was to be kept in a sacred place, usually the sanctuary of the vassal nation. This placement underscored the sacred nature of the covenant and reminded the people that the covenant was under the protection of Deity. In addition, the covenant was to be read to the people periodically. For Israel, this reading was to take place every seven years during the Feast of Tabernacles. This would revitalize the people's commitment and also teach the younger generations that they were a covenant people, bound to God by sacred promises and obligations.

This pattern of covenant making—with preamble, historical prologue, stipulations, cursings and blessings, witnesses, and deposit of the covenant—is found in several places in the scriptures, not only when God instituted a covenant but also at times of major transition or following periods of great wickedness.[10] Such was the case after the Israelites wandered for forty years in the wilderness.

Under Joshua's leadership a new generation of Israelites was prepared to enter the promised land. As they faced new leadership, a new home, and new tests of faith, it was imperative that the covenant burn brightly in their hearts and minds. Few would remember the magnificent theophany at Sinai; many had not been born. At this crucial juncture, Moses held a covenant-renewal ceremony to teach the Israelites that the Lord made this covenant not only "with our fathers, but with us, even us, who are all of us here alive" (Deuteronomy 5:3). This ceremony constitutes most of the book of Deuteronomy and follows the traditional pattern with a preamble (Deuteronomy 1:1–5; 4:44–49[11]), a historical review

(Deuteronomy 1:6–3:29; 8–10), covenant stipulations (Deuteronomy 4–7; 11–26), blessings and cursings (Deuteronomy 27–31), witnesses (Deuteronomy 30:19), and deposit and reading instructions (Deuteronomy 31).

Covenant Vocabulary

Covenants were written with a specific vocabulary. Inside the covenant/treaty context, certain words had official and legal meanings that sometimes differed from their normal, everyday use, especially as we have come to know them. For instance, both to *hate* and to *rebel* refer to breaking the terms of one's covenants. *Servant* and *son* are technical terms for a vassal. *Woe* is the pronouncement of a covenant curse, and to do *evil* is to break one's covenant (*evil* in covenant curses conveys disaster, calamity, and misfortune—not the moral opposite of righteousness). To do *good* is to keep one's covenants.[12] To *know* means to be loyal to, to recognize the legitimate suzerain, and to acknowledge the terms of a covenant or treaty as binding.[13]

Understanding the covenant meaning of these words increases our understanding of certain scriptures. For instance, in Isaiah 1:3 we read, "The ox knoweth his owner, and the ass his master's crib [manger]: but Israel doth not know [me], my people doth not consider." God's complaint about Israel's lack of knowledge refers not to her intelligence but to her loyalty. Also of interest is Isaiah 45:7, wherein God states, "I form the light, and create darkness: I make peace, and create evil." This verse does not mean that God is the author of evil. As Moroni explains, "All things which are good cometh of God; and that which is evil cometh of the devil" (Moroni 7:12). Rather, this verse explains that God will fulfill the terms of his covenant, granting covenant blessings (peace) or covenant curses (evil) as the people warrant them.[14]

Another word that has a specific covenant meaning is *love.* If a vassal abides by the terms of the covenant, he is said to love the suzerain; if he does not, he is said to rebel against him. In Deuteronomy 6:5 when man is commanded to "love the Lord thy God with all thine heart, and with all thy soul, and with all thy might," God is not requiring an emotion or a feeling of endearment. He is demanding obedience and loyalty, something a suzerain had every right to demand of his vassal and something a vassal owed to his lord. Moreover, in Hebrew thought, the heart (not the mind) was the source of thinking, willing, and deciding. Therefore, to love God with all one's heart was to make a deliberate commitment to steadfast loyalty and unwavering obedience. To love "with all thy soul" was the demand for the vassal to be prepared to die for the suzerain. It denoted full devotion. To love "with all thy might" meant that a vassal would come to the aid of the suzerain with all his force, with his army and chariots. In sum, Deuteronomy 6:5 requires a vassal to pledge complete loyalty and obedience to his suzerain and to be willing to give all that he is and all that he has as an expression of his loyalty.[15]

God's response to covenant love is *hesed.* Although it is often translated "mercy," "there is no English word that conveys the meaning of *hesed* accurately. It means loving-kindness or unfailing love. It is the kind of love that translates into action."[16] Delbert Hillers explained: "*Hesed* is the quality one wants in a partner to an alliance, hence it involves loyalty above all. But it is more than just abiding by the letter of what one is legally required to do. It is the quality shown when a man helps a partner who needs it, hence it connotes 'kindness, mercy, grace.'"[17] Such rescuing loving-kindness is the promise of Isaiah 41:10: "Fear thou not; for I am with thee: be not dismayed; for I am thy God: I will strengthen thee; yea, I will help thee; yea, I will uphold thee with the right hand of my righteousness." The right hand is the hand with which we make covenants. Thus, by covenant God has sworn that he will be there for us, that he will uphold us and strengthen us throughout this rigorous mortal experience.

President George Q. Cannon noted: "When we went forth into the waters of baptism and covenanted with our Father in heaven to serve Him and keep His commandments, He bound Himself also by covenant to us that He would never desert us, never leave us to ourselves, never forget us, that in the midst of trials and hardships, when everything was arrayed against us, He would be near unto us and would sustain us. That was His covenant."[18]

The Eternal Nature of Covenants

In most covenant treaties, the suzerain stated that the covenant was to remain effective forever. One historian studied seventy-five hundred "eternal" treaties that were signed between 1500 B.C. and 1850 A.D. and found that in reality the treaties lasted an average of only two years.[19] Like mortal suzerains, God intends his covenants to span generations and even eternities. Unlike temporal treaties, they do. In the book of Deuteronomy we learn that the children of Israel were redeemed from Egypt because of the covenants made with the fathers. Deuteronomy 4:37 states, "Because he loved *thy fathers,* therefore he chose their seed after them, and brought thee out in his sight with his mighty power out of Egypt" (italics added; see also Deuteronomy 7:8). From our latter-day perspective we see that the covenants God made with Abraham extended not only to the Exodus but even thousands of years beyond, to the current gathering of Israel.

The idea of God blessing a man's posterity because of the covenants God makes with that man also applies on a personal level. President George Q. Cannon wrote, "For be it known unto you that God makes covenants with men, and He blesses men, and He will bless their posterity. This ought to be an incentive to every man to live as he should do, not only for his own sake but for the sake of his posterity."[20] In Isaiah 41:8 God chooses and blesses Israel because she is "the seed of Abraham my friend."

Friendship is a binding of hearts and souls. We often describe this relationship with such phrases as "bosom buddies" or "soul mates." We attain a similar but far more sacred friendship with God by making covenants with him. Each covenant raises the level of our purity so we are more like him. Each covenant binds us to him in purpose and heart. This covenant unity, or sacred friendship, grants great blessings to us and our posterity. President George Q. Cannon stated:

"When my boys go out on a mission, I say to them, 'Boys, God is your father's friend; He has always been his friend; you can trust Him and can call upon Him with confidence; for I tell you that while I live and keep His commandments, God will watch over my children and will preserve and bless them.' And He has done it. So it will be with every faithful man and woman."[21]

Covenant Blessings

Ancient covenants spelled out the attending blessings and curses. Deuteronomy 28:1–14 lists seven different covenant blessings: fruitfulness (of man, flocks, and crops), rain, protection, abundance, a holy identity, land, and ascendancy over other nations. These blessings were present when the people were faithful. It is worth noting that these blessings are mostly temporal in nature. Ancient Israel was governed by the Aaronic Priesthood, which is primarily concerned with spiritual preparation and the administration of temporal affairs. Today Latter-day Saints live under the authority of the higher covenant and the higher priesthood. Not surprisingly, the blessings attending the covenants of the Melchizedek Priesthood are of a spiritual nature; still, they have a direct correlation to the blessings in Deuteronomy 28. For instance, the temporal promise of personal fruitfulness corresponds to the celestial promise of eternal increase. Ascendancy over nations is expressed in Melchizedek Priesthood blessings in terms of becoming kings and queens, priests and priestesses (D&C 76:56). The promise of land contained in the Mosaic covenant and the Nephite covenant (2 Nephi 1:5–12) is but a type and shadow of the ultimate promised land, the celestial kingdom. The promise of abundance that awaits us in the celestial kingdom is expressed well by the word *fulness*. Our celestial abundance will include a fulness of glory, light, joy, and power.

Although many of these blessings will reach their fruition in the next world, they still have a bearing on the here and now. This is particularly so with the promise of having a holy identity, which is both a blessing and an obligation. Elder Russell M. Nelson states: "For us to be identified by servants of the Lord as his peculiar people is a compliment of the highest order. When we know who we are and what God expects of us . . . we are spiritually protected."[22] This peculiarity, however, is maintained only as we keep ourselves apart from the ways of the world—in appearance, in morals, in values, in language, in behavior. We must always remember that "when individuals become like Gentiles, Israel's identity is endangered; indeed, it is lost."[23]

Covenant Cursings

Along with covenant blessings, ancient Near Eastern treaties and covenants contained covenant curses. Curses were basically a reversal of blessings, though the curses were typically far more detailed and extensive. For instance, in Deuteronomy 28, fourteen verses are dedicated to describing covenant blessings; the covenant curses go on for fifty-four verses. The curses are graphic and horrifying. They are filled with images of devouring beasts, cities that are conquered and deserted, the end of all joyous sounds, parents eating their children because of the privations of famine resulting from siege, men eating their own dung, wives being ravished, and warriors being turned into women and left unburied as food for carrion-eaters. This last was a most dreadful execration because the ancients believed that "the soul continued to feel what was done to the body."[24] "The curses aim at total destruction of the offender, all he is and all he has."[25] They were meant to strike horror and fear into the vassal, for, human nature being what it is, the loss of a blessing is not nearly as powerful a deterrent to rebellion as the fear of impending doom and the curse of the gods. Some may wonder at the appropriateness of such explicit and grisly curses in a religious record, but virtually all the curses in the scriptures represent common, ancient Near Eastern treaty/covenant curses.[26]

Understanding these curses allows us to understand the history of Israel. Covenant curses came as a consequence of Israel's apostasy, her rebellion and disloyalty toward her Suzerain and King. When Israel's apostasy was ripe, the curses were unleashed. Such was the case in 721 B.C. when Assyria destroyed the northern kingdom of Israel and carried away the ten tribes into captivity. The land was ravaged and the fruitfulness destroyed. Because Israel had so flagrantly and stubbornly violated her covenants, she lost her divine protection. She lost her ascendancy by becoming prisoner to another nation. She lost her land. And she lost her holy identity. So thorough was the loss of this identity that even today much of scattered Israel does not even know she is of Israel. These same curses happened again in 587 B.C., when the Babylonians came against Judah, and yet again in 70 A.D., except this time Israel retained her identity.

An understanding of the curses also grants us understanding of the words of the prophets. Whenever Israel was in spiritual danger (which was the precursor of temporal danger), a prophet was sent to raise a warning voice. These warnings often included a reminder of the covenant curses. As Hillers explains, "The prophets were often not arbitrary in choosing the lurid figures in which they depicted the wrath to come. They were not indulging a morbid imagination but were fundamentally like lawyers quoting the law: this is just what the covenant curses had said would happen."[27] Thus Isaiah's warnings echo the curses enumerated in Deuteronomy 28. He warns of captivity and desolation, of being "devoured with the sword" (Isaiah 1:20), and of the Israelites having "their carcases . . . torn in the midst of the streets" (Isaiah 5:25). We also read of curses being directed against Israel's enemies. In Isaiah 13:15–16 God declares, "Every one that is joined unto [Babylon] shall fall by the sword. Their children also shall be dashed to pieces before their eyes; their houses shall be spoiled, and their wives ravished." The destruction will be so complete that their cities shall be desolate and uninhabited and the wild desert animals will lodge there (Isaiah 13:20–22). In Isaiah 51:8 we read that in the last days "the moth shall eat [the wicked] up like a garment, and the worm shall eat them like wool." Moths and worms might not strike terror into our souls, but they are destructive in the functions here mentioned and thus found their way into treaty curses.

The prophets who cited covenant curses were not limited to the eastern hemisphere. Abinadi warned King Noah and his court that they "shall be brought into bondage, and shall be smitten on the cheek; yea, and shall be driven by men, and shall be slain; and the vultures of the air, and the dogs, yea, and the wild beasts, shall devour their flesh" (Mosiah 12:2). Insects shall devour their grain, and famine and hail shall smite their crops. All of these events are typical in Deuteronomic curses. Particularly interesting is the curse that "they shall also be smitten with the east wind" (Mosiah 12:6), for the east wind was the "sirocco," a scorching wind that blew in off the Arabian deserts, raising temperatures and sapping human energy. Such a wind is out of place in the lush rain forests of Central America, but Abinadi was citing covenant law, not announcing new judgments. We also read of similar curses from Nephi, son of Helaman, as he castigated the people from the tower (Helaman 7:19), from Samuel the Lamanite (Helaman 13:9), and from Alma to the inhabitants of Ammonihah (Alma 9:24). Alma's speech even includes the typical elements of a covenant speech: a historical prologue (Alma 9:9–11), the terms of the covenants (Alma 9:13–14) and the blessings and cursings (Alma 9:18–28).

Our prophets today also thunder warnings of impending destruction. President Gordon B. Hinckley boldly commands: "Avoid drugs. They will utterly destroy you. They will take from you control and discipline over your minds and bodies. They will enslave you and place a vicious and deadly grip upon you that will be almost impossible to break. Stay away from pornography. It too will destroy you. It will cloud your minds with evil and destroy your capacity to appreciate the good and the beautiful. Avoid alcohol as you would a loathsome disease. . . . Shun immorality. It will blight your life if you indulge in it. It will destroy your self-respect."[28]

The familiarity of these offenses in no way diminishes the destruction and devastation they will bring. Their consequences are every bit as fearsome and horrifying as the ancient curses.

One of the unique things about the book of Isaiah is that it includes the eventual reversal of covenant curses through divine intervention. The major covenant curse reversal is barrenness transformed into fruitfulness. When Israel broke her covenants, she was scattered. The imagery used in Isaiah to depict this scattering is a barren woman. When the gospel was not on the earth, for instance, Israel was like a barren woman with no covenant children. With the restoration of the gospel, Israel is again bearing covenant children, so many that her tent is rapidly being enlarged (Isaiah 54:2), and she rightly says in amazement, "Who hath begotten me these, seeing I have lost my children? . . . Behold, I was left alone; these, where had they been?" (Isaiah 49:21).

The Greatest Covenant Blessing

Perhaps the greatest of all covenant blessings is expressed in Isaiah 43:1 in the promise given to covenant Israel: "Thus saith the Lord that created thee, O Jacob, and he that formed thee, O Israel, Fear not: for I have redeemed thee, I have called thee by thy name; thou art mine." Jacob is one of the covenant fathers with whom God established, or reestablished, the Abrahamic covenant, and "Israel" is Jacob's covenant name. These names often signal a covenantal context.

God promises covenant Israel, "I have redeemed thee." "To the Israelites, a redeemer was a close family member responsible for helping other family members who had lost their property, liberty, or lives by buying them out of their bondage. . . . The family relationship was the reason the redeemer acted on behalf of his enslaved kinsmen."[29] It is evident that fallen man is in dire need of this redemption. Spiritual lives, liberty, and inheritances are at risk. Less evident is the implication that our Redeemer is a close family member. As our spirit brother, Jesus Christ redeemed all mankind from death, but redemption from sin requires an even closer relationship. This relationship is established by covenant when we enter the waters of baptism and thereby enter his church. We become the children of Christ, and he becomes our spiritual Father. This very special familial relationship makes us eligible for redemption from sin. In Isaiah 44:21–22 we read, "Remember these things, O Jacob, for you are my servant, O Israel. . . . I have swept away your offenses like a cloud, your sins like the morning mist. Return to me, for I have redeemed you."[30] This redemption is a supernal gift.

Anciently, when one made a covenant, one received a new name. In Isaiah 43:1 God states not only "I have redeemed thee" but also "I have called thee by thy name." This association between covenants and new names exists today, even in temporal matters. When a professional athlete signs a contract with a new team, he takes on the name of that team. When a person receives all the appropriate medical training, he takes the Hippocratic oath (a kind of covenant) and takes on the new name of a doctor. Most commonly, when a man and a woman marry, the bride traditionally takes on the name of her husband. When we enter into Christ's church by covenant, we receive the name of Christ. "In ancient times, a name was more than an identifying label. Your name was your essence, what you were all about, your identity rather than just your identification."[31] Thus, to take on Christ's name is both a privilege and an obligation. It requires us to also take on his identity, his way of being, and his mission of saving souls. The only way to accomplish this formidable task is through the covenant itself. With this covenant comes the gift of the Holy Ghost, which purifies our nature, reshapes our hearts, and fills us with the desire to live higher and holier lives. Gradually everyone that is called by his name is created, or re-created, for his glory (Isaiah 43:7). This is the whole essence of our covenants. They have been given by a loving God to strengthen our commitment and to keep us on track. They are to lift and bless, to ennoble and purify, and ultimately to help us become what he is and receive all that he has. Such is our privilege as a covenant people.

Notes

1. Brigham Young, *Journal of Discourses*, 26 vols. (London: Latter-day Saints' Book Depot, 1855–86), 9:311, as cited in Richard Neitzel Holzapfel, "Salvation Cannot Come without Revelation," *Doctrines for Exaltation* (Salt Lake City: Deseret Book, 1989), 92.

2. Robert G. Boling, *Joshua*, vol. 6 of the Anchor Bible series (New York: Doubleday, 1982), 36.

3. Delbert R. Hillers, *Covenant: The History of a Biblical Idea* (Baltimore: John Hopkins University Press, 1969), 29.

4. Lee L. Donaldson, "The Plates of Ether and the Covenant of the Book of Mormon," in *The Book of Mormon: Fourth Nephi through*

Moroni, from Zion to Destruction, ed. Monte S. Nyman and Charles D. Tate Jr. (Provo, Utah: Brigham Young University, Religious Studies Center, 1995), 70, 71.

5. Ronald Youngblood, *The Heart of the Old Testament* (Grand Rapids, Mich.: Baker Book House, 1971), 40–41.

6. Boling, *Joshua,* 540.

7. John M. Lundquist, "The Legitimizing Role of the Temple," in *Temples of the Ancient World,* ed. Donald W. Parry (Salt Lake City: Deseret Book, 1994), 220.

8. Hillers, *Covenant,* 129.

9. Donaldson, "Plates of Ether and the Covenant," 72.

10. See Exodus 19–24; Joshua 24; Mosiah 2–5; Mosiah 7; Ether 2:7–12; Moroni 4–5.

11. There are some duplications of these covenant elements. Notably, there are two preambles, two historical reviews, and two sets of covenant stipulations. Many scholars believe that the book of Deuteronomy originally began at Deuteronomy 4:44 and that the first four chapters were added later as a second introduction, accounting for the duplications. See Moshe Weinfeld, *Deuteronomy 1–11,* vol. 5 of the Anchor Bible series (New York: Doubleday, 1991), 9–10.

12. Avraham Gileadi, "Isaiah: Four Latter-day Keys to an Ancient Book," in *Isaiah and the Prophets,* ed. Monte Nyman (Provo, Utah: Brigham Young University, Religious Studies Center, 1984), 123–24.

13. Hillers, *Covenant,* 121.

14. For other examples of such words in covenant context, see Exodus 20:5.

15. Weinfeld, *Deuteronomy 1–11,* 351–52.

16. Kent P. Jackson, "The Marriage of Hosea and Jehovah's Covenant with Israel," in Nyman, *Isaiah and the Prophets,* 66.

17. Hillers, *Covenant,* 130.

18. George Q. Cannon, *Gospel Truth,* sel. Jerreld L. Newquest, 2 vols. (Utah: Zion's Book Store, 1957), 1:170.

19. Youngblood, *Heart of the Old Testament,* 42.

20. Cannon, *Gospel Truth,* 2:85.

21. Ibid., 2:88.

22. M. Russell Nelson, "Children of the Covenant," *Ensign,* May 1995, 34.

23. Ellen Juhl Christiansen, *The Covenant in Judaism and Paul: A Study of Ritual Boundaries as Identity Markers* (New York: Brill Academic Publishers, 1997), 103.

24. Roland De Vaux, *Ancient Israel, Its Life and Institutions* (Grand Rapids, Mich.: Eerdmans, 1961), 56.

25. Hillers, *Covenant,* 38.

26. Gileadi, "Isaiah," 123.

27. Hillers, *Covenant,* 134.

28. Gordon B. Hinckley, "Why We Do Some of the Things We Do," *Ensign,* November 1999, 54.

29. Jennifer Clark Lane, "The Lord Will Redeem His People: 'Adoptive' Covenant and Redemption in the Old Testament, in *Thy People Shall Be My People and Thy God My God* (Salt Lake City: Deseret Book, 1994), 49.

30. The Holy Bible, New International Version (Grand Rapids, Mich.: Zondervan, 1996), 616.

31. Harold S. Kushner, as cited in Dallin H. Oaks, *His Holy Name* (Salt Lake City: Bookcraft, 1998), 46.

3

Profiles of a Covenant People

Blair G. Van Dyke

ENTERING INTO AND KEEPING SACRED COVENANTS is vitally important to members of The Church of Jesus Christ of Latter-day Saints. They view covenants as the cohesive through which mankind may be bound to God. The roots of this view are recorded, in part, in the Old Testament books of Deuteronomy, Psalms, and Isaiah. These three books provide many insights into the significance of covenants and the distinctiveness of those who keep them.

The word *covenant* in the books of Deuteronomy, Psalms, and Isaiah is a translation from the Hebrew word *berith.*[1] The etymology of *berith* is not completely clear; however, it has been suggested that *berith* is related to two Akkadian terms: *baru,* which means "to look for and to make a fixed choice" and *biritu,* which means "to clasp, fetter, bond, or fasten."[2] In ancient times both words were used to describe terms of contractual agreements. In short, *berith* is associated with rendering clear favor toward or choosing one from

Blair G. Van Dyke teaches at the Orem Utah Institute of Religion.

many to take for your own by having it bound to you. The result of this binding selection is the creation of something more beautiful and desirable than was had in an earlier form.[3]

A contemporary illustration of this meaning of *berith* may be found in the black walnut tree President Gordon B. Hinckley planted near his home in the mid 1960s. After nearly four decades of being nurtured and cared for, the tree died. To make use of the valuable wood, President Hinckley had the tree cut down. The wood was then dried, cut into boards, and used to build the strikingly beautiful pulpit in the Conference Center of The Church of Jesus Christ of Latter-day Saints in Salt Lake City. In a word, something valuable was identified, selected, cared for, and then transformed in such a way as to enhance and embolden its already singular and precious nature.[4] This typifies an important connotation of the word *berith.*

President Hinckley's gentle and long-term labors with the black walnut tree serve as a type or shadow of what God does with his covenant children. In the Old Testament, the word *berith* suggests that God calls men and women and gives them opportunities to enter into long-term, sacred relationships with him. When the mutual agreement is entered into, the covenant individual is figuratively bound to God and cut away from worldly surroundings. Cured, honed, shaped, and refined over time, he or she becomes fit for something far more glorious than the person would have been prior to entering into a covenant with God.[5]

The faithful who desire to enter into binding agreements with their Maker have always looked to the holy prophets as the couriers of God's covenant terms. Prophetic teachings are replete with the essential elements of *berith.* One example of this covenant concept expressed in modern vernacular is provided by Brigham Young who explained that "all Latter-day Saints enter the new and everlasting covenant when they enter this Church. They covenant to cease sustaining, upholding and cherishing the kingdom of the Devil and the kingdoms of this world. They enter the new and everlasting covenant to sustain the Kingdom of God and no other kingdom. They take a vow of the most solemn kind, before the heavens and earth, and that, too, upon the validity of their own salvation, that they will sustain truth and righteousness instead of wickedness and falsehood, and build up the Kingdom of God, instead of the kingdoms of this world."[6]

Throughout the Old Testament books of Deuteronomy, Psalms, and Isaiah, covenant keeping is a salient theme. An analysis of these books shows four attributes that a covenant people have in common: 1) they love God with all their heart; 2) they are a peculiar and holy people; 3) they acknowledge the temple ordinances as essential to salvation; and 4) they make the Atonement the focal point of their worship of God. Exploring these four attributes in Deuteronomy, Psalms, and Isaiah renders a fundamental profile of a covenant member of the house of Israel, both in ancient times and today.

A Covenant People Love God with All Their Heart

Traditionally, the first words uttered by a practicing Jew in the morning and the last words uttered before sleep at night come from Deuteronomy 6: "Hear, O Israel: The Lord our God is one Lord: and thou shalt love the Lord thy God with all thine heart, and with all thy soul, and with all thy might" (Deuteronomy 6:4–5).[7] These verses are known as the *Shema'* because the first word, *hear,* is the Hebrew word *shema'*.[8] The *Shema'* clearly indicates that God requires the hearts of those blessed to have entered into covenants with him. The people of ancient Israel were commanded to keep these words in their hearts. Figuratively speaking, the heart is the seat of wisdom, intellect, feelings, emotions, and intentions.[9]

Furthermore, covenant Israelites were commanded to talk of the *Shema'* "when thou sittest in thine house, and when thou walkest by the way, and when thou liest down, and when thou risest up" (Deuteronomy 6:7). They were also commanded to figuratively bind the *Shema'* and other specified passages in the Old Testament between their eyes, suggesting that every thought and visual experience should be governed by God. They were also commanded to figuratively bind these words to their hand, suggesting that all their actions were to be in subjection to the will of God. Finally, faithful

Israelites were to figuratively bind these words to the post or door frame. This image suggests that the home is a refuge wherein no influence contrary to God's covenants and commandments should be permitted to enter (Deuteronomy 6:7–9).[10]

A covenant-keeping Israelite in the book of Deuteronomy is one whose heart is bound to God through language, sight, thought, action, and all activity conducted within and without the home. The covenant encompasses all aspects of life.

Adherence to the *Shema'* anciently and today serves as a sign from man to God that no interest, activity, passion, or pursuit will replace God in the heart of man.[11]

As in Deuteronomy, a prevalent theme in the book of Psalms is the complete submission of the heart and soul to God. For example, "Stand in awe, and sin not: commune with your own heart upon your bed, and be still. . . . Offer the sacrifices of righteousness, and put your trust in the Lord" (Psalm 4:4–5). The charge to "sin not" is reminiscent of the intent of *berith.* Therefore, consciously avoiding sin is a covenant Israelite's way of cutting himself out of and away from worldliness. Such wholehearted devotion and loyalty to God results in a greater personal capacity to keep covenants and follow a righteous course in the future (D&C 21:9).[12]

The prophet Isaiah is no less zealous in his writings concerning the surrender of the covenant heart to God: "Hearken unto me, ye that know righteousness, the people in whose heart is my law; fear ye not the reproach of men, neither be ye afraid of their revilings. For the moth shall eat them up like a garment, and the worm shall eat them like wool: but my righteousness shall be for ever, and my salvation from generation to generation" (Isaiah 51:7–8).

These verses suggest that God's law may be meshed in the human heart and become part of the very essence of a covenant Israelite. Again, the image is one of complete fidelity and is indicative of the spirit of *berith.* The will of the covenant-keeping Israelite is ultimately subsumed under the laws of God. All thoughts and actions are to be in harmony with God's commandments—the result being "salvation from generation to generation." In our day, as in antiquity, this serves as a reminder that all God truly desires of us is the only unique thing we have to give—our heart, or, as stated earlier, our deepest thoughts, feelings, emotions, intentions, and loyalties.[13]

A Covenant People Are Peculiar and Holy

The word *peculiar* is a translation from the Hebrew word *segullah* and means personal property rather than something unusual or unique.[14] As used in the Old Testament, *segullah* generally suggests the image of covenant Israelites being the personal treasure of Jehovah bought by him. They are like priceless jewels that are carefully guarded and cared for in a special fashion.[15] The word *holy* is a translation from the Hebrew *qodhesh,* which means sacred, undefiled, and set apart.[16]

We see the significance of this in Deuteronomy when Moses says, "The Lord hath avouched thee this day to be his peculiar people, as he hath promised thee, and that thou shouldest keep all his commandments; and to make thee high above all nations which he hath made, in praise, and in name, and in honour; and that thou mayest be an holy people unto the Lord thy God, as he hath spoken" (Deuteronomy 26:18–19).

A fundamental attribute of a covenant Israelite is a heightened understanding of the value God places upon his children, who have entered into sacred promises with him. They also understand that God will take particular pains to protect, honor, embellish, and enhance his covenant children wherever possible. Finally, responsibility accompanies the unique status and divine protective guardianship afforded to covenant Israelites. Whether in the days of Moses or in the last days, those honoring covenants are continually aware that they are obligated to abhor worldliness and to consecrate their lives to build the kingdom of God under all circumstances and conditions. By doing so, they become peculiar and holy and thus "all the people of the earth shall see that thou art called by the name of the Lord; and they shall be afraid of thee" (Deuteronomy 28:10).[17]

As in Deuteronomy, this theme is clearly present in the Psalms. A description of a covenant Israelite striving to become peculiar and holy is found in Psalm 101: "I will behave myself wisely in a perfect way. . . . I will walk within my house with a perfect heart. I will set no wicked thing before mine eyes: . . . A froward [perverse] heart shall depart from me: I will not know a wicked person. . . . Mine eyes shall be upon the faithful of the land, that they may dwell with me: . . . He that worketh deceit shall not dwell within my house: he that telleth lies shall not tarry in my sight. I will early destroy all the wicked of the land; that I may cut off all wicked doers from the city of the Lord" (Psalm 101:2–8).

In these verses we learn that peculiar and holy people are those who are concerned with appropriate personal behavior; their conduct within familial relationships remains above reproach; they maintain an intellectual purity that prohibits the viewing or reading of titillating or salacious media and literature; they consciously monitor personal thoughts, feelings, emotions, and intentions in an effort to maintain personal virtue; they uphold a strong link between appropriate social conduct and covenant obligations; and finally, they maintain and actively promote the highest civic and spiritual standards possible in society. These verses give timely counsel for the last days and serve as one example of many that portray covenant-keeping Israelites as peculiar and holy—always willing to be owned by God and set apart from the things of the world in hopes of further establishing the kingdom of God on the earth.[18]

Isaiah's treatment of this theme is consistent with that of Deuteronomy and Psalms.[19] Isaiah 52:11 is representative of the many times Isaiah calls for covenant Israel to maintain their peculiarity and holiness. The prophet writes: "Depart ye, depart ye, go ye out from thence [Babylon—or the world], touch no unclean thing; go ye out of the midst of her; be ye clean that bear the vessels of the Lord" (Isaiah 52:11).

The image of taking immediate and rapid flight out of Babylon is a recurring one. The commingling of peculiar and holy Israelites with Babylon is strictly forbidden. The moment a covenant people embrace worldliness in any degree they cease to be a peculiar and holy people.[20] Whether then or now, mature and committed keepers of the covenant do not consort with Babylon.

Maintaining cleanliness in order to bear the vessels of the Lord is also directly related to being peculiar and holy. Elder Jeffrey R. Holland explains that this refers to the dedicated implements, such as bowls, basins, cups, and other vessels, used in ancient temple worship. Great care was taken to keep these implements in clean and perfect condition. They were peculiar and holy in every way.

Elder Holland further explains that by permitting ancient Israelites to handle these objects, the Lord was reminding them of their need to be as clean as the ceremonial instruments themselves. Isaiah's instructions in verse eleven suggest that covenant Israelites of all dispensations must be clean, not only because of what they will be called upon to do in the name of the Lord but also, and more importantly, because of what they are to be—peculiar and holy in every way.[21]

Isaiah's cogent depiction of a covenant people was recited by the Savior during his ministry among the Nephites (3 Nephi 20:41) and included by him in two revelations given to the Saints in the last days (D&C 38:42; 133:5).

A Covenant People Acknowledge the Holy Temple As Essential to Salvation

The word *temple* does not appear in the King James version of the Old Testament until 1 Samuel 1:9. In the book of Deuteronomy, the Lord's house is known as the tabernacle. Exploring the meaning of the words *tabernacle* and *temple* in their Hebrew forms may provide a greater appreciation for the vital role that the temple plays in the lives of covenant Israel.

In Deuteronomy the word *tabernacle* is a translation from the Hebrew *'ohel.* This word describes a personal dwelling place that serves as a covert from outside intrusion. Therefore, the tabernacle is the house of the Lord.[22] In Psalms and Isaiah, the Old Testament writers maintain the imagery and meaning of *tabernacle* and also use the word *temple* to describe the house of the Lord. The word *temple* is a translation from the Hebrew word *hekhal,* which denotes a royal residence that is able to accommodate all who qualify to enter.[23]

Therefore, the temple is God's royal residence. It is a palace of no small stature, in which the evil influences of the fallen world are set at bay. God invites all qualified subjects to gather to his home, where they receive gifts from him. Specifically, God is able to grant the knowledge and power that will enable his guests to resist and overcome the evil forces that are prevalent outside the walls of the temple. It is no wonder that an Israelite acknowledges the holy temple as essential to his status under the covenant and his eternal salvation.[24]

Concerning the holy sanctuary, Moses taught: "There shall be *a place which the Lord your God shall choose* to cause his name to dwell there; *thither shall ye bring* all that I command you; your burnt offerings, and your sacrifices, your tithes, and the heave offering of your hand, and all your choice vows which ye vow unto the Lord: and ye shall rejoice before the Lord your God" (Deuteronomy 12:11–12; emphasis added).

The tabernacle is identified here as the personal residence of the Lord. Also, it is a place where indispensable covenants, or vows, are entered into, which, when honored, will cause the recipient to experience joy in this life and obtain eternal life in the next.

Furthermore, the "place specific" nature of the tabernacle and temple is clearly introduced in this verse. The Lord chooses the specific address of his royal residence, and all others must travel to that holy site to have certain rites performed in their behalf and receive certain mandatory ordinances.[25] Covenant Israelites wholeheartedly understand that there are no exceptions to this rule. The tabernacle, and later the temple, are the only places on earth where certain ordinances, covenants, and promises are offered to mankind.[26]

The Psalms also chronicle the central importance of the temple to covenant-keeping Israelites. Psalm 61 serves as an illustrative example: "From the end of the earth will I cry unto thee, when my heart is overwhelmed: lead me to the rock that is higher than I. For thou hast been a shelter for me, and a strong tower from the enemy. I will abide in thy tabernacle for ever: I will trust in the covert of thy wings. . . . For thou, O God, hast heard my vows: thou hast given me the heritage of those that fear thy name" (Psalm 61:2–5).

Being led to "the rock that is higher than I" bears obvious

allusions to Jehovah's title as the "Rock" throughout the Old Testament (Deuteronomy 32:4). This title recommends the permanence, formidability, and strength of God. In both Psalm 61 and Deuteronomy 32, the word *rock* is a translation from the Hebrew word *tsur.*[27] Rocks and rock crevices provide protection, stability, shade, and a place where people and things may hide from hostile elements. Figuratively, this word describes God's role as a guardian; he provides refuge and protection to his children.[28]

Here again, the image of the temple is consistent with those portrayed in Deuteronomy. Limited mortals must ascend to the refuge or dwelling place of God. Once there, they are fortified, protected, and promoted by receiving the heritage of those that fear or respect the King of Kings. Put another way, they are placed firmly on the path to exaltation. All covenant peoples seek this heritage.[29]

The critical role of the temple for covenant Israel is confirmed in these familiar verses from Isaiah: "It shall come to pass in the last days, that the mountain of the Lord's house shall be established in the top of the mountains, and shall be exalted above the hills; and all nations shall flow unto it. And many people shall go and say, Come ye, and let us go up to the mountain of the Lord, to the house of the God of Jacob; and he will teach us of his ways, and we will walk in his paths: for out of Zion shall go forth the law, and the word of the Lord from Jerusalem" (Isaiah 2:2–3).

The word *mountain* in these verses is a translation from the Hebrew word *har.* In this case the word is used in a poetic and figurative way that suggests an elevated place set apart for advancement.[30] This interpretation reveals a fundamental theme in the book of Isaiah. The great prophet consistently beckons to covenant Israel and, in the last days, all nations to ascend to the high place of the Lord.

As in Deuteronomy, Isaiah clearly states that the temple of the Lord is "place specific" and all nations must come to it. In this case, the temple is located high above and figuratively out of reach of the negative influences of a fallen world. Once qualified individuals enter the palace sanctuary they are taught God's ways and come to walk in the paths of the Lord. In other words, through instruction and emulation, the covenants and promises disseminated in the temple serve to promote the faithful toward a Godlike life.[31]

A Covenant People Make the Atonement the Focal Point of Their Worship of God

The word *atonement* in the Old Testament comes from the Hebrew word *kaphar*, which literally means "to cover." In context of the Savior's great sacrifice, several figurative meanings are attached to the word *kaphar* such as: to appease, expiate, cleanse, pacify, reconcile, and forgive mercifully.[32] The irony, and thus the deeper meaning, connected with the Atonement is that the recipients of its grace, mercy, and protection are not worthy of it. Striking imagery related to the Atonement and its effect in the lives of less than deserving Israelites are consistently employed by Moses, the psalmists, and Isaiah.

One such example from the book of Deuteronomy occurred when Moses reminded covenant Israel of their great rebellion at the base of Sinai when, under the direction of Aaron, they created a golden calf and worshipped it. This idolatry was repugnant to God and caused such wrath in the heart of the Almighty that he would have destroyed Aaron and the entire camp of Israel had Moses not begged the Lord to spare them (Deuteronomy 9:19–20; Exodus 32). The mercies of the Atonement were extended to Israel on this occasion. Following repentance, they were cleansed, forgiven, and, in general, received continued protection from Jehovah.

In order to leave an indelible impression in the minds of his less than worthy congregation regarding the significance of this experience, Moses used the golden calf to teach several principles about the atonement of Jesus Christ. Moses recounts: "I took your sin, the calf which ye had made, and burnt it with fire, and stamped it, and ground it very small, even until it was as small as dust: and I cast the dust thereof into the brook that descended out of the mount" (Deuteronomy 9:21).

One conclusion that may be drawn from this imagery is that sin must be purged by fire. In other words, the cleansing power of the Atonement is always accompanied by the power of the Holy Ghost.[33]

Also, the Savior has the power to take sins that are large and glaring and crush them, grind them, and wash them away. The image of grinding suggests to the mind painstaking work and stifling pressure brought to bear. In other words, the Atonement would be intensely difficult for the Savior to perform. The image of our ground and powdered sins being washed away in the currents of a river suggests that our mistakes need never return to us. It also suggests that God has the ability to forgive our sins and forget them. Therefore, peoples of the covenant should never try to relive or fall back into even a speck's worth of rebellion or sin that the Savior has cast away through his atonement.[34]

The book of Psalms also affirms the absolute dependence that covenant Israelites have on the atonement of Jesus Christ. It records the striking irony of *kaphar,* or atonement. Again, the irony lies in the fact that the recipient of the atoning mercy and cleansing is by no means worthy of it. The psalmist writes that Jehovah "hath not dealt with us after our sins; nor rewarded us according to our iniquities. For as the heaven is high above the earth, so great is his mercy toward them that fear him. As far as the east is from the west, so far hath he removed our transgressions from us" (Psalm 103:10–12).

In this verse the phrase "fear him" refers to those who reverence and honor Jehovah as the only God endowed with the power to save from sin. The expression "hath not dealt with us after our sins" is another indication that, given our sinfulness and rebellion in this life, we do not get what we really deserve. Because of the Atonement, the Savior is able and willing to give us perfect and beautiful rewards when we deserve wretchedness and misery. Finally, the phrase "as far as the east is from the west" is another way of saying that the Atonement has the power to place incalculable distance between covenant Israel and their sins when they are fully repentant. Ultimately, this is why covenant Israelites, both ancient and modern, make the atonement of Christ the focal point of their worship.[35] They clearly understand that he is the only source of power whereby cleansing of this permanent and exalting nature may occur.[36]

No Old Testament author focuses more poignantly and prophetically on the atonement of Jesus Christ than Isaiah. Of the many passages in Isaiah that capture the essential character of the Atonement, the following verses are particularly insightful: "I, even I, am the Lord; and beside me there is no saviour. . . . But thou hast not called upon me, O Jacob; but thou hast been weary of me, O Israel. Thou hast not brought me the small cattle of thy burnt offerings; neither hast thou honoured me with thy sacrifices. I have not caused thee to serve with an offering, nor wearied thee with incense. Thou hast bought me no sweet cane with money, neither hast thou filled me with the fat of thy sacrifices: but thou hast made me to serve with thy sins, thou hast wearied me with thine iniquities. I, even I, am he that blotteth out thy transgressions for mine own sake, and will not remember thy sins. Put me in remembrance; let us plead together; declare thou, that thou mayest be justified" (Isaiah 43:11, 22–26).

The Atonement has power to solve problems for which mortals have no solutions. These verses describe the perilous conditions in which covenant Israelites place themselves through rebellion, disobedience, and neglect. Isaiah explains that they repeatedly dishonor their God by refusing to repent and by so doing are cut off from his presence and blessings. Nevertheless, when covenant Israel bows in humility before the Master and begs his forgiveness, they can be saved.

Remembering that one meaning of the word *kaphar* is "to cover," we may see the significance of Isaiah's testimony that Jesus Christ has the power to blot out or cover transgressions that otherwise would cause rapid spiritual stagnation and, finally, eternal damnation. Isaiah explains that the Atonement allows an omniscient Messiah to utterly forget the errant and offensive behavior of those who approach him in humility. Finally, the Atonement has power to reconcile God and his imperfect children. Because of the atonement of Jesus Christ, the Father is able to invite repentant sons and daughters to abandon their sinfulness and reunite with him in his royal palace where he can teach them, protect them, and promote them in ways that they never thought possible given their fallen condition. As Isaiah explains, God gives them "beauty for ashes, the oil of joy for mourning, the garment of praise for the spirit of heaviness; that they might be called trees of righteousness, the planting of the Lord, that he might be glorified" (Isaiah 61:3).

With all this in mind, it is no wonder that covenant Israelites, anciently and today, make the Atonement the focal point of their worship of God the Father.[37]

Conclusion

Deuteronomy, Psalms, and Isaiah illustrate that a covenant Israelite of any dispensation will share at least four indispensable attributes: 1) They love God with all their heart; 2) they are peculiar and holy—owned by God and set apart from worldliness; 3) they acknowledge the holy temple as essential to salvation; and 4) they make the atonement of Jesus Christ the focal point of their worship of God the Father. When these four attributes are in place, covenant Israelites, regardless of the age in which they live, flourish spiritually, are blessed temporally, and are likened to "a tree planted by the rivers of water, that bringeth forth his fruits in his season; his leaf also shall not wither; and whatsoever he doeth shall prosper" (Psalm 1:3).

The image of the tree planted by rivers of water suggests a continuous link to vital nutrients. To bring forth fruits in the appropriate season suggests that the elements of the tree are ordered, governable, and productive. Leaves not withering implies that every limb and branch of the tree are properly maintained and nourished. Even its smallest and most fragile parts are cared for and nothing is overlooked. The tree prospers, not because it is never threatened or damaged, but because in the final analysis, the nourishing waters of life and the protective environment allow the net growth and productivity of the tree to overshadow occasional setbacks. As it is with the psalmist's tree, so it is with covenant Israel—then and now.

Notes

1. Francis Brown, S. R. Driver, and Charles A. Briggs, *Hebrew and English Lexicon* (Peabody, Mass.: Hendrickson, 2000), 136. See also

G. Johannes Botterweck and Helmer Ringgren, *Theological Dictionary of the Old Testament,* 10 vols. (Grand Rapids, Mich.: Eerdmans, 1975), 2:255–58.

Although the *Hebrew and English Lexicon,* by Brown, Driver, and Briggs, is a valuable resource and widely used, it is in need of being updated. Hence, the appeal to additional sources for citations dealing with Hebrew usage. The author expresses thanks to Dr. Donald W. Parry, associate professor of Hebrew in the Department of Asian and Near Eastern Languages at Brigham Young University, for guidance regarding Hebrew usage in this chapter.

2. Botterweck and Ringgren, *Theological Dictionary of the Old Testament,* 2:255–58.

3. Ibid. See also Victor L. Ludlow, "Covenant Teachings of the Scriptures," Brigham Young University Devotional Address, Provo, Utah, 13 October 1998.

4. Gordon B. Hinckley, Conference Report, April 2000, 5; or *Ensign,* May 2000, 6.

5. Brown, Driver, and Briggs, *Hebrew and English Lexicon,* 136. See also Botterweck and Ringgren, *Theological Dictionary of the Old Testament,* 2:253–67, 275–79. Given this etymological background, it should not be surprising that Jehovah prescribed circumcision as a great symbol of his covenant with faithful Israelite males. Circumcision required a binding agreement and the total physical submission of the male for the foreskin to be cut away. Every day thereafter he was reminded, literally and symbolically, that he had been spiritually selected, or cut away from the world, and had pledged total submission to the will of God. God, in turn, was happily bound to provide greater privileges and blessings for the covenant son in his kingdom. For more information and background reading on the covenant, see George E. Mendenhall and Gary A. Herion, "Covenant," in *Anchor Bible Dictionary,* ed. David Noel Freedman, 6 vols. (New York: Doubleday, 1992), 1:1179–1202. See also Ludlow, "Covenant Teachings of the Scriptures"; Lawrence O. Richards, *Expository Dictionary of Bible Words* (Grand Rapids, Mich.: Zondervan, 1991), 193–99.

6. Brigham Young, *Discourses of Brigham Young,* sel. John A. Widtsoe (Salt Lake City: Deseret Book, 1954), 160.

7. This is still the case among observant Jews. The School of Shammai explains: "In the evening one must recite the Shema' in a reclining

position, and in the morning standing up, for it is said: when you lie down and when you get up." As cited in Leo Trepp, *Judaism Development and Life,* 4th ed. (Belmont, Calif.: Wadsworth, 2000), 268. It should not be directly construed from this tradition that this was the practice of ancient Israelites. Frankly, we do not know, specifically, how ancient Israelites infused the Shema' into their daily life. Nevertheless, the enduring tradition of the Jews regarding these scriptural passages may serve as an indicator of the spiritual and cultural import of the Shema' over the centuries. Incidentally, Shammai was one of two very prominent sages teaching, interpreting, and creating rabbinic tradition near the end of the first century before Christ. His counterpart was Hillel. Robert Goldenberg, "School of Shammai," in Freedman, *Anchor Bible Dictionary,* 5:1158.

8. Brown, Driver, and Briggs, *Hebrew and English Lexicon,* 1033. See also Ernst Jenni and Claus Westermann, *Theological Lexicon of the Old Testament,* trans. Mark E. Biddle, 4 vols. (Peabody, Mass.: Hendrickson, 1997), 3:1375–80.

9. The word *heart* is a translation of the Hebrew word *leb,* which occurs alongside *lebab.* Figuratively, *leb* encompasses all dimensions of human existence. It signifies intellect, wisdom, vitality, emotion, conscience—indeed the very essence of a person lies within the *leb* (Psalm 22:15; 27:3; 33:21; 45:2). In the theological sense, one's knowledge of Jehovah's laws and deeds are to be lodged in the *leb.* From this we may conclude that the command in the Shema' to love God with all one's heart is a command rich in meaning and total commitment. See Jenni and Westermann, *Theological Lexicon of the Old Testament,* 2:638–40.

10. Nothing is known regarding the literal practice of binding the scriptural passages of the Shema' to the head or to the hand or to the doorpost in Old Testament times. It is possible that the Old Testament passages referring to the binding of the Shema' were read and applied figuratively and not literally. By the time of the Savior's mortal ministry, however, the commandment to bind the words had, without question, been taken literally. Phylacteries were the subject of a stinging rebuke by the Savior aimed at apostate scribes and Pharisees who did all their works to be seen of men (Matthew 23:5). Whatever the practice may have been among Israelites of the Old Testament, all we know concerning the matter finds its roots in Second Temple Judaism of the days of Jesus and later. Therefore, it would be prudent to view Pharisaical practices dating from these time periods with caution. Suggesting that the ritual practices of first-century Pharisees

are a clear indication of how God was worshiped centuries earlier is problematic in many ways and should be considered accordingly. See Bruce R. McConkie, *Doctrinal New Testament Commentary* (Salt Lake City: Bookcraft, 1987), 615; see also Alfred Edersheim, *The Life and Times of Jesus the Messiah* (New York: Longmans, Green, and Co., 1904; reprint, Peabody, Mass.: Hendrickson, 1999), 12–27, 755; James E. Talmage, *Jesus the Christ*, 3d ed. (Salt Lake City: Deseret Book, 1977), 565–66).

11. Other examples in Deuteronomy that a covenant people love God with all their heart include Deuteronomy 8; 10:12; 27; 29:13–14; 30; 32:1–4.

12. Other examples in Psalms that a covenant people love God with all their heart include Psalm 5:11; 6:1–9; 27:1; 31:23–24; 51:16–17; 62:5–9; 90:9–10; 111:10; 118:22–29; 139.

13. Neal A. Maxwell, Conference Report, October 1995, 30; or *Ensign*, November 1995, 24. In this talk, entitled "Swallowed Up in the Will of the Father," Elder Maxwell taught that "the submission of one's will is really the only uniquely personal thing we have to place on God's altar. The many other things we 'give,' brothers and sisters, are actually the things He has already given or loaned to us. However, when you and I finally submit ourselves, by letting our individual wills be swallowed up in God's will, then we are really giving something to Him! It is the only possession which is truly ours to give!" For other scriptures in Isaiah that a covenant people love God with all their heart, see Isaiah 2:22; 12:2; 25:1; 41:10; 43:11; 45:20–25.

14. Brown, Driver, and Briggs, *Hebrew and English Lexicon*, 688. See also Botterweck and Ringgren, *Theological Dictionary of the Old Testament*, 10:144–48.

15. Brown, Driver, and Briggs, *Hebrew and English Lexicon*, 688. See also Botterweck and Ringgren, *Theological Dictionary of the Old Testament*, 10:144–48.

16. Brown, Driver, and Briggs, *Hebrew and English Lexicon*, 871. See also Jenni and Westermann, *Theological Lexicon of the Old Testament*, 3:1103–5.

17. Other examples in Deuteronomy that a covenant people love God with all their heart include Deuteronomy 10:12–16; 12:2–3; 14; 15:19–23; 18:9–14; 23.

18. Other examples in Psalms that a covenant people love God with all

their heart include Psalm 7:9–10; 15; 23; 37:25–27; 74:2; 95; 101; 119:97–104; 125:2.

19. Although Isaiah consistently addresses this theme, there is variety in his presentation. For example, Isaiah 3 is a detailed description of the reversal of peculiarity and holiness. In this chapter the great prophet describes, in striking detail, how the Israelites appear and behave when they are *not* honoring their covenants and are, therefore, *not* peculiar and holy.

20. Hugh Nibley, *Approaching Zion* (Salt Lake City: Deseret Book, 1989), 30–31.

21. Jeffrey R. Holland, "Sanctify Yourselves," *Ensign,* November 2000, 39. Other examples in Isaiah that a covenant people love God with all their heart include Isaiah 1:16; 3; 25:7–9; 51; 46:3–4.

22. Brown, Driver, and Briggs, *Hebrew and English Lexicon,* 13–14. See also Botterweck and Ringgren, *Theological Dictionary of the Old Testament,* 1:118–130.

23. Brown, Driver, and Briggs, *Hebrew and English Lexicon,* 228, 1090. See also Botterweck and Ringgren, *Theological Dictionary of the Old Testament,* 3:382–88; Carol Meyers, "Temple, Jerusalem," in Freedman, *Anchor Bible Dictionary,* 6:351–52.

Additionally, it may be helpful to know that in Hebrew, as in English, multiple words could be used to identify the temple. The Hebrew word *mikdash* is an example. See Jenni and Westermann, *Theological Lexicon of the Old Testament,* 1:234. See also Brown, Driver, and Briggs, *Hebrew and English Lexicon,* 228.

24. This ancient conception of the temple as a residence was clearly perceived by the early leaders of the Church in this dispensation, and they taught it to the Saints of their day repeatedly. Consider the following explanation by Brigham Young as one example of many: "This I do know—there should be a temple built here. I do know it is the duty of this people to commence to build a temple. Now, some will want to know what kind of a building it will be. Wait patiently, brethren, until it is done, and put forth your hands willingly to finish it. I know what it will be. I scarcely ever say much about revelations, or visions, but suffice it to say, five years ago last July I was here, and saw in the spirit the temple not ten feet from where we have laid the chief cornerstone. I have not inquired what kind of temple we should build. Why? Because it was represented before me. I

have never looked upon that ground, but the vision of it was there. I see it as plainly as if it was in reality before me. Wait until it is done. I will say, however, that it will have six towers, to begin with, instead of one. Now do not any of you apostatize because it will have six towers, and Joseph only built one. It is easier for us to build sixteen, than it was for him to build one. The time will come when there will be one in the centre of temples, we shall build, and, on the top, groves and fish ponds. But we shall not see them here, at present.

"I have determined, by the help of the Lord and this people, to build him a house. You may ask, 'Will he dwell in it?' He may do just as he pleases; it is not my prerogative to dictate to the Lord. But we will build him a house, that, if he pleases to pay us a visit, he may have a place to dwell in, or if he should send any of his servants, we may have suitable accommodations for them. I have built myself a house, and the most of you have done the same, and now, shall we not build the Lord a house?" *Discourses of Brigham Young*, sel. John A. Widtsoe (Salt Lake City: Deseret Book, 1954), 410–11.

25. First, the author credits Dr. Andrew C. Skinner, professor of ancient scripture and dean of Religious Education at Brigham Young University, for providing clarity and scope regarding the "place specific" concept associated with temple worship.

Second, given that we do not possess complete accounts of rites and ordinances performed within the temples of the Old Testament, the following explanation from Elder Bruce R. McConkie is particularly helpful in determining the absolute need to go to the temple of God in antiquity and today. He explained:

"The everlasting gospel; the eternal priesthood; the identical ordinances of salvation and exaltation. . . . the same Church and kingdom; the keys of the kingdom, which alone can seal men up unto eternal life—all these have always been the same in all ages; and it shall be so everlastingly on this earth and all earths to all eternity. These things we know by latter-day revelation.

" . . . Do not let the fact that the performances of the Mosaic law were administered by the Aaronic Priesthood confuse you on this matter. Where the Melchizedek Priesthood is, there is the fulness of the gospel; and all of the prophets held the Melchizedek Priesthood.

" . . . Was there a Church anciently, and if so, how was it organized and regulated? There was not so much as the twinkling of an eye during the whole so-called pre-Christian Era when the Church of Jesus Christ was not upon the earth, organized basically in the same way it now is. Melchizedek belonged to the Church; Laban was a member; so also was Lehi, long before he left Jerusalem.

"There was always apostolic power. The Melchizedek Priesthood always directed the course of the Aaronic Priesthood. All of the prophets held a position in the hierarchy of the day. Celestial marriage has always existed. Indeed, such is the heart and core of the Abrahamic covenant. Elias and Elijah came to restore this ancient order and to give the sealing power, which gives it eternal efficacy" ("The Bible, a Sealed Book," in *Symposium on the New Testament,* supplement, prepared by Church Educational System, Salt Lake City: The Church of Jesus Christ of Latter-day Saints, 1984). See also D&C 132:38–39.

26. Other examples in Deuteronomy that a covenant people acknowledge the holy temple as essential to salvation include Deuteronomy 16; 31:15.

27. Brown, Driver, and Briggs, *Hebrew and English Lexicon,* 849.

28. Botterweck and Ringgren, *Theological Dictionary of the Old Testament,* 10:270–77. The word *tsur* is a derivative of the Hebrew *sela.* Both terms are used to designate Jehovah as a Rock. *Tsur* carries a stronger connotation of Jehovah's tutelary power. See also Moses 7:53.

29. Other examples in Psalms that a covenant people acknowledge the holy temple as essential to salvation include Psalm 15; 24; 27:4–5; 84; 92:13; 93; 100.

30. Brown, Driver, and Briggs, *Hebrew and English Lexicon,* 249. See also Botterweck and Ringgren, *Theological Dictionary of the Old Testament,* 3:427–37, 442–46.

31. Other examples in Isaiah that a covenant people acknowledge the holy temple as essential to salvation include Isaiah 2; 4:5–6; 6; 19; 33:20; 66.

32. Brown, Driver, and Briggs, *Hebrew and English Lexicon,* 497. See also Botterweck and Ringgren, *Theological Dictionary of the Old Testament,* 7:289–303.

33. Bruce R. McConkie, *The Mortal Messiah,* 4 vols. (Salt Lake City: Deseret Book, 1978–82), 3:40–41.

34. Other examples in Deuteronomy that a covenant people make the

Atonement the focal point of their worship of God include Deuteronomy 30:1–10; 32:1–14, 39; 33:26–29.

35. It is important to acknowledge that covenant Israelites living in different time periods in the Old Testament enjoy varying degrees of understanding regarding the Atonement. The basic idea that God has power to purge sinfulness would be held in common among all covenant peoples of the Old Testament; however, as a general rule, covenant Israelites who lived from Adam to Moses enjoyed a more detailed understanding of the Atonement of Jesus Christ than covenant Israelites living from Moses to John the Baptist. For a more detailed discussion of these differences, see Kent P. Jackson, "One Family's Testimony of Christ," *Ensign,* February 2000, 23–27.

36. Other examples in Psalms that a covenant people make the Atonement the focal point of their worship of God include Psalm 16:10; 22; 31:5; 34:20; 49; 69; 86; 124:7; 130:3–4.

37. Other examples in Isaiah that a covenant people make the Atonement the focal point of their worship of God include Isaiah 1:18; 4:6; 44:22; 50; 53.

4

Moses' Charge to Remember

Philip A. Allred

Deuteronomy is the record of Moses' last words to the Israelites before they entered the promised land.[1] They were leaving the wilderness, where they had lived in humble dependence on the Lord, for the green pastures of Canaan. Knowing that he would not be joining them, Moses warned Israel against spiritual amnesia. This great prophet repeatedly exhorted his people not to forget the covenant they had made with God. In fact, Moses employed the words *remember* and *forget* and their variants in Deuteronomy more times than in all the rest of the Pentateuch—Genesis, Exodus, Leviticus, and Numbers—combined.

If the people would remember their deliverance—even "all the great acts of the Lord" (Deuteronomy 11:7)—they would continue to receive "power to get wealth, that he may establish his covenant which he sware unto [their] fathers" (Deuteronomy 8:18). Yosef Yerushalmi, an authority on Jewish memory, has written, "Only in Israel and nowhere else is the injunction to remember felt as a

Philip A. Allred is a professor of religion at BYU–Idaho.

religious imperative to an entire people. Its reverberations are everywhere, but they reach a crescendo in the Deuteronomic history and in the prophets."[2]

To reinforce and continually nurture Israel's covenantal memory, Moses employed various mnemonic methods throughout the book of Deuteronomy. These tools of remembrance are collected as a whole only within that book, making Deuteronomy a how-to handbook for Israel's memory. The memory-aiding methods Moses marshaled in Deuteronomy include repetition, types and symbols, the Sabbath, seasonal feasts and festivals, significant years, circumcision, altars and monuments, religious attire, the "song" of Moses, and culture.

Repetition

President Ezra Taft Benson said, "Repetition is a key to learning. Our sons need to hear the truth repeated."[3] The English appellation of the book, Deuteronomy, is "repeated law," "second law," or "copy of the law." This alludes to the fact that Deuteronomy is a selective revision of the Mosiac law and history found in Exodus through Numbers. "It is not a mere repetition, however. As Leviticus was for the priests and Numbers for the Levites, so Deuteronomy is for the people. Therefore, while it is not so detailed nor technical as the books which precede it, it contains all the essential elements which the individual must obey to insure the continual blessings associated with the covenant life."[4]

Repetition and recitation help us remember. Deuteronomy, as a book, was to be taught in the home to the children (4:4–9; 6:7). It was to be meditated upon constantly (6:7). It was to be studied by Israel's king on a daily basis (17:18–19; Joshua 1:8). It was to be rehearsed to the entire population of Israel, including the resident Gentiles, every Sabbatical year during the Feast of Tabernacles (31:10–13). Repetition is utilized within the book of Deuteronomy as well. The *Shema,* or Jewish daily prayer, consists of passages from Deuteronomy (6:4–9; 11:13–21) and Numbers (15:37–41). These references contain the Lord's injunctions to teach the law in the family, as well as to talk of and ponder the law continually. One translation of Deuteronomy 6:7 renders "talk" as "recite" and notes that Moses' instruction "involves recitation and reading or murmuring" as an aid to remembering.[5] On this point, another biblical scholar has written, "Consideration of the 'memory' passages in Deuteronomy suggests that the mode of the remembrance was preaching or *sacred recital* in the sanctuaries, and *it is so prominent as to amount to a Deuteronomic presentation of remembrance.*"[6]

Moses also stressed significant parts of Israel's immediate history within the book of Deuteronomy. These specific historical references reminded the children of Israel of the Lord's delivering hand in their past.

"Not only is Israel under no obligation whatever to remember the entire past, but its principle of selection is unique unto itself. It is above all God's acts of intervention in history, and man's responses to them, be they positive or negative, that must be recalled. . . . For the real danger is not so much that what happened in the past will be forgotten, as the more crucial aspect of *how* it happened."[7]

In this way, the children of Israel would always be reminded of the Lord's miraculous measures on their behalf. "Memory of God's past course of action and anticipation of his future course of action provide the framework for the present commitment to God in the renewal of the covenant."[8] So critical is this historical awareness that Yerushalmi declared: "Ancient Israel knows what God is from what he has done in history. And if that is so, then memory has become crucial to its faith and, ultimately, to its very existence."[9] Thus, memory of the Lord's temporal deliverance served to remind the people to ponder their greater eternal salvation also available only through their true deliverer.

One final note on the virtue of repetition for memory as provided for in Deuteronomy is that the eighth chapter is arranged as a chiasmus. Chiasmus is an ancient form of poetry that serves to enhance its message through its form. John Welch noted that in a chiasmus "the repeating of key words in the two halves underlines the importance of the concepts they present. . . . The repeating form also enhances clarity and speeds memorizing."[10] Chapter 8 features the following chiastic form:

A. Obedience ensures life (8:1)
B. Wandering in the desert (8:2–6)
C. Richness of the land (8:7–10)
D. Do not forget the Lord (8:11)
C. Richness of the land (8:12–13)
B. Wandering in the desert (8:14–16)
A. Apostasy ensures destruction (8:19–20).[11]

The central idea of not forgetting the Lord highlighted by this chiastic form is further emphasized by the repetition of the words "remember" and "forget" (8:2, 11, 14, 18, 19).

Types and Symbols

The Lord has instructed his people throughout time with types and symbols. Types may be defined as "persons, events, or things" that are real "and at the same time point to qualities of Christ or his kingdom."[12] Symbolic representations are particularly proficient because "the principles of human nature render TYPES as a fit method of instruction. It tends to enlighten and illustrate, and to convey instruction with impression, conviction, and pleasure, and to help the memory."[13] Jehovah had not yet condescended as Jesus at this point in Israelite history, but the people still needed to remember the Lord and his coming sacrifice even "as though he already was" come among them (Mosiah 3:13; see also Jarom 1:11).

Deuteronomy contains several significant types for Christ. Moses himself had the supreme opportunity to be a type of the Savior. "The Lord thy God will raise up unto thee a Prophet"—in direct contrast to the charmers and wizards of their day—"from the midst of thee, of thy brethren, like unto me; unto him ye shall hearken" (18:15; see also v. 18). In Deuteronomy 25:17 the Lord interestingly commands the people to remember their battle with Amalek as recorded in Exodus 17:8–14. During this combat Moses had to keep his hands elevated for Israel to win. Justin Martyr wrote that Moses actually foreshadowed the Messiah's redemptive work on Calvary by holding his hands horizontally, thus symbolizing Jesus' future crucifixion.[14] As a reflection of the Savior, Moses provided a way for Israel to see the deliverance available through Jesus in the anticipation of his coming.

Also, being the "repetition of the law," Deuteronomy contains the text of the law of Moses, which itself served as a type of Christ. Throughout the book Moses reminds his people that "the Lord commanded us to do all these statutes, to fear the Lord our God, for our good always, *that he might preserve us alive,* as it is at this day" (Deuteronomy 6:24; emphasis added; see also 4:10, 40; 5:16, 33; 6:2–3; 8:20; 11:8–9, 22–23; 16:20; 17:20; 20:4). Moses was referring to the symbolic meaning in the manna that had sustained wandering Israel in the wilderness (Deuteronomy 8:3, 16). This unprecedented symbol of Christ as the "bread of life" (John 6:35) was to teach the people that they must come unto him daily—not relying on yesterday's portion, nor hoarding today's helping. Communion with Christ requires constant care. Obedience to the laws associated with the manna had preserved Israel. This clearly pointed to the supreme salvation available only from Israel's faithfulness to the covenant with Jehovah—the giver of the law.

As a whole, the sacrificial ordinances described in the Mosaic law display significant features designed to point to Christ. There could be no broken bones in the animals offered—typical of Jesus' literal fulfillment of Psalm 34:20 (John 19:32–36). The sacrifice had to be without blemish—representing the purity and sinlessness of the Son of God (Deuteronomy 15:21; 17:1; Hebrews 4:15; 7:25–27; 9:11–15; D&C 45:4). On the most holy day in Israel, Yom Kippur, or Day of Atonement, the priest laid his hands on the animals and dedicated them to God as his representatives and substitutes (Leviticus 1:4; 16:21; Numbers 8:10, 12). This pointed to the fact that Jesus was the Anointed One to perform the great atoning sacrifice (Isaiah 61:1–3).[15] The blood was the means of atonement (Exodus 30:10; Leviticus 8:15; 16:18; 17:11; 1 Nephi 12:10–11; Mosiah 3:11, 14–18) and was applied to all people and things in order to purify them (Exodus 24:6–8).

While sacrifice symbolized fulfilling the requirement for reunion with God, Paul taught, "The law having a shadow of good things to come, and not the very image of the things, can never with those sacrifices which they offered year by year continually make the comers thereunto perfect. . . . But in those sacrifices there is a *remembrance* again made of sins every year" (Hebrews 10:1, 3; emphasis added). President Spencer W. Kimball mused, "I suppose that is the reason the Lord asked Adam to offer sacrifices, for no other reason than that he and his posterity would remember—remember the basic things that they had been taught."[16] All of these sacrificial shadows, repeated over and over in the Israelites' daily, weekly, and yearly rituals, were to remind them of Christ and cement him in their consciousness.

The Sabbath

Moses required Israel to observe both weekly and seasonal festivals to keep them in remembrance of the Lord. The weekly reminder came in the Sabbath. Earlier in Exodus, Moses had taught that the Lord had ordained that day as a reminder of the creation of the earth. "In it thou shalt not do any work. . . . For in six days the Lord made heaven and earth, the sea, and all that in them is, and rested the seventh day: wherefore the Lord blessed the sabbath day, and hallowed it" (Exodus 20:10–11).

What is noteworthy about Deuteronomy's recitation of the Decalogue (Ten Commandments) is that Moses changed the rationale for its observance from the one given in Exodus. "And remember that thou wast a servant in the land of Egypt, and that the Lord thy God brought thee out thence through a mighty hand and by a stretched out arm: therefore the Lord thy God commanded thee to keep the sabbath day" (Deuteronomy 5:15).

Elder Bruce R. McConkie explained: "Thus when Moses received the Ten Commandments the second time, as part of the Mosaic law rather than as part of the fulness of the gospel, the reason for keeping the Sabbath was changed. No longer was it to commemorate the creation (at least not that alone), but now it was to keep the children of Israel in remembrance of the glory of their deliverance from Egypt. . . . For nearly fifteen hundred of the four thousand years that passed between Adam and Christ, the purpose of the Sabbath was to commemorate, not the creation (except incidentally), but those events of deliverance from Egyptian bondage that so exulted the feelings of all Israel."[17]

This change in Deuteronomy from Exodus further points to the need the children of Israel had to remember the Lord—to recall their deliverance from temporal bondage in Egypt as a type of Jehovah's ultimate power to redeem them spiritually. Having been freed of temporal concerns, then, how essential it was for them neither to work nor pine away for work on that day. For within the Deuteronomic conception, temporal labors symbolically correspond with slave labor in captivity! If, on the other hand, the people were preoccupied with occupation on that day, they would be substituting the mundane for the Messiah, truly missing the mark of Christ.

Seasonal Feasts and Festivals

Israel's seasonal reminders came in the triennial festivals of Passover (*Pesah*), Weeks (*Shavuot*, or Pentecost), and Tabernacles (*Sukkoth*). These were held in the spring and fall—naturally timed with the agrarian cycle of planting and harvesting (Deuteronomy 16; see also Deuteronomy 11:13–17). Not only was the timing significant, but the activities themselves "commemorated the great events of Israel's history, the occasions when in an unmistakable way God had stepped in to deliver his people."[18] These three festivals typify three roles of the Messiah: "Passover is the festival of *redemption* and points toward the Torah-*revelation* of the Feast of Weeks; the harvest festival in the autumn celebrates not only *creation*, but especially, redemption."[19]

The Passover, with its accompanying feast of unleavened bread, specifically commemorated the great deliverance of Israel out of Egypt. It was to be held the first month of spring, or *Abib*, which corresponds with late March or early April. This date pointed to Israel's exodus, which occurred during the same month (Deuteronomy 16:1, 6). Passover was to begin and end on Sabbath days, marked by solemn assembly (Deuteronomy 16:8). Thus, bracketed by Sabbaths, the people had a double opportunity to contemplate the covenant. The center of this festival was the sacrifice of the Paschal Lamb. Killed and roasted in the evening, the lamb signified that Israel's temporal deliverance had depended on the death of Egypt's firstborn. This would lead to the continual recognition and remembrance of a future and more profound deliverance through the sacrifice of the Messiah—God's Firstborn. The meal consisted of the roasted lamb along with unleavened bread and bitter herbs, tokens of the people's "affliction" in Egypt and subsequent departure in haste (Deuteronomy 16:3). They were to eat at least a part of the meal standing with their sandals on as if prepared for travel, reminiscent of the night before the historical exodus (Exodus 12:11). The eating of the unleavened bread continued all week until the closing Sabbath, further reminding them that God governs their release from bondage.

The Feast of Weeks was held seven weeks from the benedictory Passover Sabbath (Deuteronomy 16:9–12). During this "feast of harvest, the firstfruits of thy labours" (Exodus 23:16), the people were to offer a "tribute of a freewill offering . . . according as the Lord [their] God hath blessed [them]" (Deuteronomy 16:10). This festival was to be held on one day. It celebrated the beginning of Israel's harvest season. During this prosperous season, it would be particularly tempting for the people to fall prey to pride, forgetting that God had provided the land, given the rain, and flourished the crop (Deuteronomy 8:7–17).[20] Therefore, Moses again commanded Israel to "remember that thou wast a bondman in Egypt" (Deuteronomy 16:12). Sheaves of wheat were placed on the sacrificial altars to remind the participants that God had given the increase. Additionally, the number of animal offerings during Weeks was increased over the single Passover lamb (thirteen animals altogether: nine lambs, one young bull, one kid goat, and two rams; Leviticus 23:18–19). In this way the increased repetition of offerings again point to that future, ultimate sacrifice of the Savior himself.[21] Included in the celebration were meal offerings of two loaves of leavened wheat bread, representing a return of a portion in accordance with the Lord's blessings (Deuteronomy 16:10).

At the end of the harvest season, the children of Israel were to hold their third and final feast, the Feast of Tabernacles (Deuteronomy 16:13–15). This was a full seven-day festival during which Israel was to rejoice in the bounty afforded by the Lord. Elder McConkie explained: "If the beginning of the harvest had pointed back to the birth of Israel in the Exodus from Egypt, and forward to the true Passover-sacrifice in the future; if the corn-harvest was connected with the giving of the law on Mount Sinai in the past, and the outpouring of the Holy Spirit on the Day of Pentecost; the harvest-thanksgiving of the Feast of Tabernacles *reminded* Israel, on the one hand, of their dwelling in booths in the wilderness, while, on the other hand, it pointed to the final harvest when Israel's mission should be completed, and all nations gathered unto the Lord."[22]

One of the significant aspects of Tabernacles was the construction of booths, or frail huts, which the people lived in for the seven days of the festival. During this time they rehearsed the law as noted above.[23] "Ye shall dwell in booths [constructed of branches, flowers, leaves, and fruit] . . . that your generations may know that I made the children of Israel to dwell in booths, when I brought them out of the land of Egypt" (Leviticus 23:42–43). This was a time of bounty; a time described by Moses when "thou hast eaten and art full" (Deuteronomy 8:12). Comfort breeds complacency and forgetfulness. Therefore, living in crude huts offered the people the opportunity to remember their constant dependence on the Lord and the significance of spiritual things over their material possessions. It is noteworthy that the number of sacrificial offerings ordained during this week eclipses the earlier two feasts. Israel was to participate in nearly two hundred animal offerings during those seven days.[24] Obviously the richness of this sacrificial repetition offered the people a way to indelibly etch into their hearts the coming offering of Jesus as the Lamb of God.

Living in these booths served a double function: first, the memory of past trials through dramatically reenacting the forty-year wandering was designed to give Israel proper perspective during Canaan's prosperity; and second, this booth dwelling would point the people's minds forward to the time when, if they had been faithful to the covenant, the Lord would say, "There is a place prepared for you in the mansions of my Father" (Enos 1:27).

The extraordinary nature of these seasonal celebrations is truly remarkable. In the words of a Jewish scholar, "To be a classical Jew is to be intoxicated by faith in God, to live every moment in his presence, to shape every hour by the paradigm of Torah. The day with its worship morning and evening [reciting the *Shema*], the week with its climax at the Sabbath, the season marked by nature's commemoration of Israel's sacred history—these shape life into rhythms of sanctification."[25]

These instructions in Deuteronomy concerning Israel's feasts and festivals form another of Moses' prescriptions against spiritual amnesia. Thus, even their weekly and yearly calendars provided a way for Israel to remember the Lord.

Significant Years

Moses also reiterated the command to celebrate a Sabbatical year while in the promised land (Exodus 21:2; 23:11; Leviticus 25:2, 20; Deuteronomy 15:1–18). Every seventh year was to be observed in a way similar to how the weekly Sabbath was observed. The fields were to receive a rest—unplowed, unplanted, and therefore unharvested during the Sabbatical year. The people were to have faith in God for their needs rather than labor by the strength of their arms. Slaves were freed and debts were canceled. The symbolism is unmistakable. Israel was to recall, just as during the weekly Sabbath, that God is powerful to save and deliver them. The people were to totally rely on the Lord as they had done when they were bondsmen "in the land of Egypt, and the Lord [their] God redeemed [them]" (Deuteronomy 15:15).

The freeing of the Hebrew slaves and indentured servants during this special year also suggested the need for greater benevolence and charity of heart. The slave owners were to "not let him go away empty; thou shalt furnish him liberally out of thy flock, and out of thy [harvesting] floor, and out of thy winepress" (Deuteronomy 15:13–14). This would remind the people of their own exodus out of Egyptian bondage when they took with them the treasures of Egypt (Genesis 15:14; Exodus 12:35–36). This recollection of personal and ancestral slavery was calculated to keep the people mindful of the one who had unlocked their prison and thereby invite them to emulate the loving kindness of their Savior.

Circumcision

Another method of reminding the children of Israel of their covenant with God was the rite of circumcision. This was an outward ordinance, which directed attention to the inward covenant. The surgery served no revealed intrinsic value; its meaning came only as it indicated and facilitated an inner change of heart. Moses conveys the real meaning of this rite by bidding Israel to "circumcise therefore the foreskin of your heart, and be no more stiffnecked" (Deuteronomy 10:16). Deuteronomy is the only book of Moses that contains this clarification. The people were to humbly submit to God's commands—that was their part of the spiritual circumcision. When they did so in a later day, Moses promised that "the Lord thy God will circumcise thine heart, and the heart of thy seed, to love the Lord thy God with all thine heart, and with all thy soul" (Deuteronomy 30:6). Thus, when an Israelite submitted to the physical requirement, he agreed to remember the transcendent agreement he had made with God; as he strove in humility to uphold his covenant, God promised to effect a literal change in his heart. This was symbolized by the giving of a new name at the time of circumcision (Genesis 17:5; Luke 1:59; 2:21).[26] Paul taught the Romans that "he is not a Jew, . . . which is outward in the flesh: but he is a Jew, which is one inwardly; and circumcision is that of the heart, in the spirit" (Romans 2:28–29).

As one scholar has observed, "The covenant between God and Israel is not a mere theological abstraction, nor is it effected only through laws of community and family life. It is quite literally engraved upon the flesh of every male Jewish child through the rite of circumcision, *brit milah,* the covenant of circumcision."[27] In the latter days, we similarly typify our inward conversion to Christ by the outward ordinance of baptism and mark it by receiving his name.

Altars and Monuments

Another tangible reminder of the Lord's saving relationship with Israel was called for in Deuteronomy. Moses commanded Joshua that he, upon entering the promised land, "set thee up great stones, and plaister them with plaister: and thou shalt write upon them all the words of this law" (Deuteronomy 27:2–3). These were to form an altar of sacrifice unto the Lord (Deuteronomy 27:5–8). Further, these stones were not to be chiseled or shaped with iron tools, as this would pollute the altar (Exodus 20:25).[28] Moses called for this lasting memorial to jog the people's memory every time they saw it. Joshua obeyed this command as recorded in Joshua 8:30–32. When the people crossed the Jordan into the promised land, with Joshua at their head, they took twelve men—representing each tribe—who gathered twelve stones from the "midst of Jordan" to make this monument. In the years to come, when young Israelites would naturally inquire about this memorial, their fathers were to rehearse the Lord's miraculous stopping of the river when Israel was granted entrance into their inheritance.

"Not the stone, but the memory transmitted by the fathers, is decisive if the memory embedded in the stone is to be conjured out of it to live again for subsequent generations. If there can be no return to Sinai, then what took place at Sinai must be borne along the conduits of memory to those who were not there that day."[29] It should not be lost that this miracle of passing through the River Jordan is but a repetition of the Lord's powerful deliverance of their fathers through the Red Sea when their exodus actually began. Memorials like these altars and monuments serve as reminders to the observer that the Lord's mighty hand can and will deliver his children who are faithful to him.

Religious Attire

When Moses recounted the Decalogue and the great commandment, he admonished that "these words, which I command thee this day, shall be in thine heart. . . . And thou shalt bind them for a sign upon thine hand, and they shall be as frontlets between thine eyes," and "thou shalt write them upon the posts of thy house, and on thy gates" (Deuteronomy 6, 8–9; see also 11:18–20). As noted earlier, Moses required parents to teach the law in the family and to talk of and ponder the law continually (Deuteronomy 4:9). While there exists some controversy as to whether Moses meant this figuratively or literally, mnemonic devices did develop out of these instructions. Israelites began to use frontlets, or phylacteries, on their foreheads and arms (*tefillin*), and the *mezuzot,* or small containers attached to their homes' gate or doorway. These were "ordinance[s] of remembrance" (Deuteronomy 6:8b; see also 6:8–9). Inside these little boxes were tiny written portions of the law—quotations from Deuteronomy 6:4–9, 11:13–21, and Numbers 15:37–41. Using them on a daily basis reminded the people of the law and of their covenant to obey it. Also, Israel was to "make thee fringes upon the four quarters of thy vesture" (Deuteronomy 22:12). Deuteronomy contains the command to construct them, and the book of Numbers explains them as a mnemonic tool: "That ye may look upon it, and *remember* all the commandments of the Lord, and do them" (Numbers 15:39; emphasis added). Even the number of the fringes on each prayer shawl was mnemonic, numbering 613, exactly the number of Mosaic laws.

The Song of Moses

The Lord commanded Moses to compose a song for Israel. According to his directions, the song would serve the following purposes. It would stand as a witness against wickedness (Deuteronomy 31:19, 21), contain an invitation to remember the premoral life by asking the fathers and elders to teach about it (Deuteronomy 32:7–8), indict the people regarding their forgetfulness (Deuteronomy 32:18), testify that the Lord is the only power authorized to give and take away life (Deuteronomy 32:39–40), and, if followed, "prolong [Israel's] days in the land" (Deuteronomy 32:47).

According to one scholar, "The goodness of God is perceived in the gift of the song, for a part of its function would be to warn the people of their emerging intentions and *turn them back to God* before it was too late."[30] The song of Moses is also noted to have "more polished forms of poetic parallelism."[31] We should notice that songs bracket the entire Israelite exodus. Their journey began with Moses singing the praises of the Lord (Exodus 15:1–22) and concluded in Deuteronomy with Moses warning Israel not to be "unmindful" and forget the "Rock that begat thee" and the "God that formed thee" (Deuteronomy 32:18). Songs have a truly powerful effect on the memory, and Moses employs them at the close of his ministry as another mnemonic help for the Israelites in their new home.

Culture

Hugh Nibley has noted that Israel's "cultural franchise is set down in Deuteronomy."[32] As the "children . . . of the Lord [their] God," they were not to do certain things; hence the "awareness of their heavenly parentage" would set "Israel apart *culturally* as well as doctrinally."[33] Israel was to be "peculiar" and "holy" (Deuteronomy 14:2, 21). The Hebrew word for peculiar is *segullah,* which means "set apart," "sealed," "removed from the rest of the world."[34] The people were not to intermarry with Gentiles (Deuteronomy 7:3). They were required to destroy all vestiges of Gentile worship found in the promised land (Deuteronomy 7:5; 12:2–8; 16:21–22). They were prohibited from worshiping in any way like their non-Israelite neighbors; in particular, they were neither to cut themselves in self-abasement nor to remove facial hair as part of a sacrificial ritual (Deuteronomy 14:1). They had special dietary directives (Deuteronomy 14:2–21), as well as restrictions on sowing and planting (Deuteronomy 22:9–11). The effect would be that when they compared themselves with their Gentile neighbors, they would recognize cultural differences that would remind them of their covenants with the Lord.

Conclusion

Despite this Deuteronomic charge to remember, and although Moses equipped them with remarkable mnemonic devices, the people forgot, missing the Mosaic mark—fidelity to their covenant with Jehovah. Two stumbling blocks impeded Israel's ability to utilize the mnemonic structure of the Mosaic law. On one hand, the people fell short of the mark by allowing the mnemonic means to become the end itself (as with the brazen serpent and the law; see 2 Kings 18:4 and Mark 7:5–13; Gal. 2:16 respectively). On the other hand, they fell short of the mark as they "despised the words of plainness" (Jacob 4:14), missing their messianic meaning because they became bored with its repetition. The cornerstone of these stumbling blocks is pride. Pride stunts spiritual memory. President Ezra Taft Benson warned, "Pride *fades our feelings* of sonship to God and brotherhood to man"[35] (Deuteronomy 8:10–14). Memory, however, can generate humility and invite us to "Awake! And arise from the dust" (2 Nephi 1:14).

How is pride deflated, and how are humility and faith generated? Moses consistently called Israel to reflect on and live by the word of the Lord. Elder Neal A. Maxwell has observed that the scriptures are "the moral memory of mankind."[36] Both ancient and modern scriptures are devoted to calling God's people to remembrance—remembrance of his merciful deliverance and gracious covenant. The Book of Mormon attests to this by telling the tragic history of an ancient people who lost not only their language but also any belief in "the being of their Creator" because they lacked a scriptural record (Omni 1:14–18).[37] The lesson in Israel's manna should inform our modern meaning of scripture study so that we can avoid a "famine in the land" (Amos 8:11) among our personal and family lives. President Gordon B. Hinckley closed one general conference of the Church with these helpful instructions: "Perhaps, out of all we have heard, there may be a phrase or a paragraph that will stand out and possess our attention. If this occurs, I hope we will write it down and reflect on it until we savor the depth of its meaning and have made it a part of our own lives."[38]

While it is true that the Savior fulfilled the Mosaic law, making many of the Deuteronomic directives obsolete, the mnemonic qualities of the old law are encompassed in the new covenant's renewal—the sacrament. This weekly meal serves as one of our modern reminders of the Redeemer. Elder Joseph Fielding Smith wrote, "The Passover was a law given to Israel which was to continue until Christ, and was to remind the children of Israel of the coming of Christ who would become the sacrificial Lamb." The Passover was "changed by the Savior himself" during the Last Supper, and so "from that time forth the law of the sacrament was instituted. We now observe the law of the sacrament instead of the

Passover because the Passover was consummated in full by the death of Jesus Christ."[39]

We should feel renewal, not resentment, through our latter-day religious rhythms of the sacrament, family home evening, prayer and scripture study, church and temple service with their appropriate attire, and general conferences. President Kimball taught: "You will always be in your sacrament meetings so that you will *remember.* When you look in the dictionary for the most important word, do you know what it is? It could be *remember.* Because all of you have made covenants—you know what to do and you know how to do it—our greatest need is to remember. That is why everyone goes to sacrament meeting every Sabbath day—to take the sacrament and listen to the priests pray that they 'may always remember him and keep his commandments which he has given them.' Nobody should ever forget to go to sacrament meeting. *Remember* is the word. *Remember* is the program."[40]

It is our privilege to be reminded of the Savior and our covenants with him through these modern mnemonic tools provided by the Lord, so that we may receive from him "the precious things of heaven . . . and for the precious things of the earth and [the] fulness thereof" (Deuteronomy 33:13, 16).

NOTES

1. Chapters 1 through 4 contain his first speech, chapters 5 through 26 his second speech, and chapters 27 through 30 his third speech. See Keith H. Meservy, "The Good News of Moses," in *Genesis to 2 Samuel,* ed. Kent P. Jackson and Robert L. Millet, vol. 3 in Studies in Scripture Series (Salt Lake City: Deseret Book, 1989), 206.

2. Yosef Hayim Yerushalmi, *Zakhor: Jewish History and Jewish Memory* (Seattle: University of Washington Press, 1982), 9.

3. Ezra Taft Benson, "Worthy Sons, Worthy Fathers," *Ensign,* November 1985, 36.

4. Glenn L. Pearson, *The Old Testament: A Mormon Perspective* (Salt Lake City: Bookcraft, 1980), 32.

5. Moshe Weinfeld, *Deuteronomy 1–11,* vol. 5 of the Anchor Bible series (New York: Doubleday, 1991), 333.

6. *The Interpreter's Dictionary of the Bible* (New York: Abingdon Press. 1962), 345, s.v. "Memorial"; emphasis added.

7. Yerushalmi, *Zakhor,* 11.

8. Peter C. Craigie, *The Book of Deuteronomy* (Grand Rapids, Mich.: Eerdmans, 1976), 40.

9. Yerushalmi, *Zakhor,* 9.

10. John W. Welch, "A Masterpiece: Alma 36," in *Rediscovering the Book of Mormon,* ed. John L. Sorenson and Melvin J. Thorne (Salt Lake City: Deseret Book, 1991), 114.

11. Nils Lohfink, as cited in Weinfeld, *Deuteronomy 1–11,* 5:397.

12. Richard Rust, "Typology in the Book of Mormon," in *Literature of Belief,* ed. Neal E. Lambert (Provo, Utah: Religious Studies Center, Brigham Young University, 1981), 234.

13. Jonathan Edwards, *The Works of President Edwards,* 1847; reprint edition 1968, 9:493; as cited in Lambert, *Literature of Belief,* 235.

14. Justin Martyr, "Dialogue with Trypho," *Ante-Nicene Fathers,* ed. Alexander Roberts, D.D. and James Donaldson, L.L.D. (Peabody, Mass.: Hendrickson Publishers, Inc, 1994), 1:244; see also Sibylline Oracles, 8:251–52, in James Charlesworth, *Old Testament Pseudepigrapha* (New York: Doubleday, 1983), 1:424; of further symbolic interest, with Moses as a symbol of the Lord as a Lamb on the mountain, Joshua, as captain of Israel's army down in the field, may be said to symbolize the Lord as a Lion (Hosea 10:11).

15. See also LDS edition of the King James Version of the Bible, Bible Dictionary, s.v. "Anointed One."

16. Spencer W. Kimball, *The Teachings of Spencer W. Kimball,* ed. Edward L. Kimball (Salt Lake City: Bookcraft, 1982), 112.

17. Bruce R. McConkie, *The Promised Messiah* (Salt Lake City: Deseret Book, 1978), 395–96.

18. *Eerdmans' Handbook to the Bible,* ed. David Alexander and Pat Alexander (Grand Rapids, Mich.: Eerdmans, 1973), 180.

19. Cited in Jacob Neusner, *The Way of Torah: An Introduction to Judaism* (Encino and Belmont, Calif.: Dickenson Publishing, 1974), 39; emphasis added.

20. King Benjamin in the Book of Mormon helps us gain this perspective when he declares that the Lord even lends us breath! (Mosiah 2:21).

21. Another significant historical feature of the Feast of Weeks, apparently added later by the rabbis, is that it marks the anniversary of the Lord's giving the law to Moses on Sinai (Exodus 19:1). "The Pharisaic Rabbis held that the Torah was revealed on Mount Sinai on that day, and celebrated it as the 'time of the giving of our Torah'" (Hayyim Schauss, as cited in Neusner, *Way of Torah,* 38). See also Michael Strassfeld, *The Jewish Holidays: A Guide and Commentary* (New York: Harper & Row, 1985), 69–71. Although Deuteronomy does not mention the Torah in connection with Shavuot, there is an interesting tie-in with the day of Pentecost as recorded in Acts 2:1–40. On that Feast of Weeks, symbols of Sinai's supreme theophany were given—the fiery tongues were reminiscent of the Lord's descent on the mount in flames (Exodus 19:18) and the sound of rushing waters represented the Lord's voice (Exodus 19:19; 20:22). Further, Peter exhorted the people to enter the covenant through baptism (Acts 2:37–39; Exodus 24:3), an act which would facilitate their partaking of the same promises God had given his ancient "peculiar people" (Exodus 19:5).

22. Bruce R. McConkie, *The Mortal Messiah: From Bethlehem to Calvary,* 4 vols. (Salt Lake City: Deseret Book, 1979–81), 1:171–72; emphasis added.

23. "In 1972, I mentioned to President and Sister Harold B. Lee (then on a visit to Jerusalem) that our April and October conferences corresponded with the timing of the ancient festivals of Passover and Tabernacles. Sister Lee noted that she recalled, as a little girl, that the Salt Lake Tabernacle was always decorated with tree branches during October Conference. I have been yet unable to confirm this from other sources" (John Tvedtnes, "King Benjamin and the Feast of Tabernacles," in *By Study and Also by Faith: Essays in Honor of Hugh W. Nibley* (Salt Lake City: Deseret Book and Foundation for Ancient Research and Mormon Studies, 1990), 2:230, n. 20.

24. See McConkie, *Mortal Messiah,* 174–75.

25. Neusner, *Way of Torah,* 40.

26. LDS Bible Dictionary, s.v. "Circumcision."

27. Neusner, *Way of Torah,* 41.

28. This may refer to the tendency of man to get confused over means

and ends. In other words, as is so often the case, the vehicle to the Savior can become the object of adoration and worship itself. For example, the brazen serpent became an object of worship by later Israel and had to be destroyed (2 Kings 18:4).

29. Yerushalmi, *Zakhor,* 10.

30. Craigie, *Book of Deuteronomy,* 372; emphasis added.

31. Craigie, *Book of Deuteronomy,* 374.

32. Hugh Nibley, *Temple and Cosmos* (Salt Lake City: Deseret Book and Foundation for Ancient Research and Mormon Studies, 1992), 541.

33. Nibley, *Temple and Cosmos,* 542.

34. Nibley, *Temple and Cosmos,* 541.

35. Ezra Taft Benson, "Beware of Pride," *Ensign,* May 1989, 6; emphasis added.

36. Neal A. Maxwell, "Shine as Lights in the World," *Ensign,* May 1983, 10.

37. For how the Book of Mormon carries on this Deuteronomic charge to remember, see Louis Midgley, "The Ways of Remembrance," in *Rediscovering the Book of Mormon* (Salt Lake City: Deseret Book and Foundation for Ancient Research and Mormon Studies, 1991), 168–76.

38. Gordon B. Hinckley, "An Humble and a Contrite Heart," *Ensign,* November 2000, 88.

39. Joseph Fielding Smith, *Answers to Gospel Questions,* comp. Joseph Fielding Smith Jr., 5 vols. (Salt Lake City: Deseret Book, 1957–66), 5:153–54.

40. Spencer W. Kimball, "Circles of Exaltation," *Charge to Religious Educators,* 2d ed. (Salt Lake City: The Church of Jesus Christ of Latter-day Saints, 1981), 12.

5

Deuteronomy as a Constitutional Covenant

Timothy W. Durkin

The book of Deuteronomy may rightly be regarded as ancient Israel's national constitution.[1] As the supreme law of the land, it guided the civic, social, and religious life of the nation for nearly seven centuries. During the regencies of Manasseh and his successors, however, faithless leaders rejected Deuteronomy's divine codes, preferring instead their own corrupt statutes and edicts. Without the protections guaranteed by covenant faithfulness, Israel grew weak and vulnerable to militaristic and opportunistic neighbors.[2] Israel's rejection of the covenant, however, did not render the fifth book of Moses' Pentateuch a dead letter. By weaving history, prophecy, and law together into a unique, superbly fashioned literary whole, Moses preserved divinely inspired constitutional principles in a document capable of lifting modern nations, families, and individuals.

An exploration of the constitutional dimensions of Moses' Deuteronomy requires that we focus specifically on three constitu-

---

Timothy W. Durkin teaches at the Tempe Arizona Institute of Religion.

tional themes. First, the book of Deuteronomy is a constitutional document. It represents a primary text advocating a divinely inspired, governance-by-covenant political structure. Second, Deuteronomy shows us the necessity of codifying history—which plays a significant role in shaping national, family, and individual identity—to preserve national and individual freedoms. Finally, the book of Deuteronomy is a constitutional prototype, relied upon by both historic and modern nation makers and legislators.

Deuteronomy as a Constitutional Document

Constitutions are written instruments containing the basic laws, rules, and principles of a political or social group. Constitutions may be single documents drafted in contemplation of founding a new nation,[3] or they may be derived over time from multiple sources, documents, and traditions.[4] National constitutions codify the supreme law of the land, providing the template against which all other laws and practices are to be measured. Constitutions may not be changed or altered without express provisions authorizing amendment. In addition, constitutions typically articulate a set of substantive doctrines. Several features in the book of Deuteronomy distinguish it as a constitutional document, allowing it to reflect the formal and substantive features requisite in a constitution.

Deuteronomy represents an organized effort by Moses to establish a new nation around a set of fundamental principles expressly recorded in a single, national document. "And what nation is there so great, that hath statutes and judgments so righteous as all this law, which I set before you this day?" (Deuteronomy 4:8). Shortly before Moses was translated, he gathered the children of Israel together to declare unto them the law, which included "testimonies," "statutes," and "judgments" (Deuteronomy 4:45). Deuteronomy evidences Moses' clear intent that the book's text function as Israel's national governing law. Moses drafted into the law multiple recordation and recitation provisions intended to assure the law's survival into perpetuity.

Moses was emphatic in his command that Israel preserve a written record of its national law. The law itself obligated each citizen to copy specified provisions onto parchments, which were to be read from morning and evening.[5] Israel's national leaders were given the further responsibility of transcribing a fresh, personal working copy of the law, from which they were to read, teach, and govern.

"And it shall be, when he sitteth upon the throne of his kingdom, that he shall write him a copy of this law in a book out of that which is before the priests the Levites" (Deuteronomy 17:18). The law also authorized the establishment of a national monument, on which the text of the law was inscribed: "Thou shalt set thee up great stones, and plaister them with plaister: And thou shalt write upon them all the words of this law, when thou art passed over, that thou mayest go in unto the land which the Lord thy God giveth thee, a land that floweth with milk and honey; as the Lord God of thy fathers hath promised thee" (Deuteronomy 27:2–3).[6]

In addition to these multiple recordation provisions, the law provided for public readings on specified national holidays. "When all Israel is come to appear before the Lord thy God in the place which he shall choose, thou shalt read this law before all Israel in their hearing. Gather the people together, men, and women, and children, and thy stranger that is within thy gates, that they may hear, and that they may learn, and fear the Lord your God, and observe to do all the words of this law" (Deuteronomy 31:11–12).

We may conclude from these recordation and reading provisions that the Lord intended the law to be an omnipresent reminder of Israel's religious, social, and legal duties. Indeed, the law of the Lord was no obscure statutory scheme buried in some arcane legal treatise to be discovered and comprehended only through painstakingly tedious research. Parents were expected to school their children daily in the rudiments of the law. "And thou shalt teach them diligently unto thy children, and shalt talk of them when thou sittest in thine house, and when thou walkest by the way, and when thou liest down, and when thou risest up" (Deuteronomy 6:7). The law thoroughly embraced every aspect of Israelite life. It was indeed the supreme law of the land, undergirding and overarching all society.

Deuteronomy's constitutionality is further evidenced by its

no-amendment provision. Unlike common legislative acts, which may be changed or rescinded at the whim of a legislative majority, one may not amend constitutional law without express authorization. Deuteronomy contains no such authorization. The only provision hinting at amendment is the one expressly forbidding it: "Ye shall not add unto the word which I command you, neither shall ye diminish ought from it, that ye may keep the commandments of the Lord your God which I command you" (Deuteronomy 4:2). As the unalterable supreme law of the land, Deuteronomy therefore trumps any and all other man-made law.

In addition to being a recorded instrument containing the basic rules and laws of society, the Deuteronomic covenant contains substantive doctrines that reveal its constitutional character. Of particular importance are the provisions identifying the seat of sovereignty. Distribution of governmental power is a typical function of national constitutions. The book of Deuteronomy vests executive, judicial, and legislative powers in one:

"I am the Lord thy God, which brought thee out of the land of Egypt, from the house of bondage. Thou shalt have none other gods before me. Thou shalt not make thee any graven image, or any likeness of any thing that is in heaven above, or that is in the earth beneath, or that is in the waters beneath the earth: Thou shalt not bow down thyself unto them, nor serve them: for I the Lord thy God am a jealous God, visiting the iniquity of the fathers upon the children unto the third and fourth generation of them that hate me" (Deuteronomy 5:6–9). The Decalogue unambiguously declares Jehovah king of Israel. Beside him, there is no other. His word alone represents the "supreme law of the land."[7] To the extent that Deuteronomy vests any powers at all in an earthly executive or tribune, it does so only in a ministerial fashion. Israel's earthly rulers are subject to the Lord and his word.

The substantive limitation of governmental power is another hallmark of national constitutions. In a passage that anticipates the future establishment of Israel's monarchy, Deuteronomy expressly curtails the powers of the king:

"When thou art come unto the land which the Lord thy God

giveth thee, and shalt possess it, and shalt dwell therein, and shalt say, I will set a king over me, like as all the nations that are about me; Thou shalt in any wise set him king over thee, whom the Lord thy God shall choose: one from among thy brethren shalt thou set king over thee: thou mayest not set a stranger over thee, which is not thy brother.

"But he shall not multiply horses to himself, nor cause the people to return to Egypt, to the end that he should multiply horses: forasmuch as the Lord hath said unto you, Ye shall henceforth return no more that way. Neither shall he multiply wives to himself, that his heart turn not away: neither shall he greatly multiply to himself silver and gold. And it shall be, when he sitteth upon the throne of his kingdom, that he shall write him a copy of this law in a book out of that which is before the priests the Levites:

"And it shall be with him, and he shall read therein all the days of his life: that he may learn to fear the Lord his God, to keep all the words of this law and these statutes, to do them: That his heart be not lifted up above his brethren, and that he turn not aside from the commandment, to the right hand, or to the left: to the end that he may prolong his days in his kingdom, he, and his children, in the midst of Israel" (Deuteronomy 17:14–20).

This striking passage illustrates the two philosophical principles at the heart of constitutionalism: limited government and the rule of law.[8] Limited government is necessary, constitutionalists argue, because a government left unchecked and uncontrolled will inevitably encroach upon liberty. The liberty contemplated in Deuteronomy is the freedom that comes from keeping one's covenant with the Lord. Israel's national freedom was secured through the covenant between the Lord and the nation. Because the national compact centered in Israel's leaders, the greatest threat to national liberty was an unrighteous king.[9] The law, therefore, sought to limit the king's powers.

Deuteronomy established a theocratic kingdom in which the king functioned merely as a representative of God, a minister to the people, a shepherd to the flock. The law, which vested all powers in the Lord, delegated to the king only those powers necessary to the carrying out and fulfilling of his duty as a shepherd. Deuteronomy 17:16 illustrates this limitation. The law expressly forbade a king's unauthorized use of the war power. "He shall not multiply horses to himself, nor cause the people to return to Egypt, to the end that he should multiply horses." This restriction reminded Israel that the Lord alone was sovereign, and he alone could prosecute war. The law contained detailed provisions on the discharge of war.[10] In all cases, the law reminded Israel that "the Lord thy God is with thee" and that "the Lord your God is he that goeth with you, to fight for you against your enemies, to save you" (Deuteronomy 20:1, 4). History affirms the fact that as the institution of the monarchy grew, Israel's kings repeatedly ignored this constitutional limitation on a king's prerogative.[11]

The book of Deuteronomy further limits the powers of the king by forbidding the twin practices of marrying multiple wives and taxing the population. "Neither shall he multiply wives to himself, that his heart turn not away: neither shall he greatly multiply to himself silver and gold" (Deuteronomy 17:17). To secure international alliances, kings of the ancient Near East commonly married multiple wives. They also taxed the population to support a bloated administrative bureaucracy. The law expressly forbade Israel's king to engage in these practices. These restrictions had the practical effect of limiting the scope of the king's international and domestic powers. The constitutional structure given to Israel by revelation from God through Moses clearly envisioned an omnipotent, heavenly monarch whose work and word was administered by a limited earthly executive. It is difficult to envision a king who did not understand this constitutional scheme, particularly in light of the requirement that each king transcribe and read from a personal copy of the constitution daily. The blatant defiance of Israel's monarchs in the face of constitutional law justifies Moses' prophecy that foreign nations would enslave Israel (Deuteronomy 28:64; 29:24–28).

A second fundamental doctrine of constitutionalism is the rule of law, which is represented throughout the book of Deuteronomy. The rule of law contemplates the principle that nobody, not even the king, is above the law. A society built upon the rule of law recognizes a hierarchical relationship among the law, the governor, and the governed. The rule of law presupposes the governor and the governed to be on equal footing, each subject to the higher authority of the law. The rule of law protects the individual from the often unrighteous dominion of an appointed official.[12] Recognition of the higher authority of the law serves to secure and maximize individual and national liberty. The book of Deuteronomy beautifully expresses this principle by not only defining and limiting the powers of the king but also by ratifying the judicial system previously introduced by Moses while the children of Israel journeyed in the wilderness:

"And I charged your judges at that time, saying, Hear the causes between your brethren, and judge righteously between every man and his brother, and the stranger that is with him. Ye shall not respect persons in judgment; but ye shall hear the small as well as the great; ye shall not be afraid of the face of man; for the judgment is God's: and the cause that is too hard for you, bring it unto me, and I will hear it" (Deuteronomy 1:16–17).

This passage legally bound Israel to principles of equity and justice under the law. The scope of Deuteronomy's constitutional protections reached both the common citizen and the foreigner. With its myriad social duties and restrictions, the covenant protected the poor, the homeless, and the widow, assuring a peaceful, civil society.

"For the poor shall never cease out of the land: therefore I command thee, saying, Thou shalt open thine hand wide unto thy brother, to thy poor, and to thy needy" (Deuteronomy 15:11). Also: "Cursed be he that perverteth the judgment of the stranger, fatherless, and widow" (Deuteronomy 27:19). Of Deuteronomy's legal codes, Hugh Nibley reminds us that "what we are warned against more than anything else is taking advantage of those who are disadvantaged—the stranger, the orphan. . . . A list of things is given for which people are told they will be cursed. Of the nine specific crimes, all but one—the worship of graven images—are in the nature of taking advantage of weaker parties."[13]

In addition to defining the scope of government and constitutionally memorializing the rule of law, the book of Deuteronomy enshrines human rights, showing them in their proper and superior relation to property rights. At every level human rights are dignified, as illustrated by the codes specifying rights, duties, and obligations of masters and servants. Though slavery was permitted, it was tightly regulated. Domestic slaves were to be liberated every six years, whereupon their masters were to liberally provide them from their flocks, fields, and vineyards (Deuteronomy 15:13–14).

Fugitive slaves found plenary protection under Israel's constitution. If an Israelite found a runaway slave, he was expected to provide shelter and sustenance. A foreign slave was never to be extradited to his foreign master (Deuteronomy 23:15). Deuteronomy's property laws uniformly preserved the dignity and sanctity of human life. Even animal life found protection under Israel's constitution (Deuteronomy 25:4).

The book of Deuteronomy contains another substantive constitutional doctrine. The covenant manifesto expressed in Deuteronomy memorialized Israel's land conquests, legalizing the acquisition of property from those possessory nations that had no legal title, right, or claim. The Deuteronomic covenant enabled Israel to establish a nation on foreign soil free of the taint of lawless revolution. Not unlike the American revolution, which was justified by natural law and legally memorialized in the Declaration of Independence and the United States Constitution, the Lord's covenant with Israel legally authorized the acquisition of land on both sides of the Jordan River: "And because he loved thy fathers, therefore he chose their seed after them, and brought thee out in his sight with his mighty power out of Egypt; to drive out nations from before thee greater and mightier than thou art, to bring thee in, to give thee their land for an inheritance, as it is this day" (Deuteronomy 4:37–38).

Deuteronomy renewed and ratified the land covenant made between the Lord and Abraham.[14] Those nations that took possession of the covenant land of Abraham after Jacob's family left Palestine to find sustenance in Egypt did not have legal title to those lands. Because the supreme law of Jehovah made no provision to pass title to foreign nations via the law of adverse possession,[15] the children of Israel retained legal right and claim to their Canaanite lands of inheritance. The law of Deuteronomy posted on Mount Ebal by Joshua served notice to all the world that the King of Heaven had conveyed legal title and possessory right to his covenant people.

History and the Preservation of Freedom

"Remember the days of old, consider the years of many generations: ask thy father, and he will shew thee; thy elders, and they will tell thee" (Deuteronomy 32:7). Few principles bear as heavily on the preservation of individual and national freedom as does the role of history remembered. Lord Bolingbroke correctly understood the relationship between studying history and national and personal righteousness: "The true and proper object of [history] is a constant improvement in private and in public virtue. . . . The study of history seems to me, of all other, the most proper to train us up to private and public virtue."[16]

Prophets of the Lord have emphasized since the dawn of creation the relationship between personal righteousness and history remembered.[17] Latter-day prophets have taught this relationship with unmatched precision and clarity. Elder Spencer W. Kimball declared: "When you look in the dictionary for the most important word, do you know what it is. It could be 'remember.' Because all of you have made covenants—you know what to do and you know how to do it—our greatest need is to remember. . . . 'Remember' is the word. 'Remember' is the program."[18] Similarly, Elder Neal A. Maxwell urged the rising generation of the Church to "develop a keener sense of history and of [our] unique place in it. This sense of history can deepen [our] humility and persuade [us] to use [our] full capability as well as deepen [our] thirst for further spiritual knowledge."[19]

No other single book of scripture emphasizes the charge to remember as thoroughly and continuously as does Deuteronomy. The Deuteronomic covenant contains fourteen express provisions charging Israel with the duty to remember.[20] In addition to these provisions, the law provided the children of Israel with additional opportunities to remember their covenants through Sabbath worship, seasonal festivals, and sabbatical years. Moses skillfully wove a history of Israel's bondage in Egypt into the fabric of his constitutional document. Thus, each time the children of Israel commemorated their freedom, they recited a bondage narrative. Moses masterfully drafted Deuteronomy to demonstrate how closely freedom lay to bondage. Israel's freedom at the time was hemmed in on either side: The past was represented by bondage in Egypt while the future held the conditional certainty of bondage to "a nation whose tongue thou shalt not understand; a nation of fierce countenance, which shall not regard the person of the old, nor shew favour to the young" (Deuteronomy 28:49–50). The book of Deuteronomy powerfully portrays the fragility of freedom while simultaneously teaching the manner in which it may be preserved.

Moses' experience with the children of Israel and his attempts to establish a nation upon divine principles of law may serve as a reminder for modern nations. The book of Deuteronomy is a witness to the reality that a nation expecting to win favor and protection from the Lord must strictly adhere to those laws and principles designed to secure freedom. For ancient Israelites, covenant fidelity and a profound awareness of where they had come from secured their freedom. For modern Americans, freedom lies in virtuous living and fidelity to "that law of the land which is constitutional, supporting that principle of freedom in maintaining rights and privileges, [which] belongs to all mankind, and is justifiable before me" (D&C 98:5). Freedom, therefore, is only as strong as one's commitment to remembering the history that gave birth to that freedom. Like Israel of old, contemporary historical consciousness is waning, as the following accounts illustrate:

A federal district judge recently ruled that displays of certain historical documents posted in public buildings in Kentucky had to be removed because they violated the First Amendment. The objectionable documents included an excerpt from the Declaration of Independence, which reads, "All men . . . are endowed by their Creator with certain unalienable Rights," as well as the national motto ("In God We Trust"), the Ten Commandments, President

Abraham Lincoln's proclamation designating April 30, 1863, a "National Day of Prayer," and the Mayflower Compact, which preserves the colony's explanation that its journey was "for the glory of God and the advancement of the Christian faith."[21]

The results of a study conducted at the University of Connecticut further illustrate a patent disregard for American history. Researchers administered a "rather elementary" history test to seniors at the nation's top-ranked colleges and universities, including Harvard and Princeton. The test's thirty-four questions asked students to identify prominent persons and events associated with American history. Nearly eighty percent of those surveyed received either a D or an F grade. The study concluded that the reason for "this dismal showing" was that the students had not been taught. "These students are allowed to graduate as if they didn't know the past existed," one researcher lamented.[22]

This is precisely the condition Moses sought to prevent in Deuteronomy. Wisely, he drafted into his nation's constitution the specific provisions designed to prevent this tragedy. Reading, writing, teaching, and singing history were civil and religious obligations designed to facilitate memory. Sadly, after rejecting the constitution, Israel forgot the Lord, inviting the return of bondage to that "nation against thee from far" (Deuteronomy 28:49). Modern nations, families, and individuals may escape a tragic loss of freedom by applying Deuteronomy's simple yet profound charge to remember!

Deuteronomy's Modern Influence

In addition to functioning as ancient Israel's national constitution, Deuteronomy extends its influence to modern lawmakers and nation builders. One can see and feel the influence of Deuteronomy in their writings and activities. The corpus of contemporary criminal law comes largely from the Ten Commandments. Modern civil and tort law borrows heavily from Deuteronomy's emphasis on personal responsibility.[23] In addition, Deuteronomy also provided the covenant structure that served as a prototype for colonists who came to America seeking to establish new communities. The Christian lawmakers in these burgeoning communities readily identified with the children of Israel. They saw themselves as modern Israel, not just in a typographical sense but also in a literal sense.

America's early Christian colonists well understood what A. Hulst meant in his recent book on covenant Israel. Regarding the meaning of the name "Israel" in Deuteronomy, Hulst wrote: "Its concern is not with a conglomerate of different tribes and groups, not with a sum total of individuals, not—and this must be stressed—with a people as an ethnic entity beside other peoples, but rather with the 'assembly,' the religious community which finds its unity in the word and law of Yahweh, and thereby ultimately in Yahweh Himself.

"The name 'Israel' in Deuteronomy signifies, therefore, the people in their relation to Yahweh. In focus is not the people in their national aspect, not first of all as an ethnic group, but the people as a religious unit. It pertains to the purity of life."[24]

The Pilgrims and Puritans who came to Massachusetts seeking to establish a "Holy Commonwealth" identified with the people of Israel precisely because they were seeking to establish a holy community that emphasized this "purity of life." They saw the covenant manifesto in Deuteronomy as the key to social, civic, and religious life. The *Critical Bibliography of Religion in America* states:

"The covenant is the clue to the New England Puritan understanding of . . . the order of the church and society—the 'Holy Commonwealth.' . . . To the Puritan, God had always dealt with his children by covenant. . . . It was not only individual, between each man and God; it was also public, respecting the formation of Churches and of civil government. . . . [T]he state was established upon a covenant, like the Mayflower Compact of 1620. The Puritan theology therefore considered economic, political, and social affairs in a corporate sense, and the Church assumed responsibility for society because the Puritans considered both church and state as under covenant."[25]

It is not surprising that the early colonists saw the covenant as "the Lord's chosen method for social and religious combination."[26] The Bible was the single most influential source for the founders of the American Constitution, and among biblical texts, Deuteronomy was the most frequently cited.[27] A famous declaration by the Reverend Thomas Hooker demonstrates Deuteronomy's profound influence on American civil history. In the spring of 1638, three Connecticut towns held a general council meeting to choose representatives. During the opening session, Reverend Hooker preached a powerful sermon on the foundations of human authority, quoting liberally from Deuteronomy 1:13. He declared the foundation of authority to be in the free consent of the people. Eight months later Hooker's Deuteronomic thesis found its way into Connecticut's "Fundamental Orders," thought to be the first written constitution creating government.[28]

The Founding Fathers were not the only ones who found inspiration and direction in the book of Deuteronomy. Countless others have been blessed by applying its teachings. The book of Deuteronomy is not only a profound political document but also a personal manifesto on the preservation of individual righteousness and freedom. Individuals are inspired by the charge to remember their covenants and personal experiences with the Lord. Families are blessed by Deuteronomy's charge to teach the gospel "when thou sittest in thine house, and when thou walkest by the way, and when thou liest down, and when thou risest up" (Deuteronomy 6:7).

The book of Deuteronomy is, above all, a reminder of the Lord's goodness, mercy, and willingness to bless his children. Like Josiah of old,[29] we must rediscover the "words of the book of the law" and allow them to guide our personal reformations.

Notes

1. Modern Israel has no written national constitution, although its basic laws derive in part from Deuteronomy and other biblical sources.

2. Ironically, Israel's subjugation to other nations fulfilled the very prophecies Israel had rejected. See Deuteronomy 28:64; 29:24–28.

3. The Constitution of the United States of America represents this type.

4. The English constitution illustrates the point. It derives from Magna Carta (1215), the Declaration of Rights (1689), and English culture and

tradition. Magna Carta, composed by England's powerful barons and forced upon a recalcitrant King John, was originally drafted to protect the feudal rights of the English aristocracy. It took years for it to take on constitutional significance. It ultimately came to be recognized as "the fountain of all the fundamental Laws of the Realm." Sir Edward Coke, quoted in Michael Les Benedict, *Sources in American Constitutional History* (Lexington, Mass.: D. C. Heath and Company, 1996), 1.

5. In traditional Jewish practice, the transcribed portion of the law consisted of Deuteronomy 6:4–9; 11:13–21; and Numbers 15:37–41. These passages were called, collectively, the Shema, which may be translated as "Hear you" from the Hebrew. These passages were placed in phylacteries (attached to the inside of the arm and the forehead) and mezuza (attached to the doorposts of the house).

6. Joshua fulfilled this legal duty by erecting a stone altar on Mount Ebal, on which he inscribed all the words of the law.

7. United States Constitution, Article VI.

8. "The object of constitutionalism is, after all, to control or to limit governmental power." David N. Mayer, "The English Radical Whig Origins of American Constitutionalism," *Washington University Law Quarterly*, 1992, 138.

9. See Mosiah 29:21–24.

10. See Deuteronomy 20; 21:10–14.

11. Isaiah 31:1; Ezekiel 17:15.

12. See Doctrine and Covenants 121:39.

13. Hugh Nibley, *Approaching Zion* (Salt Lake City: Deseret Book and Foundation for Ancient Research and Mormon Studies, 1989), 193–94.

14. See Genesis 13:15–17; 17:8; 26:3.

15. Adverse possession is a law of property granting legal title to a party who openly and adversely possesses the land of another for a statutory period of time.

16. Lord Bolingbroke, *Letters on the Study and Use of History* (1735) in David N. Mayer, *English Legal and Constitutional History* (Columbus, Ohio: Capital University Law School, 1992), 8.

17. Adam kept a book of remembrance that his children might know the source of their freedom. See Moses 6:5–6.

18. Spencer W. Kimball, *Circles of Exaltation,* Brigham Young University Devotional Address, Provo, Utah, 28 June 1968.

19. Neal A. Maxwell, "Those Seedling Saints Who Sit Before You," in *Supplement to the Seventh Annual Church Educational System Symposium on the Old Testament* (Salt Lake City: The Church of Jesus Christ of Latter-day Saints, 1984), 2.

20. See Deuteronomy 5:15; 7:18; 8:2, 18; 9:7, 27; 15:15; 16:3, 12; 24:9, 18, 22; 25:17; 32:7.

21. Joseph Gerth, "Judge Orders Commandments Off Walls in Kentucky," *Louisville, Kentucky, Courier-Journal,* 7 May 2000, 3B, as cited in James C. Dobson, *Focus on the Family,* September 2000, 1.

22. Caren Benjamin, "College Seniors Flunk History Test," *Chicago Sun Times,* 28 June 2000, A3, as cited in Dobson, *Focus on the Family,* September 2000, 4.

23. See Deuteronomy 22:8, which required the homebuilder to take personal responsibility for the safety of his guests.

24. A. Hulst, as cited in Hans K. LaRondelle, *The Israel of God in Prophecy: Principles of Prophetic Interpretation* (Berrien Springs, Mich.: Andrews University Press, 1983), 84.

25. Nelson R. Burry, James Ward Smith, and A. Leland Jamison as cited in Lynn D. Wardle, "The Constitution as Covenant," *BYU Studies* 27, no. 3 (1987): 14.

26. Ibid.

27. A published study found the top six sources of the Founders' learning to be as follows: Bible, 34 percent; Montesquieu, 8.3 percent; Blackstone, 8 percent; Locke, 3 percent; Hume, 2.9 percent; classical thinkers combined, 9 percent. Donald Lutz, as cited in Byron Merrill, "Government by the Voice of the People: A Witness and a Warning" in *The Book of Mormon: Mosiah, Salvation Only through Christ,* ed. Monte S. Nyman and Charles D. Tate, Jr. (Provo, Utah: Brigham Young University, Religious Studies Center, 1991), 127.

28. Ibid.

29. 2 Kings 22:11; see also 22:10–20.

6

Believing in the Atoning Power of Christ

Kerry Muhlestein

THE BOOK OF DEUTERONOMY BEGINS with a striking verse: "(There are eleven days' journey from Horeb by the way of mount Seir unto Kadesh-barnea)" (Deuteronomy 1:2). Because this verse is set within parentheses and seems to relay minutia, it is easily passed over. But a close examination shows it to be one of the most thought-provoking verses in the Old Testament. Identifying two of the sites referred to in the verse makes this clear. "Horeb" is another name for Mount Sinai. "Kadesh-barnea" is the place where Moses and the children of Israel camped as they sent men into the promised land as spies. Kadesh-barnea was on the border of the promised land; from there the children of Israel were supposed to enter and inherit the land.

In other words, it eventually took the children of Israel forty years to accomplish what they could have done in eleven days. It is striking to contemplate how much easier and shorter their sojourn in the wilderness would have been had they done things according

Kerry Muhlestein is a Ph.D. candidate in Egyptology at UCLA.

to the Lord's program. As this verse relates to the personal lives of Latter-day Saints, it becomes even more profound. The full import of Israel's meandering journey comes when we realize that it serves as a typological microcosm of our mortal existence. "Israel's experiences in the wilderness are both literal and allegorical of our own experiences."[1]

In Egypt the children of Israel were in bondage, symbolic of our bondage to sin. They left Israel via a baptismlike experience in the Red Sea. It was then that they undertook their wanderings in the wilderness. The scriptures often liken the wilderness to our mortal probation (1 Nephi 8:4).[2] Not long after entering the wilderness, the Israelites were able to have a temple-tabernacle and covenant-making experience at Sinai. They then continued on with their wilderness wanderings for some time. Eventually they were brought to the River Jordan (symbolic of the veil) and crossed it, entering the promised land (symbolic of the true promised land, or the celestial kingdom). Seeing ourselves in the journey of the children of Israel should cause us to ask, "In what things am I taking forty years to accomplish an eleven-day task?"

Since the symbolic microcosm of the scriptures causes us to ask the question, we should likewise expect to discover the answer in the scriptures. Most of us find ourselves somewhere between Sinai (having made temple covenants) and the River Jordan (entering the true promised land). Thus, we should turn to this part of our scriptural story to better understand what delayed the Israelites in their journey. In turn, this will help us identify the delays of our own mortal journey.

While the Israelites had a host of problems during their wilderness wanderings, such as difficulty in following the prophet, two incidents seem to have been the deciding factors in the Lord's determining that Israel would wait forty years before entering the promised land. The common and crucial element behind both these incidents was Israel's lack of faith in the delivering power of Jehovah.

The first incident happened at Mount Sinai. The children of Israel had been promised a marvelous opportunity. They were commanded to prepare themselves, "for the third day the Lord will come down in the sight of all the people upon mount Sinai" (Exodus 19:11). As preparation for this event, Israel undertook three days of sanctification. On the third day, the mount was filled with thunderings, lightnings, a thick cloud, and the sound of trumpets. Then Moses "brought forth the people out of the camp to meet with God" (Exodus 19:17). At this point the mount was filled with more smoke and light. It quaked, and the people heard the voice of the Lord (Exodus 19:18–19).

It was then that Moses ascended the Mount and received the Ten Commandments. We learn from Deuteronomy that "these words [the Ten Commandments] the Lord spake unto all your assembly in the mount out of the midst of the fire, of the cloud, and of the thick darkness, with a great voice" (Deuteronomy 5:22). In other words, every member of the house of Israel heard the Lord pronounce the Ten Commandments.

Apparently the experience was too overwhelming. Though Jehovah had more in store for them, the Israelites sent their leaders to Moses. "And it came to pass, when ye heard the voice out of the midst of the darkness, (for the mountain did burn with fire,) that ye came near unto me, even all the heads of your tribes, and your elders; and ye said, Behold, the Lord our God hath shewed us his glory and his greatness, and we have heard his voice out of the midst of the fire: we have seen this day that God doth talk with man, and he liveth.

"Now therefore why should we die? for this great fire will consume us: if we hear the voice of the Lord our God any more, then we shall die. For who is there of all flesh, that hath heard the voice of the living God speaking out of the midst of the fire, as we have, and lived?

"Go thou near, and hear all that the Lord our God shall say: and speak thou unto us all that the Lord our God shall speak unto thee; and we will hear it, and do it" (Deuteronomy 5:23–27). Even though Moses told them to "fear not" (Exodus 20:20), "the people stood afar off, and Moses drew near unto the thick darkness where God was" (Exodus 20:21).

This is truly astonishing. The children of Israel had heard the voice of the Lord and were afraid they would die if they heard more. By then they had seen evidence of his delivering power time and again. They had witnessed the plagues in Egypt, especially the slaying of the firstborn, from which they had been saved. They had seen Jehovah's deliverance when the armies of Pharaoh were ready to crush them. They had nearly starved, and the Lord had sent quail and then manna. They had been thirsty, and the Lord delivered with water gushing from a rock. They had been saved from destruction by the Amalekites.

Despite all this they refused the presence of the Lord. In short, they did not believe he had power to bring them safely into his own consuming presence. Even after hearing his voice, they were afraid that if they heard it more the Lord would not be able to keep them from being consumed and dying. Moses' words "fear not" should have served as a forceful reminder of God's delivering power, for those were the same words he had spoken at the Red Sea (Exodus 14:13). Yet even this did not bolster the people's faith, and they went "afar off."

Joseph Smith taught that this was the great downfall of Israel. "When God offers a blessing or knowledge to a man and he refuses to receive it, he will be damned. [Such is] the case of the Israelites praying that God would speak to Moses and not to them, in consequence of which he cursed them with a carnal law."[3] And so, the Israelites were left with the lower law because they did not believe the Lord had power to bring them to "meet with God" and live.

The problem became compounded and clarified sometime later, when the children of Israel were at Kadesh-barnea. They had finally arrived at the borders of the promised land. The Lord had promised that he would bring them into this land and cause them to inherit it. Moses poignantly reminded them of this upon their arrival at the oasis: "Ye are come unto the mountain of the Amorites, which the Lord our God doth give unto us. Behold, the Lord thy God hath set the land before thee: go up and possess it, as the Lord God of thy fathers hath said unto thee; fear not, neither be discouraged" (Deuteronomy 1:20–21). Again Moses used the same words pronounced in the dramatic deliverance at the Red Sea: "Fear not." But again the faith of the children of Israel faltered.

At this time they and the Lord agreed to send twelve spies, one from each of the tribes, to perform a reconnaissance mission (Deuteronomy 1:22; Numbers 13:1–2). The result of this action is well known. All of the spies reported that the land was full of wonderful produce and was extremely fertile. But only Joshua and Caleb felt that the Israelites should go forth and take the land. The other spies were full of dread because of the military strength of the people they saw.

Years later Moses reported that the people "would not go up, but rebelled against the commandment of the Lord your God: and ye murmured in your tents, and said, Because the Lord hated us, he hath brought us forth out of the land of Egypt, to deliver us into the hand of the Amorites, to destroy us. Whither shall we go up? our brethren have discouraged our heart, saying, The people is greater and taller than we; the cities are great and walled up to heaven; and moreover we have seen the sons of the Anakims [giants] there" (Deuteronomy 1:26–28).

Simply put, the people did not believe that Jehovah could deliver them from their enemies and bring them safely into the promised land. Though they had seen the Lord defeat and destroy one of the mightiest armies on earth—the Egyptians must have made the Amorites look weak by comparison—they were afraid he could not bring them into his rest in the promised land. Again Moses tried to reassure them by using language similar to what he had used at the Red Sea. There he had proclaimed, "Fear ye not" and "the Lord shall fight for you" (Exodus 14:13–14). Here he exhorted Israel to "dread not, neither be afraid of them. The Lord your God which goeth before you, he shall fight for you, according to all that he did for you in Egypt before your eyes" (Deuteronomy 1:29–30).

Furthermore, he reminded them of the things the Lord had done for them in the wilderness: "And in the wilderness, where thou hast seen how that the Lord thy God bare thee, as a man doth bear his son, in all the way that ye went, until ye came into this place"

(Deuteronomy 1:31). Even with all of this, Israel refused to go, and in the end Moses was forced to lament that "yet in this thing ye did not believe the Lord your God" (Deuteronomy 1:32). The Lord asked Moses, "How long will this people provoke me? and how long will it be ere they believe me, for all the signs which I have shewed among them?" (Numbers 14:11).

It is clear that in the eyes of Moses and God the core problem in Kadesh-barnea was that the children of Israel did not believe the Lord when he said he would bring them into the promised land. As a result, the Lord swore that no one from that generation would enter the promised land (Deuteronomy 1:35). Hence, because of their refusal and inability to believe that the Lord could deliver them, the Israelites waited forty years before receiving their inheritance.

In our introspection, we must ask ourselves how this symbol parallels our lives. If this is the greatest problem that beset Israel, then the typological journey indicates that it is likely to be the greatest problem facing each of us on our own journeys toward the true promised land, the celestial kingdom.

Let us examine a few symbolic elements of the story to better understand the scriptural significance on an individual level. The objectives at Sinai and at Kadesh-barnea symbolize the same thing: our ultimate objective, which is entering the presence of the Lord and receiving exaltation in the celestial kingdom.

If latter-day Israel is indeed like ancient Israel, then it stands to reason that many Latter-day Saints are struggling with accepting the true redeeming powers of the Atonement. They may very well understand that Christ suffered for us all and made it possible for us to repent. But at the same time, they do not feel that they can be exalted. They simply lack faith in the atoning power of Christ. Stephen Robinson summed up this lack of faith while speaking of Christ's ability to make us clean:

"Unfortunately, there are many members of the Church who simply do not believe this. Though they claim to have testimonies of Christ and of his gospel, they reject the witness of the scriptures and of the prophets about the good news of Christ's atonement.

Often these people naively hold on to mutually contradictory propositions without even realizing the nature of the contradiction. For example, they may believe that the Church is true, that Jesus is the Christ, and that Joseph Smith was a prophet of God, while at the same time refusing to accept the possibility of their own complete forgiveness and eventual exaltation in the kingdom of God. They believe *in* Christ, but they do not *believe* Christ."[4]

It seems that many of us believe strongly in many things about the gospel while struggling with its very core: Christ can deliver us and bring us into his promised land. Some may believe that he can and will save others but not themselves. They may believe that somehow whatever they have done has put them beyond reach of the delivering powers of the Atonement.

This proposition was strengthened recently by a survey in my own stake in southern California. The survey was filled out in Priesthood and Relief Society meetings, which means that only fairly faithful and active members of the Church participated in it. One question asked those filling out the survey if they felt they could be exalted. Surprisingly, some answered no. Obviously, these people did not believe Christ could deliver them and bring them into the promised land.

In the scriptural story, the Israelites had seen the delivering power of Jehovah many times before they refused to enter the promised land. Undoubtedly, we too have many times felt the redeeming and delivering power of Christ's atonement. All of us who have been truly baptized, or born again, have felt the deliverance of Christ. All of us who have repented and felt forgiveness have experienced the delivering power of Christ. Truly, deliverance from one sin is an ample demonstration of the Lord's delivering power. The cleansing we have felt in our lives is much like the Israelites' being delivered from the Egyptians. Since we have been forgiven in the past, why could not the Lord deliver us again from all our sins and bring us into the celestial kingdom? Why, after having defeated the Egyptian army, could not the Lord defeat the Amorites and Anakim in the promised land? The answer, of course, is that he could.

To be sure, we must proceed according to the plan of the Lord. After rebuking the children of Israel, he forbade them from entering the promised land. They decided to enter anyway and were soundly defeated. When the next generation, with the Lord's blessing, entered the promised land, they were only delivered insofar as they followed his instructions. The point is that they *were* delivered; deliverance was well within the Lord's power.

We must also ask, what are the symbols behind the Israelites' fears? At Sinai they feared that coming before the Lord in an unworthy state would prove their destruction. This is a reasonable fear, since no unclean thing can survive the presence of the Lord (1 Nephi 15:34). Being unclean leads mankind to the twin monsters of death and hell (2 Nephi 9:10, 19; Alma 5:7–10). The Amorites and the Anakim of the promised land are perfect symbols for death and hell. The children of Israel, on their own, could not have overcome them, which would have prevented them from inheriting the promised land. Death and hell are to us what the Amorites and Anakim were to ancient Israel. No matter what we do or how hard we try, we will never overcome these obstacles on our own. We must rely upon the Lord to deliver us from them.

While it was true that the Israelites could not have withstood the presence of the Lord without his help, it was perfectly clear that the Lord could safely bring them before him, as he had done with Moses. And while the Israelites could not conquer the Amorites and Anakim without the Lord, it was abundantly clear that they could conquer them with his help. They had ample evidence of this. But they still refused to believe. For latter-day Israel, the important thing is that the atoning powers of Christ can overcome our uncleanness and conquer death and hell. Our choice, like ancient Israel's, is whether we will believe in the Lord's delivering power. Will we "fear not," or will we give in to our doubts about our future? Will we see only the Amorites (our own weaknesses)? Or will we remember how our shortcomings pale in comparison to Christ's atoning power?

Fortunately, the biblical story does not end at Kadesh-barnea. The Lord eventually brought Israel into the promised land. If latter-day Israel wants to overcome its lack of belief, the blueprint for doing so is found in the biblical story.

For ancient Israel, Kadesh-barnea could not be the end. The people had entered into a covenant with the Lord, and as a part of that covenant they would inherit the promised land. They would first have to be stripped of all unbelievers, however, for the Lord had promised that none of the unbelieving generation would be allowed to enter the promised land, with the exception of undoubting Caleb and Joshua. Furthermore, the upcoming generation would have to be filled with faith. Thus, the children of Israel were forced to remain in the wilderness, a place where they would have no chance of survival except through dependence on the Lord. This experience would create a generation that was raised in complete reliance on the Lord. S. Kent Brown writes of this:

"Part of the Lord's program for the Israelites was to force them to come to trust and rely upon him for all of their needs. . . . The point of the growing lesson was that the Lord could be trusted and, indeed, had to be trusted. In effect, he left the Israelites without any resource upon which to call except himself. It is my own view that the Israelites had to be brought to this state of mind and heart to become fully free. Without being able to trust in the Egyptians and now having only the Lord to rely upon, whether in Egypt or in the desert, the Israelites had to bring themselves to trust God more than man."[5]

This process—creating a generation of believers that relied so much on the Lord that they had sufficient faith to enter the promised land—took Israel forty years. But because of the covenantal love[6] of the Lord, which is one of the main themes of Deuteronomy, the Lord did not give up on Israel. Though the people did not have enough faith to enter the promised land after eleven days, the Lord worked with them and purged them in the wilderness until they were faithful enough to receive their inheritance and fulfill their part of the covenant.

Our covenantal relationship with the Lord is similar to that of ancient Israel. Indeed, has not the Lord's prophet told us that "God will have a humble people. Either we can choose to be humble or we can be compelled to be humble."[7] As members of the covenant, each of us will face the wilderness and probationary experiences we need in mortality to develop true faith in the atoning power of Christ. Just as ancient Israel had to be stripped of all her unbelievers, we have to strip ourselves of all unbelief. If we choose to do this, the Lord will be able to deliver us. Part of the Lord's covenant with the ancient Israelites was that they would inherit the promised land. Likewise, part of his covenant with us as members of modern Israel is that we will receive the inheritance of eternal life.[8]

It is difficult to believe that we will inherit all that the Father has. But continued reliance on his Son will help us see with an eye of faith that he has the ability to bring us to this inheritance. Just as he delivered Israel from bondage, Egyptian armies, starvation and Amorites, he can deliver us from sin, the forces of Satan, and even our own fallen natures. He has the power to justify and sanctify us. His atonement can change our natures and make us Christlike creatures. It is difficult to imagine ourselves thus, so it is hard to believe in this power. But to paraphrase one of Christ's questions, is it easier to deliver a nation or save a soul? Just as Israel entered the promised land, we can inherit the celestial kingdom and exaltation.

Additionally, asking the Lord for an increase in faith is helpful. This is amply demonstrated by the powerful supplication put to Christ: "Lord, I believe; help thou mine unbelief" (Mark 9:24). The Lord himself will help us lose our unbelief.

After the Israelites had purged themselves of unbelievers and had developed sufficient faith, the Lord showed unto them yet again his delivering power. Under the leadership of Joshua, a faithful generation, one which fully believed that the Lord could deliver them, came again to the borders of the promised land. This time the people arrived not at Kadesh-barnea but at the River Jordan.

As they prepared to cross over this division separating them from the promised land—highly symbolic of the veil—the Lord gave them explicit instructions. It was only by demonstrating both faith and obedience that they entered into the land of their inheritance.

As their fathers had done at Sinai, the children of Israel spent the day sanctifying themselves. They gathered their tents and belongings and arranged themselves behind the priests who bore the ark of the covenant. Again we are presented with an important symbol. The lid of the ark of the covenant was also called the "mercy seat," or "seat of atonement." There was no more poignant symbol of Christ and his delivering power than the ark of the covenant. Only by following this symbol could Israel enter the promised land.

Upon Joshua's command, the priests who carried the ark picked it up and marched toward the River Jordan. The people followed. They had been promised that they would reach the other side, but they first had to demonstrate their faith. They marched up to and then into the river. It was not until the feet of the priests bearing the ark were in the waters of the river that the Lord exerted his delivering powers and parted the water.

"And the priests that bare the ark of the covenant of the Lord stood firm on dry ground in the midst of Jordan, and all the Israelites passed over on dry ground, until all the people were passed clean over Jordan" (Joshua 3:17). After this demonstration of faith, following squarely behind the seat of atonement and trusting fully in the delivering power of him whom it symbolized, Israel entered into its land of inheritance. So it is with us. As we demonstrate faith in Christ's delivering power, even to the point of getting our feet wet, the Lord will part the waters—and the veil—and bring about our redemption.

We see in Israel's typological journey the pattern we must follow to inherit our promised land. Whether eleven days or forty years lie ahead of us, we must follow the Lord's instructions. The lesson we learn so well from the Israelites is that we must exercise faith in the delivering power of our Lord and Savior. If we do so, there is no doubt that he will bring us into the celestial kingdom, where we will enter into his rest and dwell with him. Thus, he has covenanted, and God cannot lie.

NOTES

1. M. Catherine Thomas, "The Provocation in the Wilderness and the Rejection of Grace," in *Thy People Shall Be My People, and Thy God My God*, ed. Paul Y. Hoskisson (Salt Lake City: Deseret Book, 1994), 168.

2. See also ibid., 169.

3. *Joseph Smith's Commentary on the Bible,* comp. and ed. Kent P. Jackson (Salt Lake City: Deseret Book, 1994), 29.

4. Stephen E. Robinson, *Believing Christ* (Salt Lake City: Deseret Book, 1992), 8–9.

5. S. Kent Brown, "Trust in the Lord: Exodus and Faith," in *The Old Testament and the Latter-day Saints* (Salt Lake City: Randall Book, 1986), 93.

6. This is probably the best translation for the Hebrew term *ḥesed,* which is usually translated as "loving kindness." The term denotes more than love; it denotes a love that is part of a covenant. Though the Lord loved all his children, it was this kind of love on which only Israel could lay claim.

7. Ezra Taft Benson, "Beware of Pride," *Ensign,* May 1989, 6.

8. See D&C 132:30–32; Bruce R. McConkie, "The Promises Made to the Fathers," in *Genesis to 2 Samuel,* ed. Kent P. Jackson and Robert L. Millet, vol. 3 in the *Studies in Scripture* series (Salt Lake City: Deseret Book, 1989), 54–55, 60.

7

The King's Law: A Framework of Leadership

Matthew O. Richardson

Before the children of Israel crossed the borders of the Jordan to reclaim the land of their forefathers, Moses gave a series of sermons "according unto all that the Lord had given him in commandment" (Deuteronomy 1:3). These sermons are often viewed as Moses' farewell address, since he would not enter the land of Canaan. In this light we see Moses not just as the great lawgiver but also as a father bidding farewell to parting children and offering practical wisdom, prophetic counsel, and heartfelt encouragement.

Moses' sermons in Deuteronomy were "intended as a permanent foundation for the life and well-being of the people in the land of Canaan."[1] Thus, these sermons contain principles with broad application that would benefit the people not only at the time they were given but also for many years to come. With this in mind, it is easy to see why Old Testament prophets quote Deuteronomy more than any other book in the Law (Pentateuch).

Matthew O. Richardson is an assistant professor of Church history and doctrine at Brigham Young University.

In the second of his three sermons, which is often called the "King's Law," Moses provided insight into governing the children of Israel (Deuteronomy 17:14–20). Since Moses' sermons are principle based and lend themselves to broad application, we might assume that the King's Law is still applicable today. But was the King's Law restricted to principles of monarchy, or were its principles to be applied to leadership in general? And just how do the six principles outlined in the law form part of the "permanent foundation for life and well-being" of God's people?

The Law of Leaders

"When thou art come unto the land which the Lord thy God giveth thee," Moses proclaimed, "[thou] shalt say, I will set a king over me, like as all the nations that are about me" (Deuteronomy 17:14). It is difficult to read this passage without connecting it to Samuel. Almost two hundred years after Israel entered Canaan, the elders approached Samuel and requested, "Now make us a king to judge us like all the nations" (1 Samuel 8:5). Moses' prophecy was hauntingly accurate, but it was not limited to Samuel's day. Later in the same sermon, Moses warned of multiplying horses, wealth, and wives (Deuteronomy 17:16–17). Not surprisingly, these characteristics describe Solomon's reign with pinpoint accuracy.

Making contextual connections between future and past events leads some to believe that Moses despised monarchial leadership and that the King's Law was no more than a prophetic declaration of inevitable future events. With some careful thought, however, the conclusion that Moses was antimonarchy only makes sense to those who know the entire story—both of the past (King's Law) and of the future (kingdom of Israel). Those living when the King's Law was given might have approached this sermon differently—not only because they did not know anything about Israel's future kingdom but also because Moses' sermons were considered practical, present-day guidelines. If Moses' intent was to discourage Israel from monarchy, this passage on a king might not seem to fit contextually for those without foreknowledge of the future kingdom.

Concentrating on the textual rendering of Moses' prophecy,

however, shows that his emphasis was not, as is often assumed, to prohibit monarchy as a form of future government. For example, the Greek translation of Moses' statement "Thou shalt in any wise set him king over thee" (Deuteronomy 17:15) is, "You may actually establish a king over you." Not only is this wording devoid of anti-monarchical sentiment, but it also expresses a volitional future event rather than something strictly prophetically mandated.[2] A modern translation of the same passage reads, "Go ahead and appoint a king."[3] While this translation may be too coarse and liberal for some, it demonstrates the permissive tone exhibited in the original Greek and Hebrew text. Thus, it appears that, at least textually, Israel could have a king. It is equally important, however, to understand that while Moses was not condemning monarchy, neither was he trying to establish a king. Thus, as C. F. Keil and F. Delitzsch concluded, "The appointment of a king is not *commanded,* . . . it is simply *permitted*, in case the need should arise for a regal government."[4]

If the Lord allowed Israel the option of monarchy rather than condemning the very idea, what was the whole point of Deuteronomy 17:14–20? The answer can only be fully realized when Israel's basic philosophy of leadership is considered. With this understanding, it becomes clear that the six principles Moses offered in the King's Law are actually principles that protect and preserve the very nature of leadership regardless of what we might call our leader—king, magistrate, president, prime minister, and so forth.

The Old Testament term *leader* was typically translated from four Hebrew words: *nasi, nagiyd, sar, and rosh.*[5] Together they provide a simple, albeit deep, insight into understanding Israel's Old Testament philosophy of leadership. These four terms are etymologically linked and mean "spokesman." Thus, since leaders in Israel speak for others, prestige, power, and wealth have very little to do with them personally, for everything is defined by message, theology, principles, and practice. For Israel, all is consumed in Jehovah. Thus, leaders in Israel, by any name or form, must clearly represent Jehovah and none else. If they violate this advocacy, even subtly, they are, by definition, no longer leaders.

With this in mind, it seems clear that Moses' sermon in Deuteronomy 17 is more about leadership than governmental form. Moses' counsel for governing Canaan actually concentrates more on principles of leading than on monarchies. "The aim of the law," according to Samuel Rolles Driver, "is to show how the monarchy, if established, is to conform to the same theocratic principles which govern other departments of the community; and how the dangers with which it may threaten Israel's national character and Israel's faith, may be most effectually averted."[6] With this in mind, rather than framing principles exclusive to monarchies, Moses outlined six important principles that maintain the integrity of a leader.

Principles of Leadership

1. "Set him king over thee, whom the Lord thy God shall choose" (Deuteronomy 17:15).

It was not enough for a leader in Israel to receive God's message, share it with the people, and live according to God's will with exactness. Regardless of personal talent, charisma, strength, diplomacy, or any other desirable quality, a leader's validity hinged upon his calling. Moses was a dramatic example of this principle. His success as a leader of Israel was not due to personal talent (Exodus 4:10) or confidence in his ability to lead (Exodus 3:11). The validity of Moses' leadership was established on the first day he stood before his people. Jehovah instructed Moses to tell the children of Israel, "The Lord God of your fathers, the God of Abraham, the God of Isaac, and the God of Jacob, hath sent me unto you" (Exodus 3:15). F. H. Seilhammer felt that the characteristic common to all biblical leaders was "their absolute assurance that God had called them personally into his service."[7] The Lord might have many purposes for establishing this as a principle of leadership, including the following three reasons:

First, having Jehovah select Israel's leaders was vital to the people both philosophically and theologically. "For the Israelites," I. M. Zeitlin explained, "existence in its entirety resulted from God's will and God's word."[8] Thus, God defined the Israelites, both temporally and spiritually. Because of this perspective, the Israelites considered themselves nothing more than indebted servants. Thus, if they selected their leaders independent of Jehovah, their government would be man-made and would undermine their dependence upon Jehovah in all things.

Second, this selection process defines the Lord's leader. Israel's leaders were not deified, larger than life, or indispensable. This is exhibited by the title *ish ha-'Elohim,* or a "man of God" (Deuteronomy 33:1). While Moses was the first leader to bear this title, it later became quite common for other Old Testament leaders as well.[9] Many interpret this title to mean a man who resembles God—a godly man. Under this selection standard, candidates obviously would have to meet godly standards. This term was also used to emphasize that leaders were called of God. In other words, a "man of God" was not only a godly man but also God's man—chosen by him. Nevertheless, he was still subservient to God in every way.

The third and last point of consideration is how an imperfect man is empowered as God's spokesman. When it comes to measuring up to the standards of God, our imperfections erode our confidence. Yet consider the principle that a leader is he "whom the Lord . . . choose[s]." Chooses, as used in this passage, is translated from the Hebrew *bachar,* which is also interpreted as "acceptable." Clearly, the Lord's leaders are not perfect individuals but individuals whom Jehovah finds acceptable. Thus, leaders are selected not because they deserve to lead or even because they are considered the best candidates. They lead because they are found acceptable by God. As President Spencer W. Kimball taught, "I would not say that those leaders whom the Lord chooses are necessarily the most brilliant, nor the most highly trained, but they are the chosen, and when chosen of the Lord they are his recognized authority, and the people who stay close to them have safety."[10] When the Lord chooses or accepts a leader, he also empowers that leader. As President Thomas S. Monson said, "Whom God calls, God qualifies."[11]

2. "One from among thy brethren shalt thou set king over thee: thou mayest not set a stranger over thee, which is not thy brother" (Deuteronomy 17:15).

According to Moses, the selection of a leader should fall upon "one from among thy brethren" (Deuteronomy 17:15). Moses was very clear that Israel's leader was not only to be from the community, but that he must not be a "stranger." At face value it seems that this directive is one that would protect the Israelites from foreigners that might usurp or undermine their power. A closer look, however, reveals a deeper motive. "Stranger," from the Hebrew *nokriy*, is often translated as foreigner, but *nokriy* actually favors a broader definition. Rather than just being limited to meaning foreigner, for example, *nokriy* also means alien, adulterous, or different.[12] According to Driver, "The motive of the provision is a religious one. A foreigner would not only be deficient in national feeling, and be liable to rule tyrannically, but he would be likely to endanger Israel's distinctive nationality, by introducing a heathen element into this most important dignity."[13] Thus, this principle is not just a protection of national power, but more important, it is a protection of national identity.

While this principle might appear to have been a closed, stale system of leadership, it was actually the lifeblood of Israelite representation. Always protecting their sense of identity, the Israelites needed leadership from those who reflected core Israelite theology, philosophy, and practice. C. S. Lewis once said, "I believe in Christ as I believe in the sun at noonday. Not because I can see it, but by it I can see everything else."[14] Although C. S. Lewis used Christianity as his reference point, this metaphor nicely illustrates this important leadership principle. Those of the faith see everything by the principles of the faith.

3. "But he shall not multiply horses to himself" (Deuteronomy 17:16).

On the surface, multiplying horses would seem to greatly benefit the people. Horses would ease the burden of daily chores, plough fields, provide transportation, and aid in progress. So when Moses states that the leader "shall not multiply horses to himself," it may appear that the Lord had no intention of easing the burdens of the people or helping them in their progress. Such conclusions, however, lack an understanding of the use of horses in Moses' day. In biblical times, horses were used primarily for military purposes—typically to pull chariots, the great war machines of the time.

Moses adds the seemingly puzzling phrase "nor cause the people to return to Egypt, to the end that he should multiply horses" (Deuteronomy 17:16) to this passage. Why would Israel ever be tempted to return to Egypt? In truth, Egypt was famous both for its horses and its chariots, and Moses understood that when men crave power, they are willing to undertake tremendous risks.[15]

Moses' counsel not to multiply horses may appear to be somewhat illogical, especially since Israel was instructed to inhabit the occupied land of Canaan by force. Rather than attempting to even military odds with comparable weaponry, Moses' counsel emphasized once again a critical component in Israel's philosophy—trust in Jehovah completely and comply with his will exactly.

If the children of Israel were to establish a powerful army by accepted standards of the day, they might have won many battles but they would have ultimately lost their war. "In war," Jeffrey H. Tigay observed, "reliance on [chariots] encourages the king to feel that he is self-sufficient and not dependent on God."[16] Isaiah later laments this very point: "Woe to them that . . . stay on horses, and trust in chariots, because they are many; and in horsemen, because they are very strong; but they look not unto the Holy One of Israel, neither seek the Lord!" (Isaiah 31:1).

Besides indicating military might, a horse was also the symbol of power in general (Psalm 147:10). In many ways, having a horse was somewhat of a status symbol.[17] Therefore, it really does not matter whether a leader craves physical power, social power, intellectual power, or even religious power. To this Elder Neal A. Maxwell wrote, "There is currently much fascination with empowerment but very little interest in the everlasting significance of the attribute of meekness, which was so perfectly embodied in the character of Jesus, our great Exemplar."[18] The Lord often reminds us that those who trust the power of man will be broken by those embracing the meekness of Christ. "The weak things of the world shall come forth and break down the mighty and strong ones, that man should not counsel his fellow man, neither trust in the arm of flesh" (D&C 1:19).

4. "Neither shall he multiply wives to himself, that his heart turn not away" (Deuteronomy 17:17).

In early biblical times, having plural wives was not forbidden. In fact, having plural wives was a common practice among Israel's contemporaries as well as among many of Israel's great leaders. If this practice was common, then why would Moses forbid a leader to "multiply wives to himself?" The answer is found in protecting a leader's heart from turning "away." So how does multiplying wives turn away the heart of the leader?

Before we can fully understand this leadership principle, we must again examine the "heart" of Israel. In Hebrew the heart was the center of anything and everything. The children of Israel considered their relationship with Jehovah as their heart—for them it was anything and everything. They believed their relationship with Jehovah was unique; because of this, they held to an undaunted belief that they were different from all other nations. In fact, Moses often used the term "peculiar" to describe Jehovah's people (Exodus 19:5, Deuteronomy 14:2; 26:18). That is why, when the Israelites spoke of other nations, they used the term *Gentile* as a way to describe those who were not part of their covenant identity.[19] This was such a foundational idea that if this relationship was broken or even diluted, "Israel would not be Israel."[20]

With Israel's identity in mind, connections between violating this identity and multiplying wives appear. Conspicuous harems were common to oriental and other monarchies of the time. While the harem was often considered a distraction to most kings in performing their duties,[21] the concern for Israel's leader was much deeper. If an Israelite leader were to multiply wives (acquire a harem) for political acceptance of other nations, validation, or just to be like other nations, he would compromise Israel's identity.

Another reason that multiple wives might turn a leader's heart deals with how kings typically acquired their wives. Royal marriages were often political arrangements used to facilitate treaties between nations. Israel was commanded not to enter into treaties with other nations (Judges 2:2). Thus, regardless of how a league is established, whether by deceit (Joshua 9) or through marriage (1 Kings 11:1), it would compromise Israel's intentional segregation and thus breach its identity.

Besides the political posturing and alliances made with other nations, there is a more subtle—and perhaps even more dangerous—connection between multiplying wives from other nations and compromising Israel's heart. Wives "bring the impact of foreign cultures into the palace, particularly the worship of other gods, and so lead the heart of the king astray."[22] The danger of having many wives is really the danger of embracing the seemingly innocuous cultural, philosophical, theological, and immoral influences of the wives. This would violate the essence of Israelite identity.

Such was the case in Solomon's kingdom, where his wives "turned away his heart" (1 Kings 11:3). Solomon assimilated the harems of other kingdoms in size and function, entered into political treaties with other nations through his marriages, began worshipping the gods of his wives, and even embraced the immoral sexual practices of Astheroth. His leadership led to a morally bankrupt and, eventually, a divided kingdom. What appears to be innocuous may, in reality, bear a ravenous cancer that destroys the identity of the Lord's people.

President Gordon B. Hinckley said, "With so much of sophistry that is passed off as truth, with so much of deception concerning standards and values, with so much of allurement and enticement to take on the slow stain of the world, we have felt to warn and forewarn."[23] Avoiding assimilation with the world has always been a concern for the Lord's people.

5. "Neither shall he greatly multiply to himself silver and gold" (Deuteronomy 17:17).

Practical issues are associated with this principle (taxation, greed, economic stability, and so forth). The real problem of personal gain, however, is once again connected with a change of heart. Moses warned the people against wealth, lest "thine heart be lifted up, and thou forget the Lord thy God" (Deuteronomy 8:14; Deuteronomy 6:12). Paul taught, "They that will be rich fall into temptation and a snare, and into many foolish and hurtful lusts, which drown men in destruction and perdition" (1 Timothy 6:9).

History is replete with examples of men and women who have become slaves to possessions. Paul pinpointed the source of the problem: "For the love of money is the root of all evil" (1 Timothy 6:10). Those who lead according to the Lord's principles must have an "eye single to the glory of God" and not allow their hearts to be divided. After warning his disciples about treasures upon earth, Christ taught, "For where your treasure is, there will your heart be also" (Matthew 6:21). He also taught that man cannot have two masters, "for either he will hate the one, and love the other; or else he will hold to the one, and despise the other" (Matthew 6:24). When we love the things of the world, we embrace an illusion of self-sufficiency and forfeit the love of the lord.

6. "And it [a copy of the law] shall be with him, and he shall read therein all the days of his life" (Deuteronomy 17:19).

The final, and perhaps capstone, principle of leadership required Israel's leader to devote himself to the higher law rather than "hanging his heart upon . . . earthly things."[24] Since Israel's leaders were known literally as spokesmen, it was understood that the ideology behind the leaders should be far more important than the personal talent, charisma, strength, or philosophies of the leaders themselves. Unfortunately, we often forget to remain vigilant to illuminating principles and allow men to "preach and set themselves up for a light unto the world" (2 Nephi 26:29). Such was the case with the Nicolaitanes. This heretical group in Asia Minor professed to be Christians but sought compromise with paganism. Elder Bruce R. McConkie described the Nicolaitanes as "members of the Church who were trying to maintain their church standing while continuing to live after the manner of the world."[25] John denounced this destructive philosophy as a "thing I hate" (Revelation 2:15).

Remaining true to guiding principles is the hallmark of successful leadership. Joseph Smith was once asked how he was able to govern so many people in such good order. Joseph responded that it was easy, for "I teach [them] correct principles, and they govern themselves."[26] John Taylor taught, "To do right in our present state, then, we must carry out the principle of legitimacy according to a correct rule, and, if we profess to be subjects of the kingdom of God, we must be subject to the dominion, rule, legitimacy, and authority of God."[27] In his great sermon about kings, Mosiah advised the people to seek for "just men to be your kings, who would establish the laws of God" (Mosiah 29:13). His rationale was that "the judgments of God are always just, but the judgments of man are not always just" (Mosiah 29:12).

Moses established a principle of leadership that firmly placed God's law as the law of the leader. Since the leader was the tangible representation of God's law, he must immerse himself in that law. Thus, Moses counseled, "And it [the law] shall be with him, and he shall read therein all the days of his life" (Deuteronomy 17:19).

Perhaps the most poignant part of Moses' final leadership principle is the outcome of allowing correct principles to determine our course and content. According to Moses, a leader immersed in the law will "learn to fear the Lord his God," "keep all the words of this law," "be not lifted up above his brethren," and "turn not aside from the commandment" (Deuteronomy 17:19–20). Thus, a leader will remain a true spokesman.

Conclusion

In its proper light, the King's Law in Deuteronomy 17:14–20 is clearly a law "intended as a permanent foundation for the life and well-being of the people" of God. Rather than condemning a form of government, this law reveals principles for effectively maintaining the moral and ethical identity of God's people. Historian Gertrude Himmelfarb feels that modern society has rejected conventional ethics and that now "we deliberately, systematically, divorce morality from social policy."[28] In many ways, it is eerie how the current stretching, shifting, and even rending of today's societal moral fabric parallels that of the Old Testament. Therefore, understanding the principles of leadership as outlined in Deuteronomy 17:14–20 provides insights worthy of application. Without cognizance of these principles, all leaders, whether in political forums, church governance, marriages, or families, risk removal from moral identity.

At the heart of Moses' law of leadership is a single, clear message: Jehovah is the center of all things. Thus, leadership must reflect that message. Paul taught, "For if the trumpet give an uncertain sound, who shall prepare himself to the battle?" (1 Corinthians 14:8). Leadership must provide a clear sound in all things.

Notes

1. C. F. Keil and F. Delitzsch, *Biblical Commentary on the Old Testament: The Pentateuch* (Grand Rapids, Mich.: Eerdmans, 1983), 3:270.

2. John William Wevers, *Notes on the Greek Text of Deuteronomy* (Atlanta: Scholars Press, 1995), 287.

3. This translation "attempts to capture the spirit of the King James Version in contemporary English." *Contemporary English Version of The Holy Bible* (New York: American Bible Society, 1995), 218.

4. Keil and Delitzsch, *Commentary,* 3:384.

5. A lengthy description and etymological background to this concept is discussed in Matthew O. Richardson, "The World Perspective and Its Impact on Leadership Conceptions: An Examination of Leadership in a Theocentric World Perspective," Ed.D dissertation, Brigham Young University, 1996.

6. Samuel Rolles Driver, *A Critical and Exegetical Commentary on Deuteronomy* (New York: Scribner, 1895), 210.

7. Frank H. Seilhamer, *Prophets and Prophecy* (Philadelphia: Fortress Press, 1977), 2.

8. Irving M. Zeitlin, *Ancient Judaism: Biblical Criticism from Max Weber to the Present* (Cambridge: Polity Press, 1984), 28.

9. Samuel, Elijah, Elisha, Shemaiah, and David were among those called "man of God."

10. Spencer W. Kimball, "Be Valiant," *Improvement Era,* June 1951, 432.

11. Thomas S. Monson, "Tears, Trials, Trust, Testimony," *Ensign,* September 1997, 5.

12. James Strong, *The Exhaustive Concordance of The Bible* (1890; reprint, New York: Abingdon, 1965), 78.

13. Driver, *Critical and Exegetical Commentary,* 210–11.

14. C. S. Lewis, *The Weight of Glory and Other Essays* (San Fransisco: Harper, 2001), 140

15. Neal A. Maxwell, *Lord, Increase Our Faith* (Salt Lake City: Bookcraft, 1994), 45.

16. Jeffrey H. Tigay, *Deuteronomy,* vol. 5 in the Jewish Publication Society Torah Commentary series, ed. Nahum M. Sarna (Philadelphia: Jewish Publication Society, 1996), 167.

17. Ralph Gower, *The New Manners and Customs of Bible Times* (Chicago: Moody Press, 1987), 238.

18. Maxwell, *Lord, Increase Our Faith,* 45.

19. The Latin term *Gentiles* literally means "nations," or more specifically, "other nations."

20. Walther Eichrodt, *Theology of the Old Testament,* 2 vols., trans. J. A. Baker (Philadelphia: Westminster Press, 1961), 1:14.

21. Tigay, *Deuteronomy,* 167.

22. *The Expositor's Bible Commentary,* ed. Frank E. Gaebelein, James D. Douglas, Richard P. Polcyn, 12 vols. (Grand Rapids, Mich.: Zondervan, 1976–92), 3:117.

23. Gordon B. Hinckley, "Stand Strong Against the Wiles of the World," *Ensign,* November 1995, 100.

24. Keil and Delitzsch, *Commentary,* 3:386.

25. Bruce R. McConkie, *Doctrinal New Testament Commentary,* 3 vols. (Salt Lake City: Bookcraft, 1965–73), 3:446.

26. John Taylor, *The Gospel Kingdom,* comp. G. Homer Durham (Salt Lake City: Bookcraft, 1964), 323.

27. John Taylor, *Journal of Discourses,* 26 vols. (London: Latter-day Saints' Book Depot, 1854–86), 1:231.

28. Gertrude Himmelfarb, "A De-Moralized Society?" *Forbes,* 14 September 1992, 122.

8

Jesus' Use of Deuteronomy in the Temptations

Gaye Strathearn

Elder Bruce R. McConkie taught us that after Jesus' baptism "two things happened in the life of our Lord that always come to pass in the lives of those faithful people who find their own Bethabaras and are immersed in their own Jordans by the legal administrators of their day: (1) the Spirit of God descended upon him with power, . . . and (2) greater temptations confronted him than had ever been the case before."[1] Thus, immediately (Mark 1:12) after baptism the Spirit led Jesus into the wilderness, not "to be tempted of the devil" as the King James Version reads (Matthew 4:1), but to be with God and to commune with him (JST Matthew 4:1–2). The scriptures are silent on the specific details of the events of those forty days, but Elder James E. Talmage reminds us that during the hiatus between his baptism and the commencement of his public ministry, Jesus "had much to think about, much that demanded prayer and the communion with God that prayer alone could insure."[2]

Gaye Strathearn is an instructor of ancient scripture at Brigham Young University.

Satan's entrance onto the scene occurred only after the Father had withdrawn. Yet his appearance was almost predictable. Sometime after the presence of God had withdrawn from Moses, Satan presented himself, demanding that Moses worship him (Moses 1:9, 12). Satan had either forgotten how Moses immediately dispatched him (Moses 1:16), or he had just not learned his lesson because, to an even greater extent, he tried to do with Jesus exactly what he had failed to do with Moses: have Jesus worship him instead of the Father.

It is the dialogue between Satan and Christ that is of interest. As Elder McConkie noted, all who are baptized can expect a similar confrontation at some point in their spiritual progression. That reality highlights the need for us to clearly understand the issues at stake in the conversation between Christ and Satan. It makes sense that the more we learn about Christ's actions in this confrontation, the better we can be prepared for our own inevitable encounters with the adversary. Let us, therefore, consider the kinds of demands Satan made, the scriptures Christ used to counter those temptations, and then some possible reasons why Christ cited the book of Deuteronomy in rebuking Satan.

The Role of the Temptations

Matthew describes the encounter between Satan and Christ in this way: "And when the tempter came to him, he said, If thou be the Son of God, command that these stones be made bread. But he answered and said, It is written, Man shall not live by bread alone, but by every word that proceedeth out of the mouth of God. Then the devil taketh him up into the holy city, and setteth him on a pinnacle of the temple, And saith unto him, If thou be the Son of God, cast thyself down: for it is written, He shall give his angels charge concerning thee: and in their hands they shall bear thee up, lest at any time thou dash thy foot against a stone. Jesus said unto him, It is written again, Thou shalt not tempt the Lord thy God. Again, the devil taketh him up into an exceeding high mountain, and sheweth him all the kingdoms of the world, and the glory of them; And saith unto him, All these things will I give thee, if thou wilt fall down and worship me. Then saith Jesus unto him, Get thee hence, Satan: for it is written, Thou shalt worship the Lord thy God, and him only shalt thou serve" (Matthew 4:3–10).

Jesus' encounter with Satan was an important precursor to events in his mortal ministry and is closely tied to what happened at his baptism, even though there is a chapter break between the two events in Matthew and Luke.[3] Two things should be noted about the temptations in relation to the baptism. First, when Jesus approached John seeking to be baptized, he declared that baptism is necessary to "fulfil all righteousness" (Matthew 3:15). The New Testament never explains that phrase, but Nephi teaches that it consists of two elements: to show "unto the children of men that, according to the flesh [Christ] humbleth himself before the Father," and also to "[witness] unto the Father that [Christ] would be obedient unto him in keeping his commandments" (2 Nephi 31:7). Nephi's point here is to show that when Jesus submitted to baptism, he accomplished both of these criteria. A point that Nephi does not address, but which is apparent in Matthew and to a lesser extent in Luke, is that Jesus also "fulfilled all righteousness" when he resisted Satan's temptations.[4] In other words, Jesus certainly fulfilled all righteousness by being baptized, but he also achieved that state when he rejected Satan's demands.[5] Each of the demands—to turn stone into bread, to jump from the pinnacle of the temple, and to worship Satan—was a temptation for the Savior to exalt himself above the Father and to break his commandments. If Jesus had succumbed to any of the temptations, he would have elevated his own needs above the Father's wishes. Instead of witnessing to the Father that he would obey his commandments, he would have flagrantly broken them. But the reality is that the Savior rejected each of the temptations and showed again that he was committed to fulfilling all righteousness.

A second item to note about the relationship between the baptism and the temptations is the issue of Jesus' divinity. In all three temptations, Satan not only tempts the Son but also implicitly attacks the Father. You will recall that the first two temptations begin with the challenge, "If thou be the Son of God. . . ." Elder

Howard W. Hunter suggests that "there is, of course, running through all of these temptations, Satan's insidious suggestion that Jesus was not the Son of God, the doubt implied in the tempter's repeated use of the word *if*."[6] In the first two temptations, Satan directly challenges Christ's divinity. But in a more subtle way, he is also challenging the Father. Remember that it was the Father who, at the baptism, declared Jesus to be his "beloved Son, in whom [he was] well pleased" (Matthew 3:17). By questioning whether Jesus was indeed the Son of God, Satan is also challenging the Father's declaration. Furthermore, in the final temptation when Satan offers Jesus all the kingdoms of the world and their glory if he will just "fall down and worship [him]" (Matthew 4:9), Satan sought to replace the Father as the object of Jesus' worship. In responding to Satan in these three instances, therefore, Jesus not only rejected Satan, he also reaffirmed his loyalty and commitment to the Father and to "the first and great commandment" (Matthew 22:38; see also 22:37).

Why is it important for Jesus to show us, "the children of men," that he "humbleth himself before the Father"? The answer lies in the fact that, at some time in our lives, we will all encounter Satan's insidious web. It will probably not take on the same form as the Savior's temptations, but it will nevertheless be just as real and just as potent. Speaking about Christ's temptations, President David O. McKay declared: "Nearly every temptation that comes to you and to me comes in one of those forms. Classify them, and you will find that under one of those three, nearly every given temptation that makes you and me 'spotted,' ever so little as it may be, comes to us as: (1) *a temptation of the appetite;* (2) *a yielding to the pride and fashion and vanity of those alienated from the things of God;* or (3) *a gratifying of the passion or a desire for the riches of the world or power among men.*"[7] It is therefore instructive to examine how the Savior responded to his temptations, so that we might use his example as we experience our own encounters with the adversary.

Christ's Use of Scripture

Jesus responded to each of Satan's insidious temptations with a scriptural rebuttal. In Matthew's account, the phrase "it is written" (*gegraptai*) precedes each of Jesus' pithy and powerfully disarming declarations (Matthew 4:4, 7, 10).[8] The lesson for us is clear: we should never underestimate the power of the scriptures in our need to counter the adversary. Paul described for the Ephesian Saints the armor of God that is essential for us to fight against principalities, powers, and the rulers of the darkness of this world (Ephesians 6:12).

Named in that arsenal is "the sword of the Spirit, which is the word of God" (Ephesians 6:17). Note Elder Jeffrey R. Holland's comments on this passage of scripture:

"In that description of preparing for spiritual battle, I have been impressed that most of the protection the Lord outlines for us there is somewhat defensive. The revelation speaks of breastplates and shields and helmets, all of which are important and protective but which leave us, in a sense, without an actual weapon yet. Are we only to be on the defensive? Are we simply to ward off blows and see it through and never be able, spiritually speaking, to strike a blow? No. We are supposed to advance in this and win a battle that started in heaven long ago. So we need some kind of even chance on the offense, and we are given it. You are given it. The weapon that is mentioned, the thing that allows us to actually do battle with the 'darkness of this world,' to use Paul's phrase, is 'the sword of the Spirit, which is *the word of God*' (Ephesians 6:12, 17; italics added). May I repeat that? 'The sword of the Spirit, which is the word of God.' I love that marriage of spiritual concepts."[9]

In withstanding Satan, the Savior does not just deflect his taunts, he uses the scriptures to go on the offensive. Likewise, a working knowledge of the scriptures can be a powerful weapon in our personal arsenals. That is why we have consistently been instructed to study the standard works. President Ezra Taft Benson asked, "Do we, as Saints of the Most High God, treasure the word He has preserved for us at so great a cost? Are we using these books of latter-day revelation to bless our lives and *resist the powers of the evil one?*" (emphasis added). Then he continues, "This is the purpose for which they were given."[10]

This lesson from Christ's temptations is critical and should be readily apparent to even the casual reader, but perhaps we can identify some lessons that are not so immediately evident. It is interesting that Jesus did not refute Satan with just any pastiche of scriptures. He mounted his defense by citing passages from the book of Deuteronomy.

Christ's Use of Deuteronomy

May I suggest that it was likely somewhat easier for ancient readers than it is for us in modern times to infer lessons from the scriptures. They were, after all, closer to the social and cultural contexts of the scriptures than we are. Consider two examples. In 2 Nephi 25, Nephi explains to his people that one of the reasons they were having a difficult time understanding Isaiah was because they were unfamiliar with the "manner of the Jews." In contrast, Nephi had dwelt in Jerusalem and knew "concerning the regions round about" (2 Nephi 25:6; see also 25:5). To help his people more fully understand and appreciate Isaiah, Nephi had to proceed with his own prophecy whereby he explained the intent of Isaiah's prophecies "according to [his] plainness; in the which [he knew] that no man can err" (2 Nephi 25:7).

Now for a modern example. If I were on the BYU campus and heard someone talking about "the cougars," I would immediately understand the reference was to the BYU football or basketball teams. If, however, I went home to Australia and mentioned "the cougars," the assumption would be that I was talking about the animals. If I wished to be understood there, I would have to add an explanatory phrase: "the cougars, meaning the BYU football or basketball teams." On the BYU campus, however, such an explanation would be unnecessary. Likewise, as Matthew recorded the account of Jesus' temptations for his readers, he assumed a certain awareness that may not be so evident to modern readers.

Matthew's audience primarily consisted of Jewish Christians.[11] Perhaps one of the reasons that he provided the most complete account of the temptations is precisely because he knew that his audience would recognize and appreciate the allusions to Israelite history and scripture it contained. A Jewish Christian in the first century would readily recognize the parallel between Jesus' fasting for forty days and nights in the wilderness and Israel's forty-year sojourn in the wilderness. Likewise, they would also readily recognize that Israel and Jesus were both tempted by hunger and idolatry.[12] Matthew did not need to explain such parallels to his audience because they were familiar with Israel's history. Modern readers who are conversant with that same history also readily recognize the similarities. With that background in place, let us now turn specifically to the scriptural quotations that Christ used to dispatch Satan; all of which come from the book of Deuteronomy. We will first examine them in the context of the chapter in which they are found, and then we will look at all three quotations within the greater context of the book of Deuteronomy as a whole. In examining these texts, we will do well to look for lessons that will help us in our own confrontations with the adversary.

In responding to the first temptation that he turn stone into bread, Jesus quotes Deuteronomy 8:3: "Man shall not live by bread alone, but by every word that proceedeth out of the mouth of God." Ancient readers would not only have heard the rebuke but would have been reminded of the context in which the dictum was originally given—the Lord calling upon Israel to remember how manna was miraculously provided them in their wilderness sojourn. God can certainly do what Satan demanded; he had already proved that by sustaining them during their wanderings. The whole point of that forty-year experience was for the children of Israel to humble themselves and to learn to trust and obey the Lord. The manna was evidence of his love for them and his power, and as they gratefully received it, they were to reciprocate by being obedient. In fact, the chiastic structure of chapter 8 draws the reader to verse 11: "Beware that thou forget not the Lord thy God, in not keeping his commandments, and his judgments, and his statutes, which I command thee this day."[13] Note the warning at the end of the chapter, if the house of Israel "forget the Lord thy God, and walk after other gods, and serve them, and worship them, I testify against you this day that ye shall surely perish. As the nations which the Lord destroyeth before your face, so shall ye perish; because ye would not be obedient unto the voice of the Lord your God" (Deuteronomy 8:19–20). That is why, even though God provided manna for their physical needs, he insisted that both their physical and spiritual life be governed by "every word that proceedeth out of the mouth of God." The children of Israel struggled to understand and accept this concept in the wilderness.

Unlike Israel, when he was at the point of one of his greatest physical challenges (the Atonement being the other point), the Savior did not allow his physical cravings to overpower his loyalty to God. Thus, he fulfilled all righteousness in the first temptation because he remembered God by keeping his commandments. Likewise, if we are to disarm Satan we must not only give lip service to this principle, we must actually live it.

Jesus' responses to the second and third temptations come from Deuteronomy 6. This chapter emphasizes the need for Israel to give exclusive allegiance to their God. Verse 4, known as the *Shema,* reads: "Hear, O Israel: The Lord our God is one Lord," which by the Second Temple period became an established liturgical declaration recited every morning in the temple.[14] Note the importance that Jehovah places on these verses. "And thou shalt love the Lord thy God with all thine heart, and with all thy soul, and with all thy might. And these words, which I command thee this day, shall be in thine heart: And thou shalt teach them diligently unto thy children, and shalt talk of them when thou sittest in thine house, and when thou walkest by the way, and when thou liest down, and when thou risest up" (Deuteronomy 6:5–7). Jehovah required that this verse be at the very center of everything that Israel did. To ensure they were constantly mindful of it, Jehovah commands them to put it in their phylacteries and *mezuzot.* Phylacteries are small black boxes that are worn on the inside of the left arm and on the forehead during daily prayers. The *Shema* is in this way physically close to their heart and mind as they pray. Similarly, the *mezuza* is a small box that is mounted on the lintel of the front door, serving as a visual reminder of the *Shema* as the people enter or leave their home.

When Satan asked Jesus to jump from the pinnacle of the temple so that angels could come and bear him up, Jesus responded by saying, "Thou shalt not tempt the Lord thy God." In Deuteronomy the rest of the verse says "as ye tempted him in Massah" (Deuteronomy 6:16). This refers to the time in the wilderness when the children of Israel, thirsty for water, complained to Moses. These complaints stemmed from feelings of insecurity over whether God was really with them on their journey (Exodus 17:1–7). Did Satan think that Jesus had doubts about whether the Father would be with him as he embarked upon his mortal ministry? Israel may have wavered, but the Son of God did not. He had no need to tempt God because, as one scholar noted, "Being himself full of faith, he need not try God's faithfulness."[15] Christ's faithfulness stemmed, at least in part, from his confidence that he was indeed God's "beloved Son, in whom [the Father was] well pleased" (Matthew 3:17). The Prophet Joseph Smith taught that one of the characteristics needed for an individual to "exercise faith in God unto life and salvation" was to have an "actual knowledge that the course of life he is pursuing is according to [God's] will."[16] Jesus obtained that assurance at the time of his baptism. He needed no external reassurance, and he certainly wouldn't seek it at the behest of Satan.

Of the three temptations, the final temptation—to worship Satan—was clearly the most audacious and revolting. Jesus' response, "Thou shalt worship the Lord thy God, and him only shalt thou serve" (Matthew 4:10) again hearkens back to Deuteronomy 6, where Jehovah commands Israel that they are to seek after no other gods. Israelite history is full of such indiscretions, which began with their worshipping the golden calf at Mount Sinai (Exodus 32; Deuteronomy 9:15–16). How could anyone declare the *Shema* and then worship Satan? Israel may have tried to do so, but the Son of God would not even entertain such an idea. He is, after all, committed to God and to fulfilling all righteousness.

Thus, in the context of Deuteronomy, Jesus was able to do in the wilderness what Israel had failed to do in the wilderness. If there is something for us to learn from these passages, it is that we can truly ward off Satan only by giving our love and our loyalties to the Father. If that was necessary for the Savior, it is essential for us.

We have now examined Jesus' scriptural rebukes in their

specific contexts in Deuteronomy. Our last task is to examine Jesus' choice of scriptures within the context of Deuteronomy as a whole. Deuteronomy is a unique book in the Old Testament. Although it repeats many events that we find in other books of the Torah, they are here gathered together in a way unparalleled in the other texts. The name *Deuteronomy* means "second or repeated law." It contains the words that Moses spoke to the house of Israel as they prepared to finally enter the promised land after forty years of wandering in the wilderness. At this important time, Moses wanted Israel to not only remember the covenant that they had made with God at Mount Sinai but also to renew it, to recommit themselves to the God of Israel. Thus, the book of Deuteronomy is the text of a covenant renewal ceremony.

Scholars have long noticed the similarities between this text and the ancient Hittite treaty pattern, which consists of six elements: (1) some form of preamble or introduction of the parties who will make the treaty; (2) a rehearsal of the past history between the two parties, which leads them to make the treaty; (3) the stipulations of the treaty; (4) a list of divine witnesses to the treaty; (5) a recital of the covenant; and (6) the deposit of the tablets, usually in a sacred place such as a temple or a palace.[17] An examination of Deuteronomy shows the following elements:[18] An introduction of the covenant parties, Deuteronomy 1:5; a review of history, Deuteronomy 1:6–3:29 (also 9:7–10:11); individual commandments, Deuteronomy 4–26; blessings and curses, Deuteronomy 27:9–28:68; witness and oaths of acceptance, Deuteronomy 31:19–22; 31:30–32:45; reading of the covenant and deposit of the text, Deuteronomy 27:1–8; 31:1, 9, 24–26.

It is not surprising that we find all of the scriptural references Jesus used to rebuke Satan in Deuteronomy 4–26, the portion of the text that corresponds to the individual commandments section. As we have noted, one of the major points of the temptations described in Matthew is to show that Jesus is obedient to all of the commandments. What is important here is that those commandments are part of a larger covenant renewal ceremony. Thus, Jesus obeys the commandments because he is true to the covenants that he has made with his Father. Matthew's audience would have noted this fact. We should also take note of it when Satan engages us. Christ's utilization of Deuteronomy teaches us that being true to our covenants with God is tantamount to dismissing Satan from our lives. Note the following counsel by Elder M. Russell Ballard: "Sometimes we are tempted to let our lives be governed more by convenience than by covenant. . . . But there is no spiritual power in living by convenience. The power comes as we keep our covenants."[19]

Conclusion

After Jesus dismissed Satan for the third time, Matthew records that "the devil leaveth him, and, behold, angels came and ministered unto him" (Matthew 4:11). This was certainly not the last time that Satan would approach Christ. Luke tells us that he merely departed "for a season" (Luke 4:13). But it is significant that when he did leave, angels ministered to the Savior, perhaps bringing him the food that he needed as they had done for Elijah (1 Kings 19:5–8). Just as Satan did not approach Jesus while he was in the presence of the Father, neither could the angels attend to him while Satan was present.

So what do we learn from this encounter? Is it possible for us to withstand and dispatch Satan? The answer is an unequivocal yes! To quote Elder Howard W. Hunter, "The question for us now is—will we succeed? Will we resist? Will we wear the victor's crown? Satan may have lost Jesus, but he does not believe he has lost us. He continues to tempt, taunt, and plead for our loyalty. We should take strength for this battle from the fact that Christ was victorious not as a God but as a man."[20] To succeed as the Savior did, we must respond as he responded. From this experience we learn three major lessons: (1) The scriptures are a powerful tool against Satan, and we must learn to use them. Not only must we put on the whole armor of God, but we must also take the offensive with the word of God, or the scriptures; (2) In a sense we are all the children of Israel wandering in the wilderness, searching for the promised land. As we pursue that journey we must be motivated in our thoughts and actions by our love for and loyalty to God. If we are constantly in communion with him then there is no place for Satan in our lives;[21]

(3) The making and keeping of covenants is critical in denying Satan a place in our wildernesses. Doing these things, of course, does not mean that we will be exempt from Satan's temptations. He will certainly continue to tempt us, as he did the Savior, but the lessons from the Savior teach us that we can be empowered to rebuke and to expel him from our lives.

Notes

1. Bruce R. McConkie, *The Mortal Messiah: From Bethlehem to Calvary* (Salt Lake City: Deseret Book, 1981), 408.

2. James E. Talmage, *Jesus the Christ,* 3d ed. (Salt Lake City: Deseret Book, 1983), 120.

3. In Mark there is no chapter break between the two events. From a literary perspective, Matthew has tied the baptism and the temptations together by emphasizing that it was the Spirit whom Jesus received at his baptism who then led him into the wilderness. Ulrich Luz, *Matthew 1–7: A Continental Commentary,* trans. Wilhelm C. Linss (Minneapolis: Fortress Press, 1992), 186; Birger Gerhardsson, *The Testing of God's Son: An Analysis of an Early Christian Midrash* [ConBNT 2:1; Lund: CWK Gleerup, 1966], 19). Luke makes the same association in his account, but it is not as clear because he also inserts Jesus' genealogy between the baptism and the temptations (Luke 3:21–4:13).

4. W. D. Davies and Dale C. Allison, Jr., *The Gospel According to Saint Matthew,* 3 vols. (Edinburgh: T&T Clark, 1991), 2:354.

5. "Jesus was tempted—if we may so say—to fulfill all righteousness" (McConkie, *Mortal Messiah,* 417).

6. Howard W. Hunter, "The Temptations of Christ," *Ensign,* November 1976, 18. Davies and Allison insist on the translation "since you are the Son of God" because, they say, "the introductory εἰ expresses a real condition." They therefore argue that Satan is not questioning Jesus' divine status. Instead, "Jesus' status as 'Son of God' is the presupposition for the devil's temptation" (*Gospel According to Saint Matthew,* 1:361; see also Luz, *Matthew 1–7,* 185–86). Later, however, in Matthew 14:28 (which has the same sentence structure: εἰ + present indicative in the protasis with an aorist active imperative in the apodosis) they admit that either "'if' or 'since' would be appropriate" (Davies and Allison, *Gospel According to*

Saint Matthew, 2:507). Therefore, there appears to be some flexibility in the translation in Matthew 4 that Davies and Allison do not allow for. It seems to me that the context favors a translation of "if," given Satan's role in opposition to the Father and his plan (Moses 4) and the close connection between the baptism and the temptations.

7. David O. McKay, "Individual Righteousness—The Strength of the Church," *Instructor,* September 1962, 290. See also Rudolf Bultmann, *History of the Synoptic Tradition* (New York: Harper & Row, 1976), 256.

8. See Joseph B. Fitzmyer, *Essays on the Semitic Background of the New Testament* (Missoula: Scholar's Press, 1974), 8–10.

9. Jeffrey R. Holland, "Therefore, What?" New Testament Conference, Brigham Young University, Provo, Utah, 2000, 2.

10. Ezra Taft Benson, "The Gift of Modern Revelation," *Ensign,* November 1986, 80.

11. We can discern this point from the text. Matthew makes numerous references to show that Jesus fulfills Old Testament prophecy (Matthew 1:22–23; 2:15, 17, 23; 4:14; 8:17; 12:17; 13:14, 35; 21:4; 26:54; 27:9, 35); his account of Jesus' genealogy goes back to Abraham (in contrast, Luke, writing to a Gentile audience, goes back to Adam).

12. Davies and Allison, *Gospel According to Saint Matthew,* 1:352.

13. N. Lohfink, *Das Hauptgebot,* vol. 20 of Analecta Biblica (Rome: Pontificio Instituto Biblico, 1963): 194–95.

A. v. 1: paraenetic frame
  B. vv. 2–6: wandering in the desert
    C. vv. 7–10: the richness of the land
      D. v. 11: the central idea (not to forget YHWH)
    C.' vv. 12–13: the richness of the land
  B.' vv. 14b–16: wandering in the desert
A.' vv. 19–20: paraenetic frame

14. Moshe Weinfeld, *Deuteronomy 1–11,* vol. 5 of the Anchor Bible series (New York: Doubleday, 1991), 353.

15. Davies and Allison, *Gospel According to Saint Matthew,* 1:368–69.

16. Joseph Smith, *Lectures on Faith* (Salt Lake City: Deseret Book, 1985), 38.

17. J. A. Thompson, "The Near East Suzerain-Vassal Concept in the Religion of Israel," *Journal of Religious History* 3 (1964): 1–15; George E.

Mendenhall, "Covenant Forms in Israelite Traditions," *Biblical Archeologist* 3 (1954): 49–76; Stephen D. Ricks, "Deuteronomy, a Covenant of Love," *Ensign,* April 1990, 55–59.

18. Adapted from Ricks, "Deuteronomy, a Covenant of Love," 59.

19. M. Russell Ballard, "Like a Flame Unquenchable," *Ensign,* May 1999, 86.

20. Hunter, "Temptations of Christ," 18–19.

21. That does not mean that difficult times will not come to us. Mortality is a testing ground, and we cannot attribute all difficulties to Satan.

9

The Calling of Isaiah

David E. Bokovoy

The Lord inspired the prophet Isaiah to produce a record that would provide both direction and meaning in the latter-days. "Yea a commandment I give unto you," declared the resurrected Savior, "that ye search these things diligently; for great are the words of Isaiah" (3 Nephi 23:1). The book of Isaiah fulfills a significant role in our Heavenly Father's plan. This ancient record serves as a witness of our Lord and Savior Jesus Christ. As a prophet of God, Isaiah accepted an assignment to go forth and declare God's word to the children of Israel. Isaiah shared the details of this prophetic commission in the sixth chapter of his book. A careful study of Isaiah's call narrative suggests that the prophet described his experience in a similar manner to ancient literary accounts depicting the operations of a heavenly council.[1] Significantly, the existence of a heavenly council, as featured in Isaiah chapter six, proves consistent with doctrinal truths revealed through the Prophet Joseph Smith. When analyzed with the additional insights provided

---

David E. Bokovoy teaches seminary in Grantsville, Utah.

by modern revelation and recent textual discoveries, Isaiah's call narrative contributes important information to our understanding of God's heavenly council.

As Latter-day Saints we recognize the importance of our premortal state in God's plan of salvation. In the premortal world, the Lord organized a grand assembly where Jehovah, the Firstborn Son of our Heavenly Father, received a special commission to serve as the Savior of the world. This essay demonstrates that Isaiah's call narrative functions as typology for the election of Jehovah in the premortal council. The connection between Isaiah's prophetic commission and the calling of Jehovah provides an additional witness of the momentous role played by the book of Isaiah in the latter-day restoration of religious truth.

One of the great doctrinal precepts restored through Joseph Smith is the transcendent role assumed by a prophet of God. Throughout the centuries the Lord has called prophets to serve as witnesses of our Savior Jesus Christ. As one such signatory, Isaiah had a testimony of Jesus; he openly declared that a messiah would someday come and take upon himself the sins of the world. Isaiah saw the day when the Savior would be "wounded for our transgressions" and "bruised for our iniquities" (Isaiah 53:5). "The chastisement of our peace was upon him," declared Isaiah, "and with his stripes we are healed" (v. 5). Jesus' life and mission, therefore, provide the foundation for all of Isaiah's prophetic declarations.

Due to the Savior's centrality in the plan of salvation, the Book of Mormon teaches that "all things which have been given of God from the beginning of the world . . . are the typifying of [Christ]" (2 Nephi 11:4). This declaration demonstrates one of the roles that prophets such as Isaiah fulfill. Elder Bruce R. McConkie explained, "No doubt there are many events in the lives of many prophets that set those righteous persons apart as types and shadows of their Messiah. It is wholesome and proper to look for similitudes of Christ everywhere and to use them repeatedly in keeping him and his laws uppermost in our minds."[2]

From this observation we learn that many of the events that occur in a prophet's life are meant to serve as typology of the Savior.

Elder McConkie provided additional insights into this doctrine by offering a clear definition of a prophet. "A prophet is one who has the testimony of Jesus," proclaimed Elder McConkie, "who knows by the revelations of the Holy Ghost to his soul that Jesus Christ is the Son of God."[3] Yet in addition to this inspired witness, many of the prophets "lived in special situations or did particular things that singled them out as types and patterns and shadows of that which was to be in the life of him who is our Lord."[4] Elder McConkie's statement concerning the typological role of a prophet was true for Isaiah. Isaiah's commission to the service of God symbolized the election of Jehovah, the premortal Messiah, as our Lord and Savior.

Latter-day revelation teaches that prior to the creation of the world, God called together his children in a grand assembly to discuss the details of his plan for their happiness. Joseph Fielding Smith explained, "When the time arrived for us to be advanced in the scale of our existence and pass through this mundane probation, councils were held and the spirit children were instructed in matters pertaining to conditions in mortal life, and the reason for such an existence."[5] During these meetings, "all the sons of God shouted for joy" at the prospect of obtaining a physical body (Job 38:7). Our Heavenly Father explained that he would commission a savior to overcome the effects of mortal probation that would separate us from his presence. After some deliberation Jehovah accepted a call to serve in this capacity. We know that as a prophet of God, Isaiah was familiar with these events. His own commission to the Lord's service functioned as typology for Jehovah's election in the premortal council.

Isaiah received a call from the Lord to declare God's word to the children of Israel. In biblical society the calling of a prophet often accompanied a vision of a heavenly council.[6] The earliest recorded attestation of this phenomenon is Micaiah's experience with the celestial realm (1 Kings 22:19–22). In a prophesy concerning the death of King Ahab, Micaiah declared, "I saw the Lord sitting on his throne, and all the host of heaven standing by him on his right hand and on his left" (v. 19). As one scholar has observed, "Despite the terms 'host of heaven' for the court and 'spirits' for the individual members, the functioning of the old divine council [in this passage] is obvious."[7] The "host of heaven" or in other words the heavenly council, played a significant role in the celestial events witnessed by Micaiah. In accordance with a well established pattern in antiquity, Micaiah saw the Lord petition his council for volunteers to fulfill a serious mission (v. 20). After the council had offered its various suggestions, a select individual finally came forward with an acceptable proposal (vv. 20–21). This brief outline of Micaiah's encounter with the host of heaven shares several features in common with Isaiah's narrative.

Isaiah begins his account in a manner reminiscent of the description provided by Micaiah concerning his vision of the heavenly council. "In the year that king Uzziah died," begins Isaiah, "I saw also the Lord sitting upon a throne, high and lifted up, and his train filled the temple" (Isaiah 6:1). While Isaiah's brief introduction to this experience fails to specify whether his vision involved the earthly temple at Jerusalem or the heavenly temple where God dwells, the context of the narrative seems to suggest the latter.[8] Like the prophet Micaiah, Isaiah witnessed a celestial vision of God seated upon his throne. Both of these narratives provide a description of the heavenly throne room that includes a vision of the divine council offering praises to the Lord.

The spiritual encounter described by these two prophets is sometimes called a throne theophany, which refers to an individual's ascent into the celestial world where he or she sees the throne of God.[9] The details of Isaiah's vision suggest that he, like Micaiah and many other visionaries from the ancient Near East, received an invitation to attend a meeting of the heavenly council. Ancient texts from the world of the Bible reveal that the people of the Near East believed in a heavenly council or divine assembly that governed the affairs of the universe.

The divine assembly served an important role in Near Eastern theology. Yet not only was this assembly of deities a meaningful element in Gentile mythology, but as witnessed in the book of Isaiah, the council is attested in biblical cosmology as well. So compelling is the position of the council in the Old Testament that one essay has reported that the Hebrew noun *sod* (council) "refers specifically to the divine court in four passages, implies its existence in two others, and could possibly refer to it in an additional two."[10] Among the Bible's more explicit references to the divine assembly is Psalm 82:1: "God has taken his place in the divine council," reports the psalmist, "in the midst of the gods he holds judgment."[11] Yet even obscure passages such as Isaiah 40:1, where God directs an unknown audience with the masculine plural imperative to comfort his people, are better understood when interpreted as references to the heavenly council.

For the people of the Near East, the divine assembly described by Isaiah represented the ultimate authority in the universe. The discovery of several cuneiform tablets from Ugarit and Mesopotamia has allowed scholars to retrace the central features of this institution.[12] A comparative analysis of these traditions suggests several literary motifs as commonly featured elements in the tales of the assembly. These stories often include the following scenario: first, a crisis would occur; this crisis would then force the high god to call upon the council for volunteers to resolve the dilemma; various proposals would then be considered; when at last, all hope for resolution seemed lost, a winning suggestion was made and a savior commissioned.[13] The remarkable similarity between this outline and the first prophetic encounter with the council demonstrates the extensive attestation of these popular motifs. Ultimately, this brief description applies to myths from both the eastern and western spheres of Semitic influence. For the purpose of this essay concerning Isaiah's encounter with the assembly, we will however, examine only one attestation of the above pattern from Near Eastern mythology.

The Babylonian tale of cosmic kingship known as *Enumma Elish* or "When upon High" presents the operations of the divine assembly in the midst of intense cosmic disarray.[14] According to the myth, the assembly convened in order to discuss a course of action that would successfully thwart the efforts of the primordial mother goddess Tiamat. As a result of her children's open rebellion, Tiamat had resolved to destroy her incumbent offspring. *Enumma Elish* describes how An, the high god in the Mesopotamian pantheon, called for volunteers to resolve this crisis. Prompted by the admonitions of the god Ea, Marduk, the chief deity of Babylon, offered his services to the assembly in return for a covenant that they would forever recognize him as divine sovereign. Marduk agreed to fulfill the role of savior on the condition that he would receive the glory and honor of the gods. When his plan proved acceptable to the council, Marduk received a commission to serve as savior.

This outline of events, featured in many of the tales of the assembly, proves meaningful for Latter-day Saints. The Book of Abraham presents an account of God's heavenly council that contains many of the elements featured so prominently in ancient literature. Yet these connections between ancient myth and modern revelation should not surprise Latter-day Saints. As Elder Joseph F. Smith once explained, "If the heathen have doctrines and ceremonies resembling to some extent those which are recorded in the Scriptures, it only proves, what is plain to the Saints, that these are the traditions of the fathers handed down from generation to generation, from Adam, through Noah."[15] That the story of the Heavenly Council presented in the Book of Abraham parallels many of the elements in Near Eastern mythology is a witness of the authenticity of this latter-day revelation.

The existence of a divine council of deities attested in ancient literature including the Book of Abraham proves consistent with the teachings proclaimed publicly by Joseph Smith. "The head God called together the Gods," declared the Prophet, on one such occasion, "and sat in grand council to bring forth the world."[16] From Abraham's description of these events, we learn that the Lord needed a savior to resolve the crisis that would occur as a result of humanity's mortal existence. In this grand assembly, the Lord petitioned his council with the question, "Whom shall I send?" (Abraham 3:27). Apparently, one of the sons of God volunteered in a manner reminiscent of Marduk in *Enumma Elish.* Lucifer, like Marduk, offered his services to the council in return for the power and glory of God. "Behold, here am I, send me," proclaimed Lucifer, "I will be thy son, and I will redeem all mankind, that one soul shall not be lost, and surely I will do it; wherefore give me thine honor" (Moses 4:1). However, since the Father's firstborn spirit child had offered himself without guile, saying, "Here am I, send me," the Lord declared, "I will send the first" (Abraham 3:27). Hence, in the Grand Council before the earth was organized, Jehovah, the premortal Christ, received a call from our Heavenly Father to serve as the Redeemer of the world.

The account of the premortal council and the election of Jehovah as savior proves essential in a doctrinal analysis of the commission given to the prophet Isaiah. Isaiah received his vision in the year 740 B.C. (the year King Uzziah died). This was a period of internal apostasy in the land of Israel. When Isaiah witnessed the host of heaven offering their praises to the Lord, he felt an innate desire to join them, yet he came from a people who were ripe with iniquity. As a result Isaiah felt unworthy to unite with the assembly even though he himself was a righteous man (Isaiah 6:5). Joseph Smith taught that as such, Isaiah was qualified to receive the Second Comforter, Jesus Christ.[17] The Lord had a mission in mind for this righteous servant, whom he declared worthy of entering the highest realms of the celestial kingdom.

In the process of cleansing Isaiah so that he could leave behind the impurities of his people and receive introduction into the assembly, one of the seraphim purified Isaiah's mouth with a live coal taken directly from the celestial altar (Isaiah 6:6–7). Isaiah could now fully participate with the heavenly host in offering praises to the Lord. He had become a member of the heavenly court. In the ancient Near East, mouth cleansing rituals held considerable significance.[18] In Mesopotamian ritual prayers, for example, mouth purification symbolized total and complete purity. As biblical scholar Victor Hurowitz has noted, "A large portion of the [Mesopotamian] sources . . . raise the possibility that the washing of the mouth or the purity of the mouth has independent significance as a characteristic granting or symbolizing special divine or quasi-divine status to the person or object so designated. The pure mouth enables the person or object to stand before the gods or to enter the divine realm, or symbolizes a divine status."[19]

Purity of mouth is often, therefore, but not exclusively, a divine trait. Based upon this analogy, one could argue that the purification of Isaiah's mouth symbolized his new membership in God's heavenly court.

In Isaiah's vision the assembly had presumably convened in order to discuss the crisis caused by Israel's apostasy. The Lord, therefore, needed a representative to go forth and declare his word to the chosen people. Like Jehovah before him, Isaiah was addressed by the leader of the assembly with the perennial question, "Whom shall I send?" (Isaiah 6:8). Then, with the very words used by Jehovah, the creator of the universe, Isaiah responded with the proposal, "Here am I; send me" (v. 8). This response, first articulated by Jehovah in the premortal council, is often connected with the calling of the Lord's anointed.[20] According to Rabbinic interpretation, the response *hinnehne* or "Here am I" signifies a willingness on the part of the speaker to devote his life to the individual addressed.[21] Hence, the account of Isaiah's commission, as presented in Isaiah 6:8, serves as typology for the occasion when Jehovah devoted himself to our Heavenly Father's will with the words "Here am I; send me."

The exact verbal exchange between God, Jehovah, and Isaiah during the meetings of the divine assembly parallels statements recently discovered in cuneiform tablets from Mesopotamia. An analysis of these tablets reveals that the details pertaining to Isaiah's vision, as well as those featured in the book of Abraham, reflect a well-established pattern in antiquity. In Akkadian, the language of ancient Babylon and Assyria, the phrase *mannam lušpur,* or "Whom shall I send," occurs in a number of documents. Significantly, the Lord used this same inquiry when he addressed the divine assembly in both Isaiah's narrative and the Book of Abraham. The extensive attestation of this popular expression supports the observation of Joseph F. Smith previously cited in this essay. The details concerning Jehovah's commission as savior, though perverted with time, were recognized in antiquity.

In the Babylonian antiwitchcraft compilation known as *Maqlu,* a mortal sufferer addressed the heavenly host with the statement, "Anu and Antu have sent me saying, 'Whom shall I send?'"[22] The human speaker in *Maqlu* then petitioned the deities of the assembly to purify him so that he could be introduced as one of their company.[23] Following a ritual cleansing, the council commissioned the speaker to act as a representative of the gods. This assignment was possible since the mortal sufferer had officially become a member of the divine court. The details involved in this section of the Babylonian ritual clearly reflect the account of Isaiah's prophetic commission.[24] Not only does the classic phrase "Whom shall I send" appear in both *Maqlu* and Isaiah, but the very pattern of cleansing, introducing, and commissioning provides the literary basis for the two accounts.

The Akkadian phrase *mannu lušpur* or "Whom should I send" that appears in the first tablet of *Maqlu* forms part of an ancient literary formula featured in the magical rites of Mesopotamia.[25] "Whom should I send with orders to the seven (+) seven daughter(s) of Anum?" asks one such document.[26] And yet another: "Whom should I send to the dweller of the great Apsû?"[27] From these Mesopotamian texts, it is apparent that Isaiah's experience parallels various literary elements well attested in antiquity. Latter-day Saints would argue that Isaiah's account reflects these non-Israelite documents since they in turn echo the premortal events recorded in the Book of Abraham. In a manner reminiscent of these ancient sources, Abraham described the operations of the premortal council where the Lord addressed his grand assembly with the question, "Whom shall I send?" Based upon these connections, it is apparent that Isaiah's call narrative was meant to serve as typology for a tradition that was once understood in antiquity, namely the election of Jehovah as Redeemer of the world.

One Book of Mormon passage seems to suggest that ancient prophets recognized the connection between Isaiah's prophetic commission and the premortal council. Perhaps it is significant that Nephi specifically prefaces his citation of Isaiah chapter six with his testimonial that "all things which have been given of God from the beginning of the world, unto man, are the typifying of [Christ]" (2 Nephi 11:4). A brief survey of 2 Nephi 11–19 indicates that at least one ancient prophet viewed the opening chapters of Isaiah, including his call narrative, as typology for the Messiah.

Indeed, as the Lord himself declared, the words of the prophet Isaiah are truly great. This pre-Exilic servant of God received a sacred commission to testify of Jesus Christ. Yet not only did Isaiah fulfill this assignment through his spoken words, he also bore witness of the Savior with the unique events that happened in his life. When Isaiah described the details of his call narrative, he did so in a manner that reflected various literary motifs, well established in antiquity. Isaiah's prophetic commission, as presented in the sixth chapter of his book, demonstrates the importance of his mission in the latter-day restoration of doctrinal truths taught by the prophets of old. With the additional insights provided by modern revelation and recent textual discoveries, Latter-day Saints can easily recognize the connection between Isaiah's call and the election of Jehovah in the premortal council.

Notes

1. Some scholars have argued against identifying Isaiah 6 as a "call narrative." See, for example, John D. Watts, *Isaiah 1–33* (Waco, Texas: Word Books, 1985), 70. Though I tend to agree that this vision marks the end of the Uzziah section and does, therefore, possess certain unique qualities, I still consider the similarities between Isaiah's experience and those generally labeled as call narratives sufficient to justify the traditional identification.

2. Bruce R. McConkie, *The Promised Messiah* (Salt Lake City: Deseret Book, 1981), 453.

3. Ibid., 448.

4. Ibid.

5. Joseph Fielding Smith, *Doctrines of Salvation*, comp. Bruce R. McConkie, 3 vols. (Salt Lake City: Bookcraft, 1954–56), 2:57.

6. See, for example, E. C. Kingsbury, "The Prophets and the Council of Yahweh," *Journal of Biblical Literature* 83 (1964): 279–86; John W. Welch, "The Calling of a Prophet," in *The Book of Mormon: First Nephi, The Doctrinal Foundation*, ed. Monte S. Nyman and Charles D. Tate, Jr.

(Provo, Utah: Brigham Young University, Religious Studies Center, 1988), 35–54.

7. S. B. Parker, “Council,” in *Dictionary of Deities and Demons in the Bible,* ed. Karel Van Der Toorn, Bob Becking, and Peter W. Van Der Horst (Leiden: Brill, 1999), 206.

8. See Donald W. Parry, Jay A. Parry, and Tina M. Peterson, *Understanding Isaiah* (Salt Lake City: Deseret Book, 1998), 64.

9. See Stephen D. Ricks, “Heavenly Visions and Prophetic Calls in Isaiah 6 (2 Nephi 16), the Book of Mormon, and the Revelation of John,” in *Isaiah in the Book of Mormon,* ed. Donald W. Parry, and John W. Welch (Provo: Foundation for Ancient Research and Mormon Studies, 1998), 175–81.

10. Parker, “Council,” 204.

11. This translation, taken from Wayne A. Meeks, HarperCollins Study Bible: New Revised Standard Version (New York: HarperCollins, 1989), correctly reflects the Hebrew wording. Without a full understanding of the significance of this passage, the King James translators opted for the less explicit rendering: “God standeth in the congregation of the mighty; he judgeth among the gods.”

12. See, for example, Thorkild Jacobsen, *The Treasures of Darkness: A History of Mesopotamian Religion* (New Haven, Conn.: Yale University Press, 1976), 86–91; E. Theodore Mullen Jr., *The Divine Council in Canaanite and Early Hebrew Literature* (Chico: Scholars Press, 1980).

13. Parker, “Council,” 204.

14. For an English translation of *Enumma Elish,* see Stephanie Dalley, *Myths From Mesopotamia: Creation, the Flood, Gilgamesh, and Others* (New York: Oxford Press, 1989), 228–77.

15. Joseph F. Smith, *Journal of Discourses,* 26 vols. (London: Latter-day Saints' Book Depot, 1854–86), 15: 325.

16. Joseph Smith, *Teachings of the Prophet Joseph Smith,* sel. Joseph Fielding Smith (Salt Lake City: Deseret Book, 1976), 348.

17. Ibid., 150–51.

18. See, for example, Victor Horowitz, “Isaiah's Impure Lips and Their Purification in Light of Akkadian Sources,” *Hebrew Union College Annual* 60 (1989): 39–89.

19. Ibid., 54.

20. While it is true that the statement "Here am I" is often used in a prophetic context of devotion, the same Hebrew expression is frequently used to signify a simple "yes" response. See, for example, Genesis 22:1, 7, 11; 27:1, 18; 31:11; 37:13; 46:2; Exodus 3:4; 1 Samuel 3:4–6, 8, 16; 12:3; 22:12; 2 Samuel 1:7; 15:26; Isaiah 58:9.

21. In his analysis of *hinnehne,* Rashi, for example, states that "such is the answer of the pious, the expression denoting both humility and readiness," as quoted in Meir Zlotowitz, *Bereishis: A New Translation with a Commentary Anthologized from Talmudic, Midrashic, and Rabbinic Sources* (Brooklyn: Mesorah Publications, 1988), 785.

22. The term "mannu lušpur" appears in line 53 of the first tablet of Maqlu. Gerhard Meier, *Die Assyrische Beschworungssammlung Maqlu* (AFO Beiheft 2, 1967), 2; Tzvi Abusch has remained the foremost authority on this text. For an introduction to Maqlu, see Abusch, "Maqlu' *Reallexikon der Assyriologie und vorderasiatischen Archaeologie* 7 (1989): 346–51.

23. According to Abusch, the speaker "must become a member of the company of the stars, the heavenly host or retinue of the gods of heaven Anu and Antu, for only then can he serve as their emissary." Tzvi Abusch, "Ascent to the Stars in a Mesopotamian Ritual: Social Metaphor and Religious Experience," in *Death, Ecstasy, and Other Worldly Journeys,* ed. J. Collins and M. Fishbane (Albany, N.Y.: State University of New York Press, 1995), 22.

24. Tzvi Abusch, "The Socio-Religious Framework of the Babylonian Witchcraft Ceremony Malqlu: Some Observations on the Introductory Section of the Text, Part II," in *Solving Riddles and Untying Knots: Biblical, Epigraphic, and Semitic Studies in Honor of Jonas C. Greenfield,* ed. Ziony Zevit, Seymour Gitin, and Michael Sokoloff (Winona Lake, Indiana: Eisenbrauns, 1995), 479.

25. Walter Farber, "*Mannam Lušpur Ana Enkidu:* Some New Thoughts about an Old Motif," *Journal of Near Eastern Studies* 49 (October 1990): 299–321.

26. Ibid., 306.

27. Ibid., 309.

10

"I Have Even from the Beginning Declared It"

Richard D. Draper

"No one has a crystal ball." Those who make this statement, even with resignation, are most often trying to assure themselves that we are all on an equal footing, because no one knows the future. Everyone must plan as best one can without that advantage. Interestingly, however, the statement is only partially correct. It is true that no human has access to the future, but heavenly beings do. In the Doctrine and Covenants, we learn that angels "reside in the presence of God, on a globe like a sea of glass and fire, where all things for their glory are manifest, past, present, and future, and are continually before the Lord" (D&C 130:7). Divine beings, it would seem, do have a crystal ball that allows them to see the future. God particularly has the power of prescience and from time to time manifests it to mortals in the form of prophecy. By prophecy, I mean those insights God shares with us about the future.[1]

I am intrigued not only by God's ability to foresee the future,

Richard D. Draper is a professor of ancient scripture at Brigham Young University.

but also by how jealously he guards this power, forbidding any attempt at duplication or imitation. This has caused me to wonder just how God interacts with the future: whether he creates it or reports it. Finally, I have been impressed that God has used prophecy as a means to verify himself, to prove that he is, indeed, the only true and living God. Thus, my mission here is to use the insights gained from the Old Testament, particularly Isaiah 40–48, to do three things: first, to determine why God forbids man's illicit attempts to probe into the future; second, to better understand God's relationship to the future; and, third, to ascertain how and why God has used his foreknowledge as a way to authenticate himself.

Thou Shalt Not Do after Their Abominations

Jehovah gave the Israelites a stiff warning as they prepared to launch their initial attack on Canaan: "When thou art come into the land which the Lord thy God giveth thee, thou shalt not learn to do after the abominations of those nations. There shall not be found among you any one that maketh his son or his daughter to pass through the fire, or that useth divination, or an observer of times, or an enchanter, or a witch, or a charmer, or a consulter with familiar spirits, or a wizard, or a necromancer. For all that do these things are an abomination unto the Lord: and because of these abominations the Lord thy God doth drive them out from before thee" (Deuteronomy 18:9–12).

This passage is interesting because it lists every Hebrew word related to an attempt to probe the future.[2] In it God forbade Israel to use any means of divination. He called such practices an abomination and placed it at the head of his list of reasons why the Canaanites had forfeited their right to the land. The Hebrew word translated as *abomination* is very strong. It denotes something so detestable that it kindles God's wrath and causes him to remove his Spirit.[3] As a result, the item or person so corrupted is left to destruction. In their practice of divination, the Canaanites fell under this bane, thus allowing Israel to prevail against them. The Lord was quick to warn the Israelites that they would be subject to the same doom if they fell into the same evil.

What is it about these practices that makes them an abomination in the sight of God? The answer is evident. Each represents an attempt by the faithless to get around God and his laws by seeking to know or shape the future on their own terms. "Since God is the LORD, the Maker of heaven and earth, and the determiner of all things, any attempt to know and control the future outside of God is to set up another god in contempt of the LORD."[4]

The list of prohibited things is headed by a condemnation of the despicable practice of sacrificing children by fire. Although on the surface this practice would seem to have nothing to do with divination, in reality it does. The reference is to a form of worship associated with the popular Ammonite god Moloch. In listing it the Lord reveals the connection between divination and idolatry.[5] Februation, or the purifying of children by passing them through fire, was a central practice of Moloch worship, intimately connected with soothsaying and magic more than any other form of idolatry, because "Moloch represented kingship and power."[6] Therefore, "sacrifices to Moloch represented the purchase, at the very least, of immunity or insurance and protection" against the future.[7] It represented man's supreme effort to control the future and command his own destiny, in other words, to be like God.

The northern kingdom of Israel, particularly, fell to this practice, but the southern kingdom was not exempt. Through his prophets, most notably Isaiah, Jehovah instructed Israel that he is the only God who knows and controls the future, and there is no way they can get around him or his commandments. In Isaiah, especially, Jehovah emphasizes this point, demonstrating the degree to which he knows the future. He revealed, during the eighth century before Christ, details, events, and people that would affect Judah two hundred years later, demonstrating through his display of prescience that he is not only the God of Israel but also the God of the whole world.

Before turning to that study, I would like to point out the irony that the exactness with which God prophesied in Isaiah caused one of the major debates in Isaiah studies. It began with Bishop Robert Lowth in the eighteenth century. Studying the basis of Old Testament prophetic ability, Bishop Lowth took a careful look at Isaiah. Though very favorable to the prophetic power and appreciative of the genius of what he called "the prophetic consciousness," he determined that prophets were, after all, "men of like nature with ourselves, in virtually all respects," and "only their higher moral and natural sensibility set them apart."[8] Viewing them as little more than mortals with a highly developed sense of justice and an acute ability to see where society was headed, he struggled to reconcile his theory with what he found in certain passages of Isaiah. Chapters 40 to 47 particularly bothered him. There he found a "strained temporal reference." What he meant was that he found it impossible for the eighth-century Isaiah to describe accurately sixth-century events and even name a principal player, the Persian ruler Cyrus. Acute dissonance set in. "To applaud prophetic genius in respect of ethical insight was one thing; but to claim for this same genius the ability to foresee events centuries in advance went beyond enlightened logic," he insisted.[9]

Later scholars also felt Lowth's dissonance. Over time, Isaiah as both *fore*-teller and *forth*-teller became "incompatible conceptions."[10] To resolve the dissonance, they were forced to break the book into two (and later three) distinct portions, with separate authors. Isaiah, chapters 1–39, they decided, belonged to an Isaiah living in the eighth century because the writings conformed rather closely with what was known about that period of Israel's history. They insisted that the rest of the book, chapters 40–66, was written at least two centuries later and then added to the earlier Isaiah material. What was the basis of their conclusion? That men, even prophets, cannot see beyond the horizon of their own time. Thus, the detailed prophecies concerning the Babylonian period could not have been written much before the end of that time.[11]

For emphasis, I repeat that this whole school of inquiry arose primarily because these people accepted the supposition that Isaiah could not see two or more centuries into the future. The irony is that they are correct. Neither Isaiah the man nor Isaiah the prophet would have had that ability. That is the very point God makes in chapters 40–47. There is no intelligence that can see beyond the horizon of its time, except a divine being. A portion of what God sees, however, he is willing to share with his people through his prophets.[12] These seers do not possess in themselves the gift. Rather, it comes directly from God.

Let me stress that in these chapters of Isaiah, we see God using prophecy, with which he alone can empower the prophet, as the means through which he verifies and authenticates his position as the God of Israel and of the nations. Using explicit statements about the future, Jehovah proves that he, and he alone, is God. Therefore, it is only he that should be the center of worship and obedience.

I like prophecy. I find security in its evidence. I am surprised, therefore, to find that many people are discomforted by the idea. Such discomfort usually originates from two sources: either they do not believe in prophecy or they can't see how both freewill and prescience can coexist. Since both issues lie outside the scope of this study, I will just say that both the Hebrews and early Christians believed God had the power of prophecy. They saw God's foreknowledge as being compatible with the concept of human agency.

God's Relationship with the Future

This study asks about God's relationship to the future. Alma testifies that God has "all power, all wisdom, and all understanding; he comprehendeth all things" (Alma 26:35). God himself testified that he is "the same which knoweth all things, for all things are present before mine eyes" (D&C 38:2), and that "all things are present with me, for I know them all" (Moses 1:6). How can he do this? "Except he was a God," Helaman explains, "he could not know of all things" (Helaman 9:41). Thus, prescience is an attribute of God.

The question is, does God know the future and express it, or does he engineer the future and share what he makes happen? In other words, does the future exist for God as something already concrete and unchangeable, which he can see? In that case, prophecy would be God sharing his vision with humankind, allowing us to see from his height the inevitable course of events flowing within the stream of destiny. Or is the future something fluid that God creates? In that case, God knows the future because he has predetermined the course it will flow.

Joseph Smith gave us some insights into the question. He announced that for the great Jehovah, "the past, the present, and the future were and are, with Him, one eternal 'now.'"[13] Does the phrase "one eternal 'now'" mean that time is static for God—that everything that has existed, does now exist, and that ever will exist, actually abides with God right now? Does the "eternal 'now'" freeze events into a predetermined, unbreakable whole? The Prophet went on to say that Jehovah "knew of the fall of Adam, the iniquities of the antediluvians, of the depth of iniquity that would be connected with the human family. . . . He was acquainted with the situation of all nations and with their destiny."[14]

On the surface, the Prophet's comments make it look as if God interacts with the future as an observer, but that is not the case. In the same discourse, Joseph Smith said that Jehovah "ordered all things according to the council of His own will."[15] The phrase suggests that God shapes and directs history and that prophecy is God's sharing with humans his ordering of all things. That is, God creates the channel in which history flows. History, therefore, is not inevitable or fated until God makes it so. The revelation of God in Isaiah reinforces this view.

God Reveals Himself in Isaiah

To those who would challenge Jehovah, Isaiah asked:

Have ye not known?
have ye not heard?
hath it not been told you from the beginning?
have ye not understood from the foundations of the earth?
It is he that sitteth upon the circle of the earth,
and the inhabitants thereof are as grasshoppers;
[It is he] that stretcheth out the heavens as a curtain,
and spreadeth them out as a tent to dwell in:

[It is he] that bringeth the princes to nothing;
he maketh the judges of the earth as vanity [i.e., nothing].
Yea, they shall not be planted;
yea, they shall not be sown:
yea, their stock shall not take root in the earth:
and he shall also blow upon them, and they shall wither,
and the whirlwind shall take them away as stubble.
(Isaiah 40:21–24)

Isaiah's testimony shows God active in history, creating earth and heaven and directing the course of peoples and nations. God is in charge of all because he creates all. That includes judges, rulers, and nations. It is on this basis that Isaiah castigates Judah:

Why sayest thou, O Jacob,
and speakest, O Israel,
My way is hid from the Lord,
and my judgment is passed over from my God?
Hast thou not known?
hast thou not heard,
that the everlasting God, the Lord,
the Creator of the ends of the earth,
fainteth not, neither is weary?
there is no searching of his understanding.
He giveth power to the faint;
and to them that have no might he increaseth strength.
Even the youths shall faint and be weary,
and the young men shall utterly fall:
But they that wait upon the Lord shall renew their strength;
they shall mount up with wings as eagles;
they shall run, and not be weary;
and they shall walk, and not faint.
(Isaiah 40:27–31)

For Isaiah, Jehovah is the active agent who directly shapes history. He knows the ways of humankind and will not let anyone get away with anything. He strengthens those who are his and enables them to bring forth his purposes. God's control of the future comes out very clearly in Isaiah's next prophecy. Here the emphasis is on God's shaping the future by using those who will follow him. Looking two hundred years ahead, to the conquests of Cyrus, the Persian, Jehovah asks:

> *Who raised up the righteous man [that is, Cyrus] from the east,*
> *called him to his foot,*
> *gave the nations before him,*
> *and made him rule over kings?*
> *he gave them as the dust to his sword,*
> *and as driven stubble to his bow.*
> *He pursued them, and passed safely;*
> *even by the way that he had not gone with his feet.*
> (Isaiah 41:2–3)

God, then, drives home his point with a question and answer:

> *Who hath wrought and done it,*
> *calling the generations from the beginning?*
> *I the Lord,*
> *the first, and with the last; I am he.*
> (Isaiah 41:4)

God, no doubt, views himself as the one who creates history; thus, he dares to reveal his plans to his people. In this regard he can assure Israel that

> *When the poor and needy seek water,*
> *and there is none,*
> *and their tongue faileth for thirst,*
> *I the Lord will hear them,*

I the God of Israel will not forsake them.
I will open rivers in high places,
and fountains in the midst of the valleys:
I will make the wilderness a pool of water,
and the dry land springs of water.
I will plant in the wilderness
the cedar, the shittah tree, and the myrtle, and the oil tree;
I will set in the desert
the fir tree, and the pine, and the box tree together:
That they may see,
and know,
and consider,
and understand together,
that the hand of the Lord hath done this,
and the Holy One of Israel hath created it.
(*Isaiah 41:17–20*)

Isaiah shows us that not only are people in the hands of the Lord but so are the very elements of the earth. On this basis, Jehovah can promise Judah (and future scattered Israel) that he will call them home, and when he does, nothing can stop them. He will use the very elements to assist them.

The problem Judah will face is that, due to her idolatry and violation of God's commands, she will forfeit her right to the land. Having done that, is there any way she can be redeemed? Isaiah had the answer. He assured her that

thus saith the Lord that created thee, O Jacob,
and he that formed thee, O Israel,
Fear not: for I have redeemed thee,
I have called thee by thy name; thou art mine.
When thou passest through the waters, I will be with thee;
and through the rivers, they shall not overflow thee:

when thou walkest through the fire,
thou shalt not be burned;
neither shall the flame kindle upon thee.
For I am the Lord thy God,
the Holy One of Israel, thy Saviour.
(*Isaiah 43:1–3*)

He goes on to ask Israel to

Fear not: for I am with thee:
I will bring thy seed from the east, and gather thee
from the west;
I will say to the north, Give up;
and to the south, Keep not back:
bring my sons from far,
and my daughters from the ends of the earth;
Even every one that is called by my name:
for I have created him for my glory,
I have formed him;
yea, I have made him.
(*Isaiah 43:5–7*)

These verses clearly show the three ways that God creates the future: first, through the manipulations of physical elements; second, by calling people who will do his will; and third, by giving those he calls strength and power over opposition.

Through Isaiah, God clearly sets himself up as the God who controls all history—past, present, and future—including both individuals and nations.

God's Use of Prophecy to Authenticate Himself

Having set the foundation, the Lord issues the first of his challenges to those who have been seduced away from him to believe in idols and to practice divination.

Bring forth the blind people that have eyes,
and the deaf that have ears.
Let all the nations be gathered together,
and let the people be assembled:
who among them can declare this,
and shew us former things?
let them bring forth their witnesses,
that they may be justified:
or let them hear, and say, It is truth.
(*Isaiah 43:8–9*)

God issues his challenge first to the Jews, who, by not following the prophets have made themselves deaf and blind. God, however, enlarges the circle to include all idolatrous nations. Idols must prove themselves, he insists. The litmus test is prophecy. In order to prove their god true, all the idolaters have to do is produce witnesses that their god has accurately foretold the future.

The Lord's response comes from his foreknowledge that they will fail the test. Speaking from the strength of Creator, he tells Israel:

Thus saith the Lord, thy redeemer,
and he that formed thee from the womb,
I am the Lord
that maketh all things;
that stretcheth forth the heavens alone;
that spreadeth abroad the earth by myself;
[I am the one] that frustrateth the tokens of the liars,
and maketh diviners mad;
that turneth wise men backward,
and maketh their knowledge foolish;
That confirmeth the word of his servant,
and performeth the counsel of his messengers;
that saith to Jerusalem, Thou shalt be inhabited;
and to the cities of Judah, Ye shall be built,

and I will raise up the decayed places thereof:
That saith to the deep, Be dry,
and I will dry up thy rivers:
That saith of Cyrus, He is my shepherd,
and shall perform all my pleasure:
even saying to Jerusalem, Thou shalt be built;
and to the temple, Thy foundation shall be laid.
(Isaiah 44:24–28)

The Lord grounds his argument on the fact that he created Israel. Indeed, he created all things, including the present and the future. For this reason he can frustrate the prophecies of the soothsayers and by the same token, fulfill the words of his prophets. Therefore, he assures his people that Jerusalem will be rebuilt in spite of all evidence to the contrary. Further, all Judea shall be restored.

The Lord then delivers the coup de grace to idols. To show just how well he knows and controls the future, he actually names Cyrus as the one who will be his tool in restoring Judah and rebuilding the temple.[16] When Isaiah spoke God's word sometime before 740 B.C., the northern kingdom of Israel was still intact. It would be another twenty years before she would fall to the Assyrians (721 B.C.).[17] It would then take over a hundred years before the Assyrians would fall to the Babylonians (609 B.C.). Twenty additional years would be needed before the Babylonians destroyed Judea (589 B.C.), and another forty before Cyrus would lead his successful Persian assault on the Babylonians (ca. 550 B.C.). Only after that would he free the Jews and that would take an additional twelve years (537 B.C.). Seen in this light, Isaiah's prophecy was truly remarkable. What soothsayer or idol-worshipping priest has even revealed the name of a person coming two hundred years in the future?

The specificity of the revelation does not end there. The Lord was very precise in speaking to Cyrus through Isaiah concerning the results of the Lord's assistance to the future Persian king.

Thus saith the Lord to his anointed,
to Cyrus, whose right hand I have holden,

to subdue nations before him;
and I will loose the loins of kings,
to open before him the two leaved gates;
and the gates shall not be shut;
I will go before thee,
and make the crooked places straight:
I will break in pieces the gates of brass,
and cut in sunder the bars of iron:
And I will give thee the treasures of darkness,
and hidden riches of secret places,
that thou mayest know that I, the LORD,
which call thee by thy name,
am the God of Israel.

(*Isaiah 45:1–3*)

In these verses the Lord guarantees Cyrus's success, including the fact that what he conquers will stay conquered. Further, the Lord will see to it that Cyrus will find not only the open riches but also those which have been carefully hidden. So spectacular were Cyrus's successes that it is hard to separate history from legend,[18] yet one fact is certain: through Cyrus's gifts as general and diplomat, whole nations fell to him, allowing him to create the largest empire up to his day. The Lord's promise of wealth was fully fulfilled. Cyrus accumulated the equivalent of more than two hundred and fifty million dollars from the Lydian state alone.[19]

Of course, God did not assist Cyrus just to bring the king glory. God had a higher purpose in mind. This he clearly spells out to the future ruler.

For Jacob my servant's sake,
and Israel mine elect,
I have even called thee by thy name:
I have surnamed thee,
though thou hast not known me.

I am the Lord,
and there is none else,
there is no God beside me:
I girded thee,
though thou hast not known me:
That they may know from the rising of the sun,
and from the west,
that there is none beside me.
I am the Lord,
and there is none else.
I form the light,
and create darkness:
I make peace,
and create evil:
I the Lord do all these things.

(Isaiah 45:4–7)

The Lord used these prophecies to impress the future king and push him into doing Jehovah's will. History shows that it worked. According to the Jewish historian Josephus: "In the first year of the reign of Cyrus, which was the seventieth from the day that our people were removed out of their own land into Babylon, God commiserated the captivity and calamity of these poor people. . . . For he stirred up the mind of Cyrus, and made him write this throughout all Asia: 'Thus saith Cyrus the king: Since God Almighty hath appointed me to be king of the habitable earth, I believe that he is that God which the nation of the Israelites worship; for indeed he foretold my name by the prophets, and that I should build him a house at Jerusalem, in the country of Judea.'

"This was known to Cyrus by his reading the book which Isaiah left behind him of his prophecies."[20]

The Lord did not make this display of his prescience merely to impress Cyrus. His main objective was to get Israel's attention. It was his way of bringing her to understanding, to testimony, to repentance, and to him. In the above scripture, the Lord clearly stated his message: he is the only God. He alone was the creator of light and dark, of blessing and cursing, his point being that Judah had to recognize him as the only God and come back into his circle.[21]

This is where God's appeal to prophecy came in. Here was evidence of power that could not be denied. A God who knew the future was a God who controlled the future. To have faith in any other being was both foolish and damnable.

The nature of Jehovah's appeal shows that his target audience was Israel. His logic, though very appealing, would not particularly persuade pagans. Judah, however, was another matter. She had her records and at least gave lip service to them. That meant she could not deny the prophecies found in them. We see this particularly in his encouragement to her when the Lord said:

> *Remember this, and shew yourselves men:*
> *bring it again to mind,*
> *O ye transgressors.*
> *Remember the former things of old:*
> *for I am God, and there is none else; I am God,*
> *and there is none like me,*
> *Declaring the end from the beginning,*
> *and from ancient times the things that are not yet done,*
> *saying, My counsel shall stand,*
> *and I will do all my pleasure:*
> *Calling a ravenous bird from the east,*
> *the man that executeth my counsel from a far country:*
> *yea, I have spoken it,*
> *I will also bring it to pass;*
> *I have purposed it,*
> *I will also do it.*
> *Hearken unto me, ye stouthearted,*
> *that are far from righteousness:*
> *I bring near my righteousness;*

it shall not be far off,
and my salvation shall not tarry:
and I will place salvation in Zion
for Israel my glory.
(*Isaiah 46:8–13*)

The Lord clearly pointed out that, in leaving him, Israel had proven herself faithless. She had forgotten her own history, in which God had proved she could trust him through his display of foreknowledge. He now commands her to remember the former things, for what he has declared will continue to come to pass. He assures her that even though she is yet far from righteous, he fully intends to save her.

The Lord concludes this line of reasoning in Isaiah 48. Here, we see his entire argument. In it he reminds Israel of the lessons he tried to teach her in the past through prophets and their prophecies. He begins by castigating the people, saying:

Hear ye this, O house of Jacob, which are called by the name of Israel,
and are come forth out of the waters of Judah,
which swear by the name of the Lord,
and make mention of the God of Israel,
but not in truth, nor in righteousness.
(*Isaiah 48:1*)

Israel's problem was not that she knew not God, but that she would not honor his ways. She would swear oaths to him, but then turn to other gods. Therefore, he turned to prophecy as a means of reclaiming her from the idols.

I have declared the former things from the beginning;
and they went forth out of my mouth, and I shewed them;
I did them suddenly, and they came to pass.
Because I knew that thou art obstinate,

and thy neck is an iron sinew,
and thy brow brass;
I have even from the beginning declared it to thee;
before it came to pass I shewed it thee:
lest thou shouldest say, Mine idol hath done them,
and my graven image, and my molten image, hath commanded them.
Thou hast heard, see all this; and will not ye declare [that is, admit] it?

(Isaiah 48:3–6)

Jehovah explains that a number of his prophecies came suddenly, without being asked for or anticipated. He had to do it this way, he laments, otherwise, Israel would have attributed the foreknowledge to her idols. Just in case she was not impressed with the past, the Lord goes on to say, he will now display this same power again.

I [will show] . . . thee new things from this time,
even hidden things, and thou didst not know them.
They are created now,
and not from the beginning;
even before the day when thou heardest them not;
lest thou shouldest say, Behold, I knew them.
Yea, thou heardest not; yea, thou knewest not;
yea, from that time that thine ear was not opened:
for I knew that thou wouldest deal very treacherously,
and wast called a transgressor from the womb.

(Isaiah 48:6–8)

Even as he speaks to Israel, God shows forth his power over the future. He declares that new things "are created now," meaning that his divine word, now being spoken through Isaiah, has set the future on its divine course. The prophecies he refers to, which take up much of the rest of Isaiah's book, are the fall of Babylon, the redemption of Judah, and the future gathering of Israel. Jehovah clearly expresses his reason for telling Judah what is to come: he knew just how treacherous, how faithless, and how given to apostasy and idolatry she was. Thus, he manifested his power as a hedge against this. If Israel will now respond to his renewed show of power, he goes on to say, he will receive her and bless her.

> *For my name's sake will I defer mine anger,*
> *and for my praise will I refrain for thee, that I cut thee*
> *not off.*
> *Behold, I have refined thee, but not with silver;*
> *I have chosen thee in the furnace of affliction.*
> *For mine own sake,*
> *even for mine own sake,*
> *will I do it:*
> *for how should my name be polluted?*
> *and I will not give my glory unto another.*
> *(Isaiah 48:9–11)*

As we see, God set up this whole display of his power in order to dissuade Israel from ascribing knowledge of that which is to come to her idols, and also to prove, once and for all, that he alone is Israel's God. He has not forsaken her—though she deserved his doing so. If she learns the lesson that God allowed "the furnace of affliction" to force upon her, Jehovah will take her back. His glory will not be given to any but Israel.

Summary

The message of hope and testimony was not lost on the sixth-century Jews, and many did return to God. Once Cyrus found out that Jehovah had been assisting him, he also responded to God's will. The Jews returned, Jehovah's temple was rebuilt, the waste places of Judah were renewed—all exactly as Isaiah had foretold. History itself bears out how perfectly God knows and can reveal the future from the ever-present "now." It is little wonder that he has singled out prophecy of Israel and of the cosmos as the ultimate test of his exclusive position as God.

In this light it is easy to see why he forbids all illicit attempts at probing the future. In the best case, they are a waste of time. In a moderate case, they are acts of extreme faithlessness. They reveal the belief that one can create his own future outside of God and his laws. In the worst case, they are acts of sheer hubris, attempts to reorder the universe according to one's designs or, in other words, attempts to become god. Jehovah will not tolerate such an abomination.

In the end only God can know the future. He can know it because he sets its course, acting within the present to assure the future. He sends forth his disciples, gives them instructions, strengthens them, and, finally, manipulates nature to their advantage. Therefore, their future is secure in him.

It is now easy to see how God used prophecy in the Old Testament period to authenticate himself. He prophesied, waited for fulfillment of his prophecies, challenged idols to do the same, and when they could not, revealed that they were nothing. He then demanded obedience.

We can also see why he used prophecy. It is a power only he possesses; nothing can duplicate it. Thus, he could use it to build the faith of others in him and demand their allegiance. Prescience and prognosis as attributes of God describe more than a very accurate ability to predict. God knows the future not just because he "ordered all things according to the council of his own will" but also because he is actively involved in it moment by moment. There is, however, even more to it than that.

I have often heard people say that God's foreknowledge is solely a function of his prolonged and discerning familiarity with us in the premortal world. This, no doubt, forms part of his ability, but it goes beyond that. Elder Neal A. Maxwell has said that we must see it in terms of "the stunning reality that the past and present and future are part of an 'eternal now' with God!"[22] He simply has knowledge and vision beyond anything we, trapped in our three-dimensional box, can have. Prophecy does not refer to the human ability to extrapolate, guess, deduce, or conjure what is coming. The word denotes a knowledge possessed by God, given to prophets through the Spirit, by which the future is known. Prophecy is not God's guessing about or predicting the future, but his sharing with us an absolute and concrete reality. One thing we can do is trust in that foreknowledge, allowing its display to do that which God designed: build faith in him as the one and only true and living God.

Notes

1. The word *prophecy* derives from the Greek προφήτης, which has much the same meaning as in English: the authorized speaking of the divine purpose or will. Thus, prophecy is any expression of and witness to God's will. This is sometimes called "forth-telling." Bearing testimony is the purest kind of prophesying (Revelation 19:10). Foretelling the future is only a small subset of prophecy.

2. See also Leviticus 19:26, 31; Deuteronomy 12:29–32.

3. The Hebrew word is הוֹעֵבָה and the Greek is βδελύγμα. Both these words convey essentially the same meaning, something so detestable that it must not be brought before God. To do so would arouse his wrath. The translations of all Greek words in this paper, unless noted otherwise, come from Walter Bauer, *A Greek-English Lexicon of the New Testament and Other Early Christian Literature,* trans. William F. Arndt and F. Wilber Gingrich, 2d ed. (Chicago: University of Chicago Press, 1979). All Hebrew translations come from William Gesenius, *A Hebrew and English Lexicon of the Old Testament,* trans. Edward Robinson, ed. Francis Brown (Oxford: Clarendon Press, 1978).

4. Rousas John Rushdoony, *The Institutes of Biblical Law* (n.p.: The Presbyterian and Reformed Publishing Company, 1973), 30.

5. See 1 Kings 11:7, 33. The word *Moloch* is the Hebrew mispronunciation of the name of this idol. The Hebrews misvocalized the word by mixing the consonants of "king" with the vowels for "shame." Rushdoony, *Institutes,* 32.

6. Rushdoony, *Institutes,* 32.

7. Rushdoony, *Institutes,* 32–33.

8. David Noel Freedman, ed., *The Anchor Bible Dictionary: H–J,* 6 vols. (New York: Doubleday, 1992), 3:472.

9. *Anchor Bible Dictionary,* 3:472–73.

10. *Anchor Bible Dictionary,* 3:473.

11. Out of this has grown three schools of thought which try to make sense of Isaiah without having to deal with his foretelling abilities: the "direct referential," "the form and traditional critical," and "the redactional." For a brief but comprehensive explanation, see Freedman, *Anchor Bible Dictionary,* 3:475–77. Though the scholars using these methodologies cannot agree on what constituted the original text of Isaiah, they do agree that the later prophetic portions cannot belong to the eighth-century Isaiah. Chapters 40 through 66, the most cohesive portion of the book, they agree, were definitely written after the rise of Cyrus.

12. This is the pattern the Lord gave to Israel through Moses. In the same passage in which God forbade Israel to use divination, he also promised them that "I will raise them up a prophet from among their brethren, like unto thee, and will put my words in his mouth; and he shall speak unto them all that I shall command him" (Deuteronomy 18:18).

13. Joseph Smith, *Teachings of the Prophet Joseph Smith,* sel. Joseph Fielding Smith (Salt Lake City: Deseret Book, 1976), 220.

14. Ibid.

15. Ibid. The word *council* here should probably be *counsel.* The popular dictionary of the Prophet's day (Noah Webster, *An American Dictionary of the English Language,* 1828; reprint, electronic edition, Salt Lake City: Deseret Book, 1998) makes it clear that a *council* is a group of people of equal rank appointed for some duty and that the word is often, but should not be, confused with *counsel*. Though the word *council* may be used for the deliberations of a council (see *Webster's New Collegiate Dictionary* [Springfield, Mass.: G. & C. Merriam Company, 1973], s.v. "Council"), the context suggests that God moved according to his own designs or purposes, that is, his own counsel.

16. According to Josephus, when Cyrus read this passage (Isaiah 44:24–28), he determined he would do Jehovah's will and sent the Jews back to the Holy Land (Flavius Josephus, *Jewish Antiquities, Books IX–XI,* trans. Ralph Marcus, vol. 6 [Cambridge, Mass.: Harvard University Press, 1987], 11.2). The history of Cyrus's name is given in Franz Delitzsch, *Biblical Commentary on the Prophecies of Isaiah,* trans. James Martin, 2 vols. (Edinburgh: T. & T. Clark, 1872), 2:217. Some say his name means "the sun" and is derived from *char.* His monuments, however, refer to him

as *Kuru* or *Khuru* (the Hebrews Hebraized it as *Kōresh.* Greeks spelled it κύρος. Strabo notes that Cyrus took his name from the river *Kur.* "There is also a river called Cyrus, which flows through the so-called cave of Persis near Pasargadæ, and whence the king took his name, changing it from Agradates into Cyrus" (Strabo 15.3, 6). There could be a connection between the name and the Indian princely title of *Kuru.*

17. Dates used here follow those of the Dictionary in the LDS edition of the KJV.

18. Xenophon's *Cyropaedia* is a good example of the combining of truth and myth. See also Jarem 1.37.

19. Jarem 1.37, 11.13; Xenophon, *Cyropaedia* 7.2, 11; Carl F. Keil and Franz Delitzsch, *Commentary on the Old Testament,* trans. James Martin, et al., 10 vols. (Grand Rapids, Mich.: Eerdmans, 1983), 7:219.

20. Flavius Josephus, *The Life and Works of Flavius Josephus,* trans. William Whiston (New York: Holt, Rinehart and Winston, n.d.), 321.

21. Though God spoke specifically to Cyrus, the king never did get the message. Throughout his life he remained a polytheist, championing the gods of the lands he conquered and restoring shrines and idols. He seems to have felt a special place for Jehovah, but he also claimed assistance from the Babylonian god Marduk. See M. J. Dresden, "Cyrus," *The Interpreter's Dictionary of the Bible,* 4 vols. (Nashville, Tenn.: Abingdon Press, 1962), 1:754–55. Cyrus did not have to convert to be God's anointed one. His position seems to have been foreordained. See Joseph Smith, *History of The Church of Jesus Christ of Latter-day Saints,* ed. B. H. Roberts, 2d ed. rev., 7 vols. (Salt Lake City: The Church of Jesus Christ of Latter-day Saints, 1932–51), 4:257. What Cyrus had to do in mortality was favor Jehovah, see that the Jews returned, and provide the means for building Jehovah's temple. He succeeded admirably in all these things.

22. Neal A. Maxwell, *All These Things Shall Give Thee Experience* (Salt Lake City: Deseret Book, 1979), 8.

11

Isaiah's Vision of God's Plan to Fulfill His Covenant

Michael L. King

As the house of Israel was in the midst of destruction and dispersion, the Lord promised through his prophet Isaiah that in an "acceptable time," he would hear them, and "in a day of salvation," he would help them and preserve them, give them "for a covenant of the people," and cause them to "inherit the desolate heritages." The Lord promised them, "I will make all my mountains a way, and my highways shall be exalted" (Isaiah 49:8, 11). The "mountains" of the Lord would provide "a way" for all of Israel to one day receive the covenant.

Having seen many of their people die, however, members of the house of Israel could not understand how they could still receive the promised blessings and lamented, "The Lord hath forsaken me, and my Lord hath forgotten me" (Isaiah 49:14). To those who did not understand the Lord's plan, the fact that many of the house of Israel died without receiving the promised blessings was evidence that God had forgotten his covenant and forsaken his people. Similarly,

Michael L. King is Church Educational System coordinator and director of the Corpus Christi Texas Institute of Religion.

many who destroyed the Nephites, a remnant of the house of Israel, believed that they had destroyed "the work of the Lord, and the Lord will not remember his covenant." As a witness of the destruction, but being one who understood the covenant, Moroni boldly declared: "The eternal purposes of the Lord shall roll on, until all his promises shall be fulfilled. Search the prophecies of Isaiah" (Mormon 8:21–23). Moroni saw in the writings of Isaiah the Lord's plan to keep his covenant with a people that had been defeated and destroyed. Nephi, Jacob, and the Savior also used the writings of Isaiah to explain God's intent to fulfill his covenant with the house of Israel.

The Message of Isaiah

Many, if not all, students of the scriptures find Isaiah difficult to understand. This is due in part to the fact that Isaiah intimately interweaves details from his own time with his prophecies of the latter days and of the time of the Savior. Like a master weaver of fabric, Isaiah uses a multitude of threads that combine to form the final tapestry. The threads are so tightly woven that it becomes difficult to separate each individual thread. This is especially true in relation to the fulfilling of the covenant with the house of Israel. While telling of the destruction coming upon the house of Israel, Isaiah blends the imagery of the tabernacle from his day, the mortal and postmortal mission of Christ, and the restoration of the gospel and construction of temples in the latter days to reveal the Lord's plan for restoring the children of Israel to the covenant. Isaiah blends these ideas over and over, going back and forth in both time and event, leaving readers to engage themselves more in the finished tapestry than to look for each individual thread.

A study of Isaiah and the commentary provided by Book of Mormon prophets shows that four main threads are instrumental in the Lord's plan to fulfill his covenant. First, many of the house of Israel will die before receiving the covenant; second, Christ must come and open the way for all people to be taught the gospel and enter into the presence of God; third, "mountains" will provide a way whereby all, including the dead, may be brought forth to receive the covenant; and fourth, the Gentiles of the latter days will be instrumental in helping ancient Israel receive the covenant. While most Latter-day Saints are familiar with God's covenant with Israel, a brief summary may be helpful before looking at Isaiah's prophecies regarding its fulfillment.

The Covenant

Since the fall of Adam, the prophets and patriarchs have been promised that they and their future posterity would one day return to the presence of God. Abraham, a man who "sought for the blessings of the fathers" (Abraham 1:2), received a renewal of this promise, which became known as the Abrahamic covenant (Genesis 17:7–9).

The Lord's promises to Abraham can be loosely summarized into three main ideas, captured in the letters LDS, representing land, deliverance (through Christ and God's priesthood), and seed (Genesis 17: 5–9; Abraham 2:6–11). The promise was that Abraham would have countless seed, a place to raise that seed, and power through a deliverer to lift his seed from the corruption of a telestial world. Neither Abraham, though faithful and righteous, nor successive prophets saw the fulfillment of the covenant during their lifetimes. Speaking of Abraham, Isaac, and Jacob, the apostle Paul wrote, "These all died in faith, not having received the promises, but having seen them afar off, and were persuaded of them, and embraced them, and confessed that they were strangers and pilgrims on the earth" (Hebrews 11:13; see also 11:10–16).

The seed of Abraham, Isaac, and Jacob, known as the house of Israel, journeyed from one land to another in search of their promised blessings, but because of disobedience to God, they were continually scattered and destroyed. It was during a time of dispersion and destruction among the house of Israel that Isaiah was called to prophesy. Watching the fall and scattering of the house of Israel, Isaiah was keenly aware of the need to provide hope to Israel that God's promises would be fulfilled, though many of Israel's people had died.

There Shalt Thou Die

From the beginning of his writings, Isaiah makes it clear that he understands the fallen condition of the children of Israel. He speaks of a people who have forgotten and forsaken the Lord. They are sick, have fainted, and are full of wounds, bruises, and sores. He speaks of their desolate country that has been burned, devoured, and overthrown by strangers. He tells them that in that day, the Lord will make a "call to weeping, and to mourning, and to baldness, and to girding with sackcloth." Israel will not listen but will say, "Eat and drink; for to morrow we shall die." So the Lord will tell Israel, "Surely this iniquity shall not be purged from you till ye die." Isaiah is commanded to tell Israel that "the Lord will carry thee away with a mighty captivity, and . . . will surely violently turn and toss thee like a ball into a large country: there shalt thou die" (Isaiah 22:12–14, 17–18; see also 22:2–7). Later, Isaiah calls Israel "a people robbed and spoiled" and "hid in prison houses," because "they would not walk in his ways, neither were they obedient unto his law" (Isaiah 42:22, 24). Isaiah makes it clear that the children of the house of Israel were to die and be shut up in prison.

A Savior, Redeemer, and High Priest

While dead and in prison, Israel is not left without hope. Isaiah prophesied that after the "prisoners are gathered in the pit, and shall be shut up in the prison, . . . after many days shall they be visited" (Isaiah 24:22). When they are visited, the Lord will say, "I will preserve thee, and give thee for a covenant of the people . . . that thou mayest say to the prisoners, Go forth; to them that are in darkness, Shew yourselves" (Isaiah 49:8–9). Isaiah repeatedly promises Israel that the Lord will be their savior and redeemer (Isaiah 43), "will swallow up death in victory," and "will wipe away tears from off all faces" (Isaiah 25:8). "Thy dead men shall live, together with my dead body shall they arise. Awake and sing, ye that dwell in dust" (Isaiah 26:19). "Awake, awake; put on thy strength, O Zion; put on thy beautiful garments, O Jerusalem. . . . Shake thyself from the dust; arise, and sit down, O Jerusalem: loose thyself from the bands of thy neck, O captive daughter of Zion. . . . Ye have sold yourselves for nought; and ye shall be redeemed without money" (Isaiah 52:1–3). The Lord further promises Israel, "The earth shall wax old like a garment, and they that dwell therein shall die in like manner: but my salvation shall be forever, and my righteousness shall not be abolished" (Isaiah 51:6). Christ's covenant to provide salvation for Israel was to go beyond the veil and take place "in an acceptable time . . . and in a day of salvation . . . that thou mayest say to the prisoners, Go forth" (Isaiah 49:8–9).

Through the ages of the earth, the percentage of God's children that has heard Christ's teachings during mortality has been relatively small. Until the dead have an opportunity to hear the gospel and receive eternal life, the plan is not acceptable to God, for he takes no "pleasure at all that the wicked should die" (Ezekiel 18:23; see also 18:30–32).

Providing redemption for the dead was to be one of the Savior's key roles as the Messiah. President Joseph F. Smith, in his marvelous vision concerning the redemption of the dead, recognized that Isaiah was referring to the Savior's role in the work for the dead when Isaiah stated, "The Lord hath anointed me to preach good tidings unto the meek; he hath sent me to bind up the brokenhearted, to proclaim liberty to the captives, and the opening of the prison to them that are bound" (Isaiah 61:1; see also D&C 138:42). Using these statements of Isaiah as a helpful template, we can see Christ's role in fulfilling the covenant with the house of Israel in four ways. First, binding up the brokenhearted may be compared to Christ's atonement for the sins of those who have a broken heart and a contrite spirit.[1] Second, Christ opened the prison to them who are bound by opening the way for the preaching of the gospel to the spirits in prison.[2] Third, through his resurrection, Christ proclaimed liberty to the captives of death and hell.[3] Fourth, through his restored Church, the Savior, who was given the priestly mantle to part the veil and allow all to enter celestial glory, declares the good tidings that he has made possible celestial exaltation.[4]

In order to illustrate Christ's role in opening the way into the celestial presence of God, Isaiah draws upon the imagery of the ancient tabernacle. Isaiah tells us that Christ would be similar to the high priest in Israel, being "clothe[d]" with the "robe" and the "girdle" (Isaiah 22:21; see also Isaiah 22:20, 20a), as the priest was clothed anciently (Leviticus 8:7). Christ would also be given the "key of the house of David," and it would be laid "upon his shoulder; so he shall open, and none shall shut" (Isaiah 22:22).[5] Isaiah then blends this tabernacle imagery with a powerful scene from the Savior's ministry, telling us that Christ would be fastened "as a nail in a sure place; and he shall be for a glorious throne to his father's house. And they shall hang upon him all the glory of his father's house" (Isaiah 22:23–24; see also 22:25).

A second witness to Isaiah's imagery of Christ as the high priest is found in the epistle of Paul to the Hebrews. As one of the great temple texts of ancient scripture, the book of Hebrews sheds additional light on "the Apostle and High Priest of our profession, Christ Jesus" (Hebrews 3:1). Christ could enter into the holy of holies, "being come an high priest of good things to come, by a greater and more perfect tabernacle . . . neither by the blood of goats and calves, but by his own blood he entered in once into the holy place" (Hebrews 9:11–12; see also 5:1–6; 7:15–17). Prior to the time of Christ, only the high priest of Israel was allowed to enter the Holy of Holies, and then only once a year on the Day of Atonement.[6] To ancient Israelites, the Holy of Holies represented the dwelling place of God, and they could not enter therein. The high priest had to perform ordinances on their behalf. As both great high priest and the sacrificial lamb, however, Christ opened the way so that all men could enter with "boldness . . . into the holiest by the blood of Jesus" (Hebrews 10:19; see also 4:14–16; 10:12–22). Christ administered the ordinances necessary to allow entrance into the Holy of Holies, not for himself alone, but also "having obtained eternal redemption for us" as well (Hebrews 9:12).

In the Garden of Gethsemane, Christ offered "the High-Priestly prayer"[7] on behalf of all his brothers and sisters. Then, through his crucifixion, he offered himself as the great and last sacrifice in order to place blood upon the doorposts (Exodus 12:7)[8] so that all might enter the Holy of Holies. At Christ's death, the "veil of the temple was rent" (Matthew 27:51), thus symbolizing that the way had opened for all men to enter into the presence of God.

Christ made it possible for all mankind to be taught the gospel, forgiven of sin, resurrected, and brought back into the presence of God through the ordinances of godliness. A way now had to be provided whereby those who had died could receive the ordinances of salvation along with the living.

I Shall Make All My Mountains a Way

The Lord tells Israel, "I will make all my mountains a way, and my highways shall be exalted" (Isaiah 49:11), and he promises, "Even them (Israel) will I bring to my holy mountain, and make them joyful in my house of prayer" (Isaiah 56:7). Isaiah tells Israel, "Ye shall be gathered one by one, O ye children of Israel . . . and shall worship the Lord in the holy mount" (Isaiah 27:12–13). Isaiah paints the image of mountains as the place for a joyful return of Israel to their God. "In the last days," he prophesies "that the mountain of the Lord's house shall be established in the top of the mountains," and "all nations shall flow unto it." It is here that "many people shall go and say, Come ye, and let us go up to the mountain of the Lord, to the house of the God of Jacob; and he will teach us of his ways, and we will walk in his paths" (Isaiah 2:2–3).

Prophets and righteous men from the beginning have been called to mountains to meet with God and receive instructions from him. Enoch was called up to mount Simeon, which means "hearing" in Hebrew, to hear God's word and be "clothed upon with glory" (Moses 7:2a, 3). The brother of Jared went up to Mount Shelem, where the veil was parted and he saw God (Ether 3). The Lord told Moses when he stood upon the mountain, "Put off thy shoes from off thy feet, for the place whereon thou standest is holy ground" (Exodus 3:5). Moses was called up to a mountain on several occasions, where he was clothed with the glory of God and received instructions regarding the creation, fall, and salvation of the world (Moses 1–4). It was to a mountain that Christ took Peter, James, and John during his mortal ministry in order for them to be endowed with the keys of the kingdom (Matthew 17:1–9).[9]

Just as mountains have served as meeting places between God and man throughout history, ancient tabernacles and latter-day temples have been built to provide man-made mountains where man and deity may meet (D&C 97:12–16). They are designed in both architecture and imagery to lift one's thoughts toward God. Much of the imagery used by Isaiah reflects an intimate understanding of the ceremony and symbolism of the tabernacle as well as of latter-day temples. Isaiah uses this understanding to teach the ordinances of the temple that are necessary so that God may fulfill his covenant with members of the house of Israel and provide them a way to return to him.

At the beginning of his ministry, Isaiah was taken to the temple to meet the Lord and receive his commission to teach the people. He "saw the Lord sitting upon a throne" surrounded by seraphim, or cherubim. As "the posts of the door moved," Isaiah became self-conscious and felt unworthy to enter into the Lord's presence. Isaiah no doubt had an understanding of the tabernacle and knew that only the high priest, on the Day of Atonement, was allowed to enter the Holy of Holies. As the high priest approached the entrance of the Holy of Holies, he encountered the veil, on which were embroidered cherubim, which symbolized sentinels to guard the way into the presence of God. In order to enter, the priest would strike the posts with blood from an animal that had been slain as atonement for the sins of the people.[10] Perhaps this was what Isaiah witnessed as he described the posts of the door moving. He realized that he was being invited to enter into the presence of the Lord. It is no wonder that he would exclaim, "Woe is me! for I am undone; . . . for mine eyes have seen the King, the Lord of hosts" (Isaiah 6:5).

Isaiah is symbolically cleansed when one of the angels takes a coal from the altar of sacrifice, a symbol of Jesus' sacrifice, and places it upon the prophet's mouth. Isaiah is told, "Thine iniquity is taken away, and thy sin purged" (Isaiah 6:7). Having been cleansed by the Atonement, Isaiah is now prepared to go forth into the presence of the Lord. Similarly, those who come to the covenant of Israel must first be cleansed through the atonement of Christ, representing the first step leading back into the presence of God.

Isaiah shows another step in the path back to God by stating that those who are called the house of Israel are those who have "come forth out of the waters of Judah, or out of the waters of baptism" (1 Nephi 20:1; see also Isaiah 48:1). Baptism provides a necessary step for all who desire to return to the presence of God (2 Nephi 31:4–18; D&C 128:13–18).

Once they have been cleansed by the Atonement and have entered into the covenant through baptism, the covenant people are "called by a new name, which the mouth of the Lord shall name" (Isaiah 62:2; see also Revelation 2:17; D&C 130:10–11). This new name will be given to those who "take hold of my covenant," and they shall receive "in mine house and within my walls a *place* and a name better than of sons and of daughters: I will give them an everlasting name" (Isaiah 56:4–5; emphasis added). The word "place" is derived from the Hebrew word *yad,* which is more commonly translated "hand."[11]

Those who accept this hand and name in the house of the Lord shall be "named the Priests of the Lord" and those of the covenant "shall be joyful in [their] God; for he hath clothed [them] with the garments of salvation, he hath covered [them] with the robe of righteousness" (Isaiah 61:6, 10). The Lord calls these his "sanctified ones" and commands them, "Lift ye up a banner upon the high mountain, exalt the voice unto them, shake the hand, that they may go into the gates of the nobles" (Isaiah 13:2–4). They are to "go through, go through the gates; prepare ye the way of the people; cast up, cast up the highway; gather out the stones; lift up a standard for the people" (Isaiah 62:10). Symbolically, it is through the gates of the nobles that one must pass in order to enter into the presence of God. Those who have thus entered must in turn help others to enter through the gates and lift up a standard for others to follow.

Gentiles Set Up for a Standard

Isaiah tells us that the Lord will "lift up [his] hand to the Gentiles, and set up [his] standard to the people: and they shall bring thy sons in their arms, and thy daughters shall be carried upon their shoulders" (Isaiah 49:22). When questioned by his brothers concerning these verses, Nephi explained that after Israel was "scattered and confounded," the Lord would "raise up a mighty nation among the Gentiles" and "set them up for a standard." God would "proceed to do a marvelous work among the Gentiles," which would be of worth not only to the Gentiles but also "unto all the house of Israel, unto the making known of the covenants of the Father of heaven unto Abraham, saying: In thy seed shall all the kindreds of the earth be blessed" (1 Nephi 22:6–9). Isaiah tells us that this marvelous work would take place when "the vision of all is become unto you as the words of a book that is sealed," which shall "speak out of the ground" (Isaiah 29:4, 11).

The coming forth of the Book of Mormon and the restoration of the gospel in the latter days marked the beginning of the marvelous work to restore Israel to the covenant and give all men the chance to feast at the table of the Lord. Isaiah prophesied that it was to be "in this mountain" that the Lord would "make unto all people a feast of fat things, a feast of wines on the lees." He would also "destroy in this mountain the face of the covering cast over all people, and the vail that is spread over all nations." He would "swallow up death in victory" and "wipe away tears from off all faces . . . for in this mountain shall the hand of the Lord rest" (Isaiah 25:6–8, 10). The Lord has told the Saints of the latter days that it is their honor to prepare this feast for all to come and partake. It is the "supper of the house of the Lord, well prepared, unto which all nations shall be invited" (D&C 58:9; see also 58:7–13).

The feast or supper of the Lord's house could not be served until a house of the Lord, or mountain, was built. Before temples could be brought forth upon the earth, however, the people had to be gathered. Both a spiritual gathering and a physical gathering had to occur before the work of the temple could proceed. Ezekiel speaks of this gathering that had to occur before "dry bones" could live (Ezekiel 37:2; see also 37:1–14), and Isaiah states that Israel must be gathered before she can "shake [herself] from the dust" (Isaiah 52:2; see also 51; 52).

In the latter days, the Prophet Joseph Smith taught, "What was the object of gathering the Jews, or the people of God in any age of the world? . . . The main object was to build unto the Lord a house whereby he could reveal unto His people the ordinances of His house and the glories of His kingdom, and teach the people the way of salvation; for there are certain ordinances and principles that, when they are taught and practiced, must be done in a place or house built for that purpose.

"It was the design of the councils of heaven before the world was, that the principles and laws of the priesthood should be predicated upon the gathering of the people in every age of the world. . . . It is for the same purpose that God gathers together His people in the last days, to build unto the Lord a house to prepare them for the ordinances and endowments, washings and anointings, etc."[12]

The gathering for the purpose of building temples is compared in both ancient and modern scripture to the spreading of a tent. Isaiah used this imagery to describe Zion and the establishment of the tabernacle (Isaiah 33:20). Isaiah told Israel to "enlarge the place of thy tent, and let them stretch forth the curtains of thine habitations: spare not, lengthen thy cords, and strengthen thy stakes" (Isaiah 54:2). In the latter days, the Lord has told the Saints to "arise and shine forth, that thy light may be a standard for the nations; And that the gathering together upon the land of Zion, and upon her stakes, may be for a defense." Zion was to be called "most holy . . . ground," a place to "build a house unto me, for the gathering together of my saints, that they may worship me" (D&C 115:5–8).

Using an analogy of circus workers raising the big top may help to understand the raising of Zion. Before the center pole can be raised, the canvas must be spread to its full capacity. The ropes or cords are drawn out to their full length, and then stakes are driven to hold the tent in place. After enough stakes have been placed, the center pole is raised, and the stakes are driven in further to keep the canvas tight and secure. Additional stakes follow until the tent is standing firm.

Similarly, in the building of temples, the gospel must first be spread out to its full capacity. Stakes are established in an area to help the members stay firm in the faith and enjoy a measure of the gospel blessings. When enough stakes are established, the center point, or the temple, is raised to complete the work of gathering all to Zion. The Lord referred to Zion as a "center place" where a temple would be erected (D&C 57:3; see also 57:1–2). The living must be physically brought together so that enough stakes can be laid to allow the center point to be raised. A spiritual gathering must also occur in order to bring people to an understanding of the covenant and in order to generate sufficient desire for the promises made to the fathers (Malachi 4:5–6; Abraham 1:1–4). A great preparatory work had to occur before the first temples of the last dispensation could be built.

The long wait between the Savior's mission among the living and the dead and the establishment of temples to provide a way for the dead to be redeemed left many wondering if God had forgotten his covenant with the house of Israel (Isaiah 64:6–12). "Zion said, The Lord hath forsaken me, and my Lord hath forgotten me." But the Lord replies, "Can a woman forget her sucking child, that she should not have compassion on the son of her womb? Yea, they may forget, yet will I not forget thee. Behold, I have graven thee upon the palms of my hands; thy walls are continually before me" (Isaiah 49:14–16). The Lord tells Israel, "For a small moment have I forsaken thee; but with great mercies will I gather thee" (Isaiah 54:7). He goes on to promise Israel that "thy children" will "gather themselves together," and he will "clothe" them. They will be so numerous that the "desolate places, and the land of thy destruction, shall even now be too narrow by reason of the inhabitants." This will leave Israel to exclaim, "Who hath begotten me these, seeing I have lost my children, and am desolate, a captive, and removing to and fro? and who hath brought up these? Behold, I was left alone; these, where had they been?" (Isaiah 49:17–19, 21). The Lord then tells Israel that he will use the Gentiles to bring back Israel's lost children to the covenant.

The Latter-day Work

All the multitudes of God's children have eagerly awaited the day when the fullness of temple work would be established so that the dead, as well as the living, could receive the covenants made available through Christ's ministry. From the first visit of Moroni to the Prophet Joseph, the Lord pointed to the time when temple work could begin. On a September evening in 1823, Moroni quoted to the boy prophet the words of Malachi, who testified that Elijah would reveal the priesthood so that the "promises [that were] made to the fathers" would be planted in the hearts of the children (Joseph Smith–History 1:39). Elder John A. Widtsoe stated, "It is sufficient for us to remember that temple work for the living and for the dead was the burden of the thought and labors of the Prophet Joseph Smith from the day when the Angel Moroni first stood before him and told him of the things that were to be up to the last day of the Prophet's life."[13]

The sealing keys of Elijah, along with other priesthood keys, were finally restored to the earth in April 1836 following the dedication of the Kirtland Temple (D&C 110:13–16). The Kirtland Temple, however, was only a preparatory temple, and the work for the dead could not begin in earnest. In 1838 the Lord told Joseph Smith, "There is not a place found on earth that he may come to and restore again that which was lost unto you, or which he hath taken away, even the fulness of the priesthood" (D&C 124:28). The Lord asked the Saints if the ordinances of baptism for the dead, washings, anointings, and endowments could be acceptable "except ye perform them in a house which you have built to my name?" He then commands the Saints, "Let this house be built unto my name, that I may reveal mine ordinances therein unto my people" (D&C 124:37, 40).

Joseph Smith told the Saints that the "great and grand secret" and the "summum bonum" of the whole matter was in obtaining the powers of the priesthood so that the ordinances and covenants of the Lord could be extended to all people, living and dead (D&C 128:11; see also 128:12–15). He pleaded, "Let us, therefore, as a church and a people, and as Latter-day Saints, offer unto the Lord an offering in righteousness; and let us present in [God's] holy temple, . . . a book containing the records of our dead, which shall be worthy of all acceptation" (D&C 128:24).[14]

The fully acceptable day of the Lord has come at last in the final days of the earth. Temples are being built on every continent and beginning to go to every nation. Regarding the 1978 revelation on the priesthood, the First Presidency stated, "The long-promised day has come when every faithful, worthy man in the Church may receive the holy priesthood, with power to exercise its divine authority, and enjoy with his loved ones every blessing that flows therefrom, including the blessings of the temple" (Official Declaration–2). All peoples from all times and nations can now have access to the covenants of the temple and enter into the "holy place," which was made possible through the Great High Priest. Speaking of the latter-day temples, President James E. Faust stated, "The acceleration of temple building in our time has been marvelous. . . . All of these exquisite holy edifices are a testimony of our belief that the Savior broke the bonds of death and opened up the way for us to enter into covenants which will be binding in another world."[15]

In order for the Lord's covenant to be fulfilled with the house of Israel, temple work must be done for all those who have died without the opportunity to receive covenants for themselves. Elder Widtsoe stated, "To understand the meaning of temple worship, it is necessary to understand the plan of salvation. . . . God's work with respect to this earth will not be complete until every soul has been taught the gospel and has been offered the privilege of accepting salvation and the accompanying great blessings which the Lord has in store for his children. Until that is done the work is unfinished.[16]

With so much work to be done, the prophets of the last days continually invite the Saints to increase their temple attendance. President Howard W. Hunter urged, "I also invite the members of the Church to establish the temple of the Lord as the great symbol of their membership and the supernal setting for their most sacred covenants. . . . Let us be a temple-attending and a temple-loving people. Let us hasten to the temple as frequently as time and means and personal circumstances allow. Let us go not only for our kindred dead, but let us also go for the personal blessing of temple worship, for the sanctity and safety which is provided within those hallowed and consecrated walls. The temple is a place of beauty, it is a place of revelation, it is a place of peace. It is the house of the Lord. It is holy unto the Lord. It should be holy unto us."[17]

Because Isaiah was dualistic in most of his writing, perhaps he was referring not only to the rebuilding of Jerusalem but also to the prolific temple building among the Latter-day Saints when he prophesied to Israel, "Sons of strangers shall build up thy walls. . . . Thy gates shall be open continually; they shall not be shut day nor night" (Isaiah 60:10–11). Some temples sponsor "fill the temple" days, conducting sessions around the clock. Perhaps Isaiah foresaw these days as common occurrences of the latter days.

Conclusion

When the day comes that all of God's children have been given the opportunity to hear and receive the gospel and the ordinances of exaltation, then is the day that God has fulfilled his promises to the house of Israel. Surely it was this day Isaiah saw when he proclaimed, "How beautiful upon the mountains are the feet of him that bringeth good tidings, that publisheth peace; that bringeth good tidings of good, that publisheth salvation; that saith unto Zion, Thy God reigneth!" (Isaiah 52:7). In that day, Zion will "awake, awake; . . . put on [its] beautiful garments, . . . shake [itself] from the dust; arise, and sit down" (Isaiah 52:1–2; see also 52:8–9) with all the holy fathers.

The dead bones seen by Ezekiel, which are "the whole house of Israel," will live and be clothed upon, not only with flesh and sinew (Ezekiel 37:11; see also 37:1–14; 2 Corinthians 5) but also with the "garments of salvation" and the "robe of righteousness" (Isaiah 61:10) in the temple. Then they will know that the God of Israel keeps his covenants.

Notes

1. Regarding the Savior, Isaiah taught, "He hath borne our griefs, and carried our sorrows. . . . He was wounded for our transgressions, he was bruised for our iniquities: the chastisement of our peace was upon him; and with his stripes we are healed" (Isaiah 53:4–5). To provide redemption for

the dead, Christ had to first pay the price of sin whereby all mankind, living and dead, could be cleansed from sin through his atoning blood and experience the mighty change of heart that comes through repentance. The Savior promised, "I dwell in the high and holy place, with him also that is of a contrite and humble spirit, to revive the spirit of the humble, and to revive the heart of the contrite ones" (Isaiah 57:15). Isaiah tells us, "He was their Saviour. In all their affliction he was afflicted. . . . In his love and in his pity he redeemed them; and he bare them, and carried them" (Isaiah 63:8–9). Lehi tells us that it is "unto all those who have a broken heart" that the "ends of the law" are answered (2 Nephi 2:7). The Savior told the Nephites that they must offer "a broken heart and a contrite spirit" in order to receive redemption from the world of sin (3 Nephi 9:20). It is the brokenhearted who will have the wounds of their soul bound up through the healing balm of the Savior's atonement.

2. Following Jesus' redeeming act of love in the garden and on the cross, his spirit did not immediately return to the Father but instead went to the world of spirits in order to continue fulfilling his mission as the savior of all mankind (1 Peter 3:18–20; 4:6; D&C 138:11–29). At his death, Jesus told the thief on the cross, "To day shalt thou be with me in paradise" (Luke 23:43). As the Prophet Joseph Smith pointed out, the Savior was referring not to the presence of God but to the world of spirits (*History of The Church of Jesus Christ of Latter-day Saints*, ed. B. H. Roberts, 2d ed. rev., 7 vols. [Salt Lake City: The Church of Jesus Christ of Latter-day Saints, 1932–51], 5:424–25). See also Bible Dictionary, s.v. "Paradise."

At his resurrection, Christ told Mary, "I am not yet ascended to my Father" (John 20:17). During the intervening time between his death and his resurrection, the Lord went to open the prison to those who were bound. Christ's personal work among the living having come to an end, his work in the spirit world was just beginning (Isaiah 24:22). The work of preaching the gospel to those in prison could not begin before the Savior's visit to the spirit world, though Christ himself would not go among those in prison (Bible Dictionary, s.v. "Temple").

While in the world of spirits, Christ "organized his forces and appointed messengers, clothed with power and authority, and commissioned them to go forth and carry the light of the gospel to them that were in darkness, even to all the spirits of men; and thus was the gospel preached to the dead" (D&C 138:30).

3. The Lord declared, "Shall the prey be taken from the mighty, or the lawful captive delivered? . . . Even the captives of the mighty shall be taken away, and the prey of the terrible shall be delivered: for I will contend with him that contendeth with thee, and I will save thy children" (Isaiah 49:24–25). What is mightier than death, which has taken captive all who are subject to the Fall? Jacob, the brother of Nephi, used these verses along with two chapters from Isaiah to clarify the doctrine of resurrection. He taught, "Death and hell must deliver up their dead, and hell must deliver up its captive spirits, and the grave must deliver up its captive bodies, and the bodies and the spirits of men will be restored one to the other; and it is by the power of the resurrection of the Holy One of Israel" (2 Nephi 9:12; see also 2 Nephi 6–8). Through his resurrection from the dead, the Savior set the captives free from death and hell and made the way possible for men to return to God. Without bodies, the spirits of men were truly captive and could not return to the presence of God. Heber C. Kimball said no man will enter into the presence of God without a body (*Journal of Discourses,* 26 vols. [London: Latter-day Saints' Book Depot, 1854–56], 3:112–13).

Perhaps that is why the dead look "upon the long absence of their spirits from their bodies as a bondage" (D&C 138:50; see also 45:17).

4. If the meek are to inherit the earth (Matthew 5:5; D&C 88:17–19; 130:7–9), then the good tidings to the meek would be that the way has been opened for them to dwell on a celestial earth in the presence of God.

5. The language here is similar to the language of Matthew 16:19. The keys of the kingdom, referring to the sealing keys, are given to bind on earth and in heaven.

6. Bible Dictionary, s.v. "Fasts."

7. William Frederic Farrar, *The Life of Christ* (1874; reprint, Salt Lake City: Bookcraft, 1998), 580.

8. *Old Testament: Genesis–2 Samuel,* student manual, 2d. ed. (Salt Lake City: Corporation of the President of The Church of Jesus Christ of Latter-day Saints, 1981), 176–77.

9. Joseph Fielding Smith, *Doctrines of Salvation,* comp. Bruce R. McConkie, 3 vols. (Salt Lake City: Bookcraft, 1954–56), 2:170.

10. *Old Testament: Genesis–2 Samuel,* 176–77.

11. James Strong, *The Exhaustive Concordance of the Bible* (New York: Abingdon Press, 1890), 47, and ref. 3027.

12. Smith, *History of the Church,* 5:423–24.

13. John A. Widtsoe, "Fundamentals of Temple Doctrine," Address Delivered at the Liberty Stake Genealogical Convention, 24 May 1922, 129.

14. Noting the language used by the Prophet Joseph Smith, it would appear that the work of the dead done in temples is at least a partial fulfillment of the prophecy made by John the Baptist during the restoration of the Aaronic Priesthood that the "sons of Levi do offer again an offering unto the Lord in righteousness" (D&C 13).

15. James E. Faust, "A Growing Testimony," *Ensign,* November, 2000, 59.

16. John A. Widtsoe, "Symbolism in the Temples," in Archibald F. Bennett, *Saviors on Mount Zion,* (George Richard Hill of the Deseret Sunday School Board, 1950), 163.

17. Jay M. Todd, "President Howard W. Hunter, Fourteenth President of the Church," *Ensign,* November 2000, 59.

12

Isaiah and the Gentiles

Terry B. Ball

On the second day of the resurrected Savior's ministry among the descendants of Lehi, he quoted several passages from Isaiah (3 Nephi 20:36–38/Isaiah 52:1–3; 3 Nephi 20:40/Isaiah 52:7; 3 Nephi 20:41–45/Isaiah 52:11–15; 3 Nephi 22/Isaiah 54) and then gave Isaiah's writings his divine endorsement: "And now, behold, I say unto you, that ye ought to search these things. Yea, a commandment I give unto you that ye search these things diligently; for great are the words of Isaiah" (3 Nephi 23:1).

Christ then explained why Isaiah's writings deserve such special attention: "For surely he spake as touching all things concerning my people which are of the house of Israel; therefore it must needs be that he must speak also to the Gentiles. And all things that he spake have been and shall be, even according to the words which he spake" (3 Nephi 23:2–3).

The Savior's observation that because Isaiah spoke "all things concerning" the "house of Israel; therefore . . . he must speak also to the

Terry B. Ball is an associate professor of ancient scripture at Brigham Young University.

Gentiles" suggests that the Gentiles are to play a significant role in the future of the Lord's covenant people. A survey of Isaiah's teachings and prophecies concerning the Gentiles and their part in fulfilling God's covenants with his people helps explain this teaching of the Savior.

Who Are the Gentiles?

Interpreting Isaiah's prophecies concerning the latter-day Gentiles requires an understanding of the term "Gentiles." Initially the term Gentile (from the Hebrew *goyim,* literally meaning "the nations") appears to have been used by the descendants of Jacob to refer to those not of the nation or house of Israel (Genesis 10:5). Thus Gentiles were defined by default—those who were not Israelites were Gentiles. This simple genealogical difference adequately distinguished between peoples in the earliest of Old Testament times, but eventually the distinction appears to have become obscure, for it grew increasingly difficult to clearly identify who was a blood descendant of one of the tribes of Israel and who was not.

For example, during King Solomon's reign (ca. 1015–975 B.C.) tribal affiliations in Israel began to be obscured as the king divided the kingdom into twelve administrative districts that were not strictly based on old tribal boundaries (1 Kings 4:7–19). Subsequent political blunders by Solomon's heir, Rehoboam, divided the house of Israel into two combative kingdoms: Israel, composed primarily of the ten northern tribes, and Judah, composed primarily of the remaining two tribes (Judah and Benjamin) in the south (ca. 975 B.C.). Within a few centuries of the division, the location and identity of the northern tribes was entirely lost. About 721 B.C. the king of Assyria besieged Samaria, the capital of the northern kingdom, and "carried Israel away into Assyria" (2 Kings 17:6; see also 17:5–23). Those carried away were not heard from again in the biblical text and today are referred to as the "Lost Ten Tribes."

Elder Joseph Fielding Smith gave some hint of what became of those tribes as he discussed the purposes for the scattering of Ephraim. He declared that the scattering of Ephraim, among other reasons, "was for the purpose of blessing the people of other nations with the blood of Israel among whom Ephraim 'mixed' himself. The scattering of other Israelites answered the same purpose."[1] Apparently, then, after being carried away from the Holy Land all or at least part of the Ten Tribes dispersed themselves among the nations and were assimilated by or mixed in with them.

The inhabitants of the kingdom of Judah who were not carried away but rather remained in the Holy Land, and those who had fled to Judah from Israel, referred to themselves simply as Jews either because they literally descended from the tribe of Judah or because they lived in the political kingdom of Judah. For example, Lehi and his family sometimes identified themselves as those who "came" from the Jews and as "descendants of the Jews" (2 Nephi 30:4; see also 33:8), although they knew that genealogically they were descendants of Joseph rather than Judah (1 Nephi 5:14). The designation of Jew, then, became not only a genealogical distinction but also a geographical and political one as well.

Because the inhabitants of the kingdom of Judah considered the "Jews" the only certain remnant of the house of Israel, by the seventh century B.C. they came to view all others as Gentiles. Thus, through time, their paradigm for classifying people shifted from the dichotomy of "Israelite or Gentile" to that of "Jew or Gentile."

Around 587 B.C. the kingdom of Judah, as the kingdom of Israel before it, suffered conquest and deportation at the hands of an invading foreign nation, this time the Babylonians. Prior to the Babylonian captivity, the Jews struggled to maintain faith in Jehovah their God, often apostatizing to worship the gods of other nations (2 Kings 21:1–6; Jeremiah 1:16; 2:11; 7:31). Realizing that their captivity had come as a result of apostasy, as prophets had warned (Jeremiah 21; Ezekiel 6), many Jews determined to never again forsake their God. They became fiercely determined to live the law of Moses and serve Jehovah.

Consequently, during their captivity in Babylon, living the law of Moses and being part of the culture associated with their understanding of the law became an important distinguishing attribute of the Jews, especially in the absence of a political kingdom or land to which they could anchor their heritage. Even those who later returned to the land of Judah (ca. 537 B.C.) and occasionally enjoyed some degree of political autonomy still relied on their faith as a distinguishing criterion of a Jew.[2] From then on, to be a Jew was not only a genealogical distinction but also perhaps even more a cultural and theological one. Accordingly, any who did not live the Mosaic law and culture or who could not trace their lineage to the tribe, land, or kingdom of Judah could be viewed as a Gentile.

The "Jew or Gentile" paradigm of distinction persists today. Thus, as one reads prophecies dealing with latter-day Gentiles, one should remember that the designation "Gentile" may be as much a cultural, political, and theological distinction as a genealogical one. Indeed, the development of the somewhat narrower "Jew or Gentile" classification paradigm has led to many people being considered Gentiles who are in fact literal descendants of one of the tribes of Israel. For example, while Joseph Smith would be considered a Gentile by the latter-day "Jew or Gentile" paradigm, modern revelation confirms that he descended from the "loins" of Abraham through Joseph (D&C 132:30; 113:3–6; 2 Nephi 3:7). Likewise, the Lord has assured other latter-day "Gentiles" by the "Jew or Gentile" designation that they are indeed the "seed of Abraham" (D&C 103:17) and "lawful heirs, according to the flesh," to the "priesthood" that "hath continued through the lineage" of their fathers (D&C 86:8–10). Thus these, and in fact most members of the Church, are in reality literal blood descendants of the covenant lineage of Israel, though in the latter-days they "are identified with the Gentiles" (D&C 109:60; see also 109:58–59). As blood descendants of Israel they are heirs, provided they live righteously, to all the blessings and responsibilities promised to Abraham, Isaac, and Jacob.

The Book of Mormon also frequently employs the "Jew or Gentile" paradigm with regard to the latter days. For example, the title page, written by Mormon, declares that one purpose of the book, which would "come forth in due time by way of the Gentile," is to convince "the Jew and Gentile that Jesus is the Christ." Elder Bruce R. McConkie explained that from the Book of Mormon's "Jew or Gentile" perspective, "Joseph Smith, of the tribe of Ephraim, the chief and foremost tribe of Israel itself, was the

Gentile by whose hand the Book of Mormon came forth, and the members of The Church of Jesus Christ of Latter-day Saints, who have the gospel and who are of Israel by blood descent, are the Gentiles who carry salvation to the Lamanites and to the Jews."[3]

In summary, the definition of a Gentile has been dynamic. While initially a genealogical distinction, at different times and among different peoples "Gentile" has become a geographical, political, cultural, and theological classification as well. Accordingly, as one seeks to understand prophecies about Gentiles in order to identify the people to whom the prophecy applies, one must consider how the term "Gentile" is understood in the day of the prophecy's fulfillment. Generally, as the term is used in latter-day contexts, a Gentile is anyone who is without the gospel or who cannot trace his or her heritage to the tribe, land, nation, or religion of Judah.[4]

The Gentiles and the Wrath of God

Isaiah's writings also refer to the Gentiles as "the nations" (Isaiah 5:26; 14:18; 17:13; 29:7)[5] and "strangers" (Isaiah 1:7; 2:6; 5:17). The Lord used the Gentile nations to chastise, humble, and correct his rebellious covenant people in Isaiah's day. For example, through Isaiah the Lord warned his apostate people that invading "strangers" would "devour" their land (Isaiah 1:7; see also 5:17), and that conquering "nations" would come "swiftly" to carry them away (Isaiah 5:26).[6] He spoke of the Assyrians—"the rod of [his] anger," "the staff" of his "indignation" (Isaiah 10:5), and the "razor that [he] hired" (Isaiah 7:20)[7]—who would "overflow" Judah in a decimating deluge (Isaiah 8:8). He foretold of the Egyptians, who would invade and fill the "desolate valleys" and the "holes of the rocks" (Isaiah 7:19; see also 7:18), and of the Babylonians, into whose merciless hands the Lord in his wrath would deliver his people (Isaiah 47:6). Fulfillment of these prophecies of invasion by Gentile nations includes the Assyrian conquest and deportation of Israel (ca. 722–21 B.C.), the subsequent Assyrian invasion of Judah (ca. 701 B.C.), and the Babylonian conquest and deportation of Judah (ca. 587–86 B.C.).

Isaiah's prophecies teach that although the Lord used the

ancient Gentile nations as a tool to chastise and humble his rebellious people, God would eventually punish the wicked of those nations as well. Through Isaiah the Lord declared, "I will break the Assyrian in my land, and upon my mountains tread him under foot" (Isaiah 14:25). He promised that though Assyria may appear formidable, the Assyrian armies would disappear suddenly like chaff before the wind, or like "a rolling thing [a tumbleweed-like plant] before the whirlwind" (Isaiah 17:13, see also 17:12).[8] This prophecy found a fulfillment in the conquest of the besieging Assyrians at Jerusalem in 701 B.C. when the "the angel of the Lord went forth, and smote in the camp of the Assyrians a hundred and fourscore and five thousand: and when they arose early in the morning, behold, they were all dead corpses" (Isaiah 37:36).[9] Through Isaiah the Lord further promised the boastful and arrogant Assyrians that they would experience his anger and know "leanness" and "terror" and be hewn down (Isaiah 10:16, 33; see also Isaiah 10:5–34). The Assyrians saw this prophecy fulfilled at the fall of Nineveh to the Medes and Babylonians (ca. 607 B.C.) and the subsequent swift demise of their empire.

Isaiah promised that the haughty and merciless Babylonians also would experience the Lord's "wrath and fierce anger" (Isaiah 13:9) and be left conquered and desolate (Isaiah 13, 14, 21, 47). Notably, more than a century and a half before the event, he even identified the Medes as a nation, and Cyrus as a king who would conquer Babylon (ca. 538 B.C.; Isaiah 13:17; 44:28–45:13). Likewise, the Egyptians, who frequently marauded through Judah and Israel (1 Kings 14:25–26; 2 Kings 23:29–30), and who, contrary to the prophet's warnings, fomented rebellion against Babylon and Assyria in Judah with hollow promises of military support (Isaiah 30:2–3; 31:1–3; 36:6, 9), would also experience destruction, suffering, and captivity (Isaiah 19, 20).

The destruction of these ancient Gentile nations that were enemies and oppressors of the covenant people are a type for the destruction of those in the latter-days who will fight against the Lord and his people as well. In fact, the Lord warned through Isaiah that every "nation and kingdom" that rejects the Lord and his covenant people will be "utterly wasted" (Isaiah 60:12; see also 29:7–8; 34:1–2).

The Gentiles, the Covenants, and the Covenant People

While Isaiah makes it clear that the Lord intended to punish the wicked of the Gentile nations both anciently and in the latter days, he also testifies that the Lord did not intend to exclude them from his covenants. This was a concept the early Church in the meridian of time had difficulty understanding. Christ himself testified, "I am not sent but unto the lost sheep of the house of Israel" (Matthew 15:24).[10] Such statements may have contributed to the belief among early Church leaders that the Gentiles were not to enjoy the blessings of gospel covenants.

It took a special revelation to Peter, the head of the early Church, followed by an outpouring of the Spirit to the Gentile Cornelius before Peter came to understand that "God is no respecter of persons" (Acts 10:34). When Peter returned to Jerusalem after baptizing Cornelius, his brethren wanted to know if it was true that he had been fraternizing with the Gentiles. When Peter told of his experience with Cornelius, they wondered, "Then hath God also to the Gentiles granted repentance unto life" (Acts 13:18). Even after Peter declared that Gentiles were indeed to be included in the gospel, the Church struggled to decide how to integrate them into the faith (Acts 15), and the issue persisted as a source of contention even among the Church hierarchy (Galations 2:11–15).

While Church leaders struggled with the doctrine, Isaiah understood and taught clearly that Jehovah was God of the Gentiles as well as of the Jews. He understood that eventually not only would the Gentiles be invited into the covenants but also that they would accept the invitation, help restore the covenants and the covenant people in the latter-days, and even be numbered among them.

Jehovah, the God of All Nations

In the ancient Near East of Isaiah's day, the pagan nations commonly believed that every land had a patron deity, and the people living in that land were to worship whatever god ruled the region (1 Kings 20:23–28; 2 Kings 17:24–28). Isaiah taught, however, that the Lord was not just the God of the Jews or of the lands of Judah and Israel. In the name of Jehovah, Isaiah delivered prophecies concerning the nations of Assyria (Isaiah 10; 14:24–27; 17:12–13), Babylon (Isaiah 13–14, 21, 47), Moab (Isaiah 15), Syria (Isaiah 17:1–2), Egypt (Isaiah 19–20), Phoenicia (Isaiah 23), Palestina (Isaiah 14:29–32), the people of Dumah, Arabia, Tema, Kedar (Isaiah 21:11–17), and others. He testified that the millennial Messiah would "judge among the nations" (Isaiah 2:4), "gather all nations and tongues" to see his glory (Isaiah 66:18), and cause all to "fear" him (Isaiah 25:3; see also 64:2). Thus, whether they accepted the Lord as their God or not, they could not escape the fact that he is indeed the God of the whole earth.

Gentiles to Accept the Covenants

Isaiah understood that while the wicked of the Gentiles would eventually be forced to accept Jehovah as their God, other Gentiles would willingly accept the gospel covenants and its blessings. For example, Isaiah testified that the Messiah was not only to "raise up the tribes of Jacob" but also be a "light to the Gentiles" so that he could provide "salvation unto the end of the earth" (Isaiah 49:6; see also 42:1, 6; 52:10).[11] He boldly declared that the "ensign," which Latter-day Saints understand to be the gospel and its covenants,[12] was to be lifted up "to the nations" (Isaiah 5:26; see also 11:12) and that "to it shall the Gentiles seek" (Isaiah 11:10). Through Isaiah the Lord promised to send ministers to "declare my glory among the Gentiles" to those "that have not heard my fame, neither have seen my glory" (Isaiah 66:19).

Isaiah promised that not only would the invitation to worship Jehovah and accept his covenants be extended to the Gentiles, but also that they would respond to the invitation in large numbers. He foretold of the day of apostasy and ignorance, when "darkness shall cover the earth, and gross darkness the people," but he promised that "the Lord shall arise," bringing "light" that would dispel the darkness (Isaiah 60:1–2). He further promised that as the covenant people began to shine forth, the Gentiles would be drawn to the light, and he referred to them as "sons" and "daughters" who would come from afar to be "nursed" (Isaiah 60:4; see also 60:3, 5).[13] He promised that even Gentile "kings" and "princes" would arise and worship "because of the Lord that is faithful" (Isaiah 49:7; see also 52:15; 60:3).[14]

These "strangers" who would be "joined" with the covenant people (Isaiah 14:1) would embrace the gospel in such large numbers that the original covenant people, when faced with the mass influx of newcomers to their family, would be left to exclaim, "The place is too strait [narrow or small] for me: give place to me that I may dwell. . . . Who hath begotten me these, seeing I have lost my children, and am desolate, a captive, and removing to and fro? And who hath brought up these? Behold, I was left alone; these, where had they been?" (Isaiah 49:20–21). With the addition of so many new children to the covenant family, totaling even more than the original family, Isaiah advised that the family "enlarge the place of thy tent, and let them stretch forth the curtains of thine habitations: spare not, lengthen thy cords, and strengthen thy stakes; For thou shalt break forth on the right hand and on the left" (Isaiah 54:2–3).

Isaiah likened the gathering of all these individuals into the covenant to a bride putting on her wedding attire (Isaiah 49:18), suggesting that bringing new souls into the gospel will be one way the covenant people will prepare for the coming of the bridegroom—even the Millennial Messiah. Once again these newly recognized and accepted children of the covenant are called strangers and Gentiles, not because they lack the blood of Israel but because they cannot be called Jews by the cultural, political, geographical, genealogical, or theological standards of the day. In reality most, if not nearly all, are indeed blood descendants of Israel, currently from the tribes of Ephraim and Manasseh as latter-day patriarchal blessings so frequently declare.[15]

Gentiles to Enjoy All the Blessings of the Covenant People

As the Gentiles flock to the gospel, they will not be second-class citizens in the covenant family but, Isaiah predicted, will have full access to all its blessings. In speaking of the mission and ministry of Jesus Christ, Isaiah prophesied that the Messiah's "visage" would be "marred more than any man, and his form more than the sons of men" (Isaiah 52:14; see also D&C 122:8) so that thereby he could "sprinkle many nations" (Isaiah 52:15). In certain types of sacrificial rites under the Mosaic law, the priest was to "sprinkle" the blood of the sacrificial animals as part of the purification and cleansing process (Leviticus 4:6, 17; 5:9; 14:7, 16, 27; 16:14). Thus, the imagery of Isaiah teaches that the marring or suffering of the Messiah would purify and cleanse not just the Jews but other nations as well.[16] In the Joseph Smith Translation of Isaiah 52:15, the verb "sprinkle" is changed to "gather," clarifying that the Messiah's suffering would bless and restore many nations.

Isaiah further taught that Gentiles would be allowed to participate in temple worship. Such promises would have seemed strange indeed to Isaiah's contemporaries, for the Mosaic laws under which they lived allowed only the descendants of Levi to perform temple ordinances. But Isaiah declared that in "the last days," when the temple, or "the mountain of the Lord's house shall be established in the top of the mountains, . . . and all nations shall flow unto it" (Isaiah 2:2).[17]

Latter-day Saints understand modern temples to be places where the worthy can receive an endowment or gift. The gift is essentially twofold—a gift of knowledge and a gift of power. The gift of knowledge comes in the form of special ordinances, instructions, and doctrines that "enable" one to enter "back to the presence" of our Heavenly Father.[18] The gift of power comes as one keeps covenants made in the temple; keeping covenants empowers one with the ability to put the gift of knowledge to use.

The language of Isaiah suggests that those of the nations going to the house of the Lord will be doing so to be endowed with just those two gifts, for they will be going with the hope that the Lord "will teach us of his ways," which is how they obtain the gift of knowledge, "and we will walk in his paths," which is how they will obtain the gift of power (Isaiah 2:3). This spiritual feast, which again is to be extended "unto all people" at the mountain of the Lord, will be so abundant that it is called in the language of Isaiah's time a "feast of fat things, a feast of wines on the lees, of fat things full of marrow, of wines on the lees well refined." Through it the Lord will "destroy . . . the face of the covering cast over all people, and the vail that is spread over all nations. He will swallow up death in victory; and the Lord God will wipe away tears from off all faces" (Isaiah 25:6–8; see also 2 Corinthians 3:14).[19]

To those "strangers" willing to accept the gospel, the Lord promises to "give in mine house and within my walls a place and a name better than of sons and of daughters: I will give them an everlasting name" (Isaiah 56:5).[20] As the Lord brings them to his "holy mountain," he assures them that there he will "make them joyful in my house of prayer" and promises that they will be able to participate in temple ordinances, for "their burnt offerings and their sacrifices shall be accepted upon mine altar; for mine house shall be called an house of prayer for all people" (Isaiah 56:7).

Gentiles to Acknowledge and Assist the Covenant People

As the Gentiles receive the gospel, they will be moved to acknowledge, respect, and help restore covenant Israel, both spiritually and physically. Isaiah promised that the Gentiles will "acknowledge . . . the seed which the Lord hath blessed" (Isaiah 61:9), "nations that knew not thee shall run unto thee because of the Lord thy God, and for the Holy One of Israel" (Isaiah 55:5), and even kings will "come . . . to the brightness" of Israel's rising (Isaiah 60:3; 52:15; 62:2).

As these latter-day Gentiles and kings come to the gospel, they will in turn play a vital role in gathering others of scattered Israel back to the covenants. Through Isaiah the Lord declared, "I will lift up mine hand to the Gentiles, and set up my standard to the people: and they shall bring thy sons in their arms, and thy daughters shall be carried upon their shoulders. And kings shall be thy nursing fathers, and their queens thy nursing mothers" (Isaiah 49:22–23). Latter-day Saints understand that the "standard" or, as it is more frequently translated in the King James Version of the Bible, "ensign," the Lord will set up is the gospel of Jesus Christ restored among the Gentiles through Joseph Smith.

As these Gentiles who accept the gospel take it to the rest of the world, they are indeed finding sons and daughters of covenant Israel and are "carrying" them back to the covenant. These "strangers" will "build up [Israel's] walls" (Isaiah 60:10), "feed [Israel's] flocks" (Isaiah 61:5), and be joined with the rest of the house of Israel as "servants and handmaids" in the land of the Lord (Isaiah 14:2; 2 Nephi 24:2; see also Isaiah 14:1; 2 Nephi 24:1).[21] While these prophecies of restoration and gathering are often properly interpreted in a physical sense to mean that the Gentiles will assist with restoring scattered Israel to its promised lands, Latter-day Saints understand that the restoration is more appropriately understood in a spiritual sense. Those who are blessed with the gospel have a responsibility to help restore scattered Israel to the Lord's covenants and to help bring about a physical gathering as well (2 Nephi 9:1–3).

Conclusion

Isaiah's understanding of the Gentiles and their role in God's eternal plan is profound. Of the entire canonized corpus written by ancient prophets, only the Book of Mormon offers such in-depth understanding of the role of the Gentiles. Like Isaiah, Book of Mormon prophets knew that God would sometimes use the Gentiles as a tool to humble his rebellious and apostate people and that God would in turn punish the wicked of the Gentiles (1 Nephi 13:14, 34; 14:6; 15:17; 2 Nephi 26:15, 19). They further understood that in the latter days the gospel of Jesus Christ would be restored among the Gentiles, and that those Gentiles would then be numbered among the house of Israel and assist in gathering and restoring others of scattered and lost Israel to the gospel (1 Nephi 14:1–7; 15:13–18; 2 Nephi 30:2–8).

Perhaps this shared understanding of the Gentiles' destiny was a contributing factor to the Book of Mormon prophets' relying so frequently on the writings of Isaiah in their teachings. That reliance certainly helps us understand why, when the resurrected Lord declared that Isaiah "spake as touching all things concerning my people which are of the house of Israel," the Lord concluded that "therefore it must needs be that he must speak also to the Gentiles" (3 Nephi 23:2). The Savior knew that the future of the house of Israel was inseparably intertwined with the future of the Gentiles.

NOTES

1. Joseph Fielding Smith, *Doctrines of Salvation,* comp. Bruce R. McConkie, 3 vols. (Salt Lake City: Bookcraft, 1954–56), 3:252.

2. The Jews of the Diaspora have continued to use their faith as one of their distinguishing attributes. Those who convert to Judaism consider themselves Jews as well.

3. Bruce R. McConkie, *The Millennial Messiah* (Salt Lake City: Deseret Book, 1982), 233; D&C 109:60; 1 Nephi 13:38–40; 15:13–14; 22:7–12.

4. Latter-day Saints recognize a third category of individuals, the Lamanites, who are neither Jews nor Gentiles but descendants of Lehi and thus descendants of Joseph through Manasseh.

5. While the plural *nations* usually refers to Gentile kingdoms, often the singular *nation* refers to Israel or Judah (Isaiah 1:4; 10:6; 18:2; 26:2).

6. Isaiah 5:26–30 can be seen as an example of a dualistic prophecy. A dualistic prophecy applies to more than one time period or people or has more than one fulfillment or interpretation. Elder LeGrand Richards taught that Isaiah 5:26–30 can be understood in the latter days to refer to the restored gospel to which nations would speedily come using modern means of transportation (*A Marvelous Work and a Wonder* [Salt Lake City: Deseret Book, 1950], 229–30). In its ancient context, the passage can also be understood as a prophecy of ancient nations being called and coming swiftly to punish the apostate covenant people (Victor L. Ludlow, *Isaiah: Prophet, Seer, and Poet* [Salt Lake City: Deseret Book, 1982], 122).

7. Apparently the Assyrians shaved off the body hair of their captives to humiliate, sanitize, and mark them (Ludlow, *Isaiah,* 145).

8. That this passage is a prophecy concerning Assyria is suggested by the use of the imagery "rushing of many waters" (Isaiah 17:13), the same imagery used for Assyria earlier in the text (Isaiah 8:7–8). The word translated in the King James Version as "rolling thing," *galgal,* is also often translated as "tumbleweed" (New International Version) and has been

identified with *Gundelia tournefortii.* For a discussion of the imagery used in this passage, see Terry Ball, "Isaiah's Imagery of Plants and Planting," in *Thy People Shall Be My People and Thy God My God* (Salt Lake City: Deseret Book, 1994), 26.

9. The Joseph Smith Translation clarifies this passage: "The angel of the Lord went forth, and smote in the camp of the Assyrians a hundred and four-score and five thousand, and when *they who were left* arose, early in the morning, behold, they were all dead corpses" (JST Isaiah 37:36; emphasis added; see also 2 Kings 19:35).

10. While Christ ministered primarily to the Jews, he also blessed and rewarded the faith of Gentiles whom he encountered (Mark 7:25–30; Matthew 8:5–13).

11. These verses are part of a series of passages in Isaiah that are collectively called the "servant songs" (Isaiah 42:1–4; 49:1–6; 50:4–9; 52:13–15; 53). These passages all speak of a servant or servants who, though they may suffer or appear insignificant, will yet do a great work for the people. The exact identity of the servant or servants is never clearly stated, but various commentators have suggested a number of different people who could fulfill the prophecies, including the prophet Isaiah himself, the nation of Israel as a whole, the benevolent conqueror Cyrus, and the Prophet Joseph Smith. Certainly no one fulfills these prophecies better than does Jesus Christ, and Isaiah likely viewed any other servants who would suffer as types of Christ. For a discussion of the identity of the servant, see commentaries on the servant song passages in Donald W. Parry, Jay A. Parry, and Tina M. Peterson, *Understanding Isaiah* (Salt Lake City: Deseret Book, 1998); Monte S. Nyman, *Great Are the Words of Isaiah* (Salt Lake City: Bookcraft, 1980); and Ludlow, *Isaiah.*

12. See Bruce R. McConkie, *Mormon Doctrine,* 2d ed. (Salt Lake City: Bookcraft, 1966), 228.

13. The context of this passage does not make it clear whether the "sons" and "daughters" referred to are already covenant children or Gentiles who become covenant children as they gather, but the expression that they "come from far" suggests that they are not individuals already assembled with the covenant people. Isaiah 60:7 clearly makes the point that Gentiles will find "acceptance" at the Lord's altars in that day, again suggesting that they become children of the covenant.

14. In Isaiah's writings the plural *kings* generally refers to kings of Gentile nations.

15. For an insightful discussion of this concept, see Mark E. Petersen, *Joseph* (Salt Lake City: Deseret Book, 1981), 11–17.

16. This passage is one of the servant songs discussed in note 11 above. The resurrected Savior used similar language to describe a latter-day servant who would be marred as he did the Father's work (3 Nephi 21:10). That latter-day servant has been identified as Joseph Smith (Parry et al., *Understanding Isaiah,* 469).

17. A mountain is a wonderful and appropriate metaphor for the temple. It draws the eye upward, as does a temple, and it is where ancient prophets traditionally went to receive revelation and make covenants, as we do in a temple. It takes a lot of effort to get to the top of a mountain. The physically flabby do not make it, just as the spiritually flabby do not make it to the house of the Lord. Mountains are enduring, as are temple covenants. Once at the top of a mountain, we have a broader perspective, being able to see where we have been and where we can go. In the temple, likewise, we gain an eternal perspective and learn where we came from, where we can go, and the path we must follow to get there.

18. Brigham Young, *Discourses of Brigham Young,* sel. John A. Widtsoe (Salt Lake City: Bookcraft, 1998), 416.

19. The mountain of the Lord referred to in this passage can be interpreted dualistically. On one level it seems to be referring to the literal Mount Zion, where the Millennial Messiah will reign and reward the faith of the righteous with a great banquet (D&C 58:3–12); on another level, in view of Isaiah's frequent use of mountains as a metaphor for temples, understanding the feast to be the blessings of the temple also seems to be appropriate.

20. The phrase "place and a name" may more accurately be translated "hand and a name."

21. The text of Isaiah quoted in 2 Nephi 24:1–2 contains important additions and wording that make it clear that the Gentiles will join with Israel as servants in the land of the Lord rather than be simply servants to Israel in the land.

13

Images of Mercy in the Writings of Isaiah

Mark Elbert Eastmond

ISAIAH IS A PROPHET OF PARADOX. To the casual reader, his writings are among the most difficult and confusing found in scriptural canon. His poetic style and ubiquitous imagery is often seen as a black hole from which no reader may emerge—not awake, anyway. Yet his powerful use of imagery lends shades and nuances to otherwise abstract doctrines, revealing meaning that extends far beyond what the written word conveys. Imagery gives us something to envision and relate to—a place to hang our hat as we ponder the eternal and the divine. Moreover, once the lesson has been learned, the imagery serves as a memory mechanism by keeping the doctrine in our thoughts, where we may continue to ponder the multilayered meanings couched in the image. Thus, the very style which so often *confuses* and *conceals* meaning from us can be a tool to *reveal* and *clarify* some of the most essential doctrines of the kingdom. And never does Isaiah use his imagery more powerfully than when he expounds the most fundamental of doctrines: the merciful nature of God.

Mark Elbert Eastmond teaches seminary in Cedar City, Utah.

Knowing God

During the closing hours of his mortal ministry, the Savior reminded his apostles of a linchpin in their quest for eternal life. The doctrine was not new, nor would it vanish into obscurity thereafter. Indeed, every prophet from Adam to the present day has centered his teachings on this one pivotal truth, a truth that perhaps has never been so simply put as on that Passover night in Jerusalem two millennia ago. "This is life eternal," Christ prayed, "that they might know thee the only true God, and Jesus Christ, whom thou hast sent" (John 17:3). Two years earlier he had first publicly taught this doctrine on the Mount of Beatitudes when he told his assembled disciples that many would profess their rights to the kingdom of heaven by pointing out deeds done in his name. To them he would say, "Ye never knew me; depart from me ye that work iniquity" (JST Matthew 7:33).

The Prophet Joseph Smith affirmed that truly knowing the Lord—knowing what he is like in personality and character—is a prerequisite to exercising veritable faith in him and gaining salvation. "Let us here observe," he said, "that three things are necessary in order that any rational and intelligent being may exercise faith in God unto life and salvation. First, the idea that he actually exists. Secondly, a correct idea of his character, perfections and attributes. Thirdly, an actual knowledge that the course of life which he is pursuing is according to his will."[1]

Clearly then, a correct knowledge of God's character traits and attributes, his *personality* and *disposition*, is of vital import in mankind's quest for exaltation. Indeed, this knowledge is the very seedbed of our faith and must be germinated if you and I are to ever progress beyond it. We must know the Being who asks our all before we can place trust, faith, and, ultimately, our complete submission on the altar.

Isaiah addresses this theme at the very onset of his writing and weaves it as a cord throughout. The Israel[2] of his time knows neither the Lord nor his disposition and is therefore struggling in its faith. In the opening chapter of Isaiah's work, he scarcely does more than introduce himself before invoking an image illustrating the dire condition of Israel's relationship with its Maker. The scene he calls to mind is one that many have witnessed, even in our modern, urban society. One need not live on a farm to know that domesticated animals of any kind are capable of forming a bond of familiarity with humans, knowing their masters' voices and responding to them over strangers. Using this familiarity as a metaphor, Isaiah points out the Lord's chief concern for his people: "The ox knoweth his owner, and the ass his master's crib: but Israel doth not know [me], my people doth not consider" (Isaiah 1:3).

The Great Jehovah, who has taken such a personal role in nurturing and molding his covenant children, is as much of an enigma to them as the silent, stone gods of their pagan neighbors. Thus, we find Isaiah pleading with Israel to come to know the God whom they outwardly worship but inwardly alienate. In so doing he uses potent imagery to help them not only *see* what he is like but *feel* it as well.

The Warning or "Angry" Passages

Many see the Lord depicted by Isaiah as the antithesis of merciful. This erroneous notion can easily be reached by a scattered reading. Several selected passages, if considered alone, cause the Lord to appear angry or even vengeful. Such phrases as "They have provoked the Holy One of Israel unto anger" (Isaiah 1:4), "I will punish the world for their evil" (Isaiah 13:11), "his anger is not turned away" (Isaiah 5:25), and "the indignation" and "fury" of the Lord (Isaiah 34:2) are enough to strike consternation into anyone's heart. Add to that the Lord's warning that he will "number you to the sword, and ye shall all bow down to the slaughter: because when I called, ye did not answer; when I spake, ye did not hear; but did evil before mine eyes, and did choose that wherein I delighted not" (Isaiah 65:12). After such a scathing rebuke, it is not surprising that some mistakenly view the Lord with fear rather than with faith.[3]

Upon closer reading, however, we find that the opposite view is true. While anger and vengeance are terms used by the Lord, Isaiah provides both a background and a sequel to these characteristics with beautiful, metaphorical language. Taken in context, Isaiah's writing again becomes paradoxical as the very phrases that can make the Lord sound vengeful and full of malice in fact help demonstrate the depth of his love.

The Background

Just as someone who inadvertently eavesdrops on a small portion of a conversation can come away with a distorted view of what was being said, so can those who lack the reasons and methods behind the Lord's chastisement misjudge his intent. Knowing the background behind his actions helps us to see clearly his intentions and thus his heart. Isaiah is therefore deliberately careful to reveal to us both *why* the Lord chastises his people and *how* he does so.

Punishment is often seen as the motive behind negative divine intervention in our lives or in the lives of the ancients. In a prophecy concerning the destiny of Egypt, Isaiah dispels this myth by revealing the Lord's true intent in chastening his people. In response to the idolatry of Egypt, Isaiah begins what he titles a "message of doom 'lifted up' against Egypt" (Isaiah 19:1).[4] After setting "the Egyptians against the Egyptians" and turning "every one against his brother, and every one against his neighbor; city against city, and kingdom against kingdom" (Isaiah 19:2), the Lord will finally "give [them] over into the hand of a cruel lord; and a fierce king shall rule over them" (Isaiah 19:4). Then, after describing their calamity, Isaiah unveils the purpose behind the aforementioned events: "And the Lord shall smite Egypt: he shall smite and heal it: and they shall return even to the Lord, and he shall be intreated of them, and shall heal them" (Isaiah 19:22). Moreover, Isaiah takes us a step further by pointing out that through this process a change will occur in the relationship between the Lord and these people: "And the Lord shall be known to Egypt, and the Egyptians shall know the Lord in that day" (Isaiah 19:21). The idols will be no more, for Egypt through its adversity will be ameliorated of its malady—estrangement from a loving God, a God who loves his children enough to chasten them that they might know him, return to him, and be healed.[5]

Equally important as knowing *why* the Lord chastens his people is understanding *how* he does so, for there is great mercy in his method. In what has been termed the "song of the vineyard," Isaiah composes a parable illustrating how the Lord often chooses to get the attention of those who turn away from him. In comparing the children of Israel to a vineyard, the prophet first points out the care and nurture they have received from the great husbandman Jehovah: "My wellbeloved hath a vineyard in a very fruitful hill: And he fenced it, and gathered out the stones thereof, and planted it with the choicest vine, and built a tower in the midst of it, and also made a winepress therein" (Isaiah 5:1–2). Yet as the Lord realizes that his efforts have been for naught, that Israel has repaid his nurturing with apathy and brought forth nothing but "wild grapes," he chooses to respond in an interesting manner. And while the resultant action brings suffering and hardship upon his vineyard, it is done in a manner meant to teach rather than punish. "I will tell you what I will do to my vineyard," reveals the Lord, "I will take away the hedge thereof, and it shall be eaten up; and break down the wall thereof, and it shall be trodden down: And I will lay it waste: it shall not be pruned, nor digged; but there shall come up briers and thorns: I will also command the clouds that they rain no rain upon it" (Isaiah 5:5–6). Notice that the Lord does not choose to personally destroy his vineyard. Rather he forsakes it. He removes his sustaining help and protection and leaves it to fend for itself.[6]

The resultant image is a vivid one to those who have dabbled in home gardening. Left alone and void of a protecting fence, the original plants will be trampled, desolated by wind, and plundered. Soon they will wither and weeds will spring up and choke out the already weakened and starving vines. It will not be long before the original occupants of the garden, or the vineyard, have been supplanted by competing plants or nations. How well Isaiah foretold the eventual fate of ancient Israel and, in so doing, unveiled the lesson taught by the Lord's abandonment. By being left to ourselves we learn, *by loss,* of the blessings, guidance, and divine intervention we had so casually taken for granted.

Furthermore, the Lord does not leave the chastened to kick against the pricks indefinitely. Using yet another image drawn from agriculture, Isaiah demonstrates that the Lord's reproof is mercifully suited, in duration and intensity, to the individual needs of his children. "Doth he who plows for sowing plow continually? Doth he continue to plow and harrow his ground after it is smooth?" he asks, posing the idea that a farmer will not keep breaking the soil after it is prepared to receive seed but will harrow it only long enough to soften it and make it receptive (Isaiah 28:24 Amplified Version).[7] Similarly, the chastening of the Lord's plow does not last forever. When the field of our heart has been loosened and opened, the painful process is ended.

Isaiah further compares Israel to the fruits of that field once they have been harvested and are ready to be trodden upon on the threshing floor. Does the Lord thrash each person with the same severity? Isaiah unfolds the answer by reminding us that "fitches are not threshed with a threshing instrument, neither is a cart wheel turned about upon the cummin; but the fitches are beaten out with a staff, and the cummin with a rod" (Isaiah 28:27). Fitches, or black poppy seeds,[8] and cummin are delicate and could not withstand the force of a sharp threshing sled. Rather, they must be separated carefully from their husk by being beaten with a stick.[9] Grain such as corn or wheat, however, must be threshed as more weight is necessary to separate the chaff from the seed. Yet, even in this case, only enough force is used to accomplish the refining process. "Grain for bread is crushed, indeed, he does not continue to thresh it forever. Because the wheel of his cart and his horses eventually damage it. He does not thresh it longer" (New American Standard Version, Isaiah 28:28). Isaiah presents this wise husbandman's treatment of his field and crops as a type of the Lord's treatment of his children. When it is necessary to separate the sinful parts of our nature from the divine, he will shake us, but with as little severity as possible to achieve the desired outcome. Even those with hearts hard enough to require threshing receive the merciful assurance that while the

Lord may thrash, he will not injure or damage his harvest. Such are not the actions of a God blinded by rage but rather of a merciful teacher tailoring the lesson with patience and concern for each individual.

The Sequel

When we know the background of the "angry" passages and warnings given through Isaiah, we begin to sense God's mercy rather than his malice. If we add to that Isaiah's sequel to the story—how the Lord responds to those he has chastened—our vision of his compassion is deepened beyond measure. This response to the reproached is driven home by the prophet's persistent repetition of a single scene. Early in his writings, Isaiah recounts to Israel the sins they are wallowing in. Charges of pride, greed, drunkenness, and dishonesty are all laid at their feet (Isaiah 5:11–23). The Lord answers such gross iniquity by expressing that "for all this his anger is not turned away, *but his hand is stretched out still*" (Isaiah 5:25; emphasis added). One can't help but picture a person in desperate need, perhaps drowning or mired in quicksand and sinking fast. A passerby notices this person's plight and, in a mighty effort to save, stretches out his hand the full length he can muster. If the floundering individual chooses to ignore the offered help and fend for himself, will the stranger retract his offer and proceed on his way? Not in the case of God and his children. For until the flailing soul has utterly perished, that hand will be stretched out—*still.*[10]

Isaiah is not content to leave it at that, however. In the mind of a true poet, it is not enough to emphasize the enduring arm of the Lord with words. If the patience of the Lord is that continual, it must be underscored in like manner. Consequently, in the ensuing chapters, a rare thing in scripture occurs. The prophet repeats the phrase, not once or twice but a total of five times: "For all this his anger is not turned away, but his hand is stretched out still" (Isaiah 5:25; 9:12; 9:17; 9:21; and 10:4). Soon the reader almost finds himself saying, "*Again?!* You mean he has still got his hand reaching out there? You've got to be kidding me—he is far more patient than I would be!" This is exactly the point Isaiah wants to indelibly imprint upon our minds.

To help us envision the ultimate result of the Lord's chastening when we are willing to respond, Isaiah summarizes the "angry" passages with an image of a forsaken widow and a loving husband. Because of rebellion, Jehovah's bride—the House of Israel—was separated from him for a time, as a widow from her husband. But in her distress he consoles, "Fear not; for thou shalt not be ashamed . . . for thou shalt forget the shame of thy youth, and shalt not remember the reproach of thy widowhood any more. For thy Maker is thine husband; the Lord of hosts is his name" (Isaiah 54:4–5). Then, with all the love inherent in the image of a husband and wife reuniting, the Great Husband reminds his bride that although her actions brought momentary estrangement, through his mercy she will be eternally reconciled with him. "For a small moment have I forsaken thee; but with great mercies will I gather thee. In a little wrath I hid my face from thee for a moment; but with everlasting kindness will I have mercy on thee, saith the Lord thy Redeemer" (Isaiah 54:7–8).

Could there be a more tender symbol for Isaiah to attribute to the Lord and his people than that of husband and wife sealed by covenant? In so doing he reminds us that we are intimately loved by the Lord, even when we distance ourselves from him. For those who accept the Lord's instructive rebuke, which is meant to draw us back to his protective, outstretched arms, the metaphor of eternal union is especially sweet: "For the mountains shall depart, and the hills be removed; but my kindness shall not depart from thee, neither shall the covenant of my peace be removed, saith the Lord that hath mercy on thee" (Isaiah 54:10).

Mercy to the Sinner: Images of Reconciliation

To the repentant sinner, Isaiah's images of mercy are particularly heartening. They lend hope to those who need God's mercy the most but feel least deserving of it. For them Isaiah writes, "Come now, and let us reason together, saith the Lord: though your sins be as scarlet, they shall be as white as snow; though they be red like crimson, they shall be as wool" (Isaiah 1:18). While this symbolism of the cleansing power of the Atonement is compelling, equally appealing is the tone of the invitation—to come, sit, and reason *together.* Whereas our sins had once cast up a wall between us, the Lord invites us back to his table to be reconciled. There he proposes an exchange: our crimson guilt for his snow-white innocence. Anciently, this transfer of guilt was symbolized in the sacrifice of a lamb by the transgressor. As the jugular was severed by the presiding priest, the blood would stain the unspotted coat of the lamb but bring cleansing to the soul of the sinner for whom the lamb stood proxy.[11] In like manner the Lamb of God will take our blood-red sin upon him, and through the shedding of his blood the pure white of his wool will come upon us. Our robes, stained with iniquity, will be washed and made "white in the blood of the Lamb" (Revelation 7:14).[12]

Because the Lord paid this awful price, his mercy becomes both infinite and intimate[13]—infinite in its scope and endurance but intimate in its application. For in standing proxy for the individual transgressor, the Savior's relationship with the sinner became ever more personal, his understanding enhanced with experience. Isaiah best illustrates this deepened tie with a scene set in despondency. Languishing in the consequences of sin, Israel cries out in her aloneness that "the Lord hath forsaken me, and my Lord hath forgotten me" (Isaiah 49:14). Isaiah answers this cry of distress with a moving question: "Can a woman forget her sucking child, that she should not have compassion on the son of her womb?" (Isaiah 49:15). That question might cause reflection in anyone but a nursing mother, who instinctively responds "No!" Surely the special bond formed between mother and infant would prevent such a lapse. And even if inadvertent preoccupation caused her to momentarily forget her hungry charge, the babe would see to it that she was reminded in no uncertain terms! Yet, to his own question, the Lord replies: "Yea, they may forget, yet will I not forget thee" (Isaiah 49:15).

Isaiah's message is three-dimensionally clear. It would be more likely for a nursing mother to completely forget that her hungry, screaming child was in the room—to just suddenly, and quite accidentally, fall oblivious—than for the Lord to forget even one of us. And in beautiful imagery he tells us why: "Behold, I have graven thee upon the palms of my hands; thy walls (i.e. sins—that which blocks our path) are continually before me" (Isaiah 49:16). The word *graven* could likewise be rendered "engraven" or "carved."[14] Either will suffice to describe the scene of cruel nails piercing Christ's hands and wrists as a propitiation for our iniquity. Significantly, the tokens of that sacrifice are still borne by the Lord,[15] serving as a witness to us of who he is but also as a *reminder to him of who we are.* How many times in a given day do you think your hands pass before your eyes? Fifty? A hundred? *"Continually"?* Each time the Savior catches sight of his hands, there, in perfect clarity, is a reminder of you and me. The walls to our eternal happiness—our sins, weaknesses, and imperfections, and thus our desperate need for his redemptive mercy—are permanently etched before his view. As we covenant to "always remember him," we can be assured that the reciprocal is, and always will be, true. "Indeed, we are in His hands," taught Elder Neal A. Maxwell, "and what hallowed hands!"[16]

Mercy to the Sufferer: Images of Succoring

Because not all that is difficult in mortality is caused by sin, the far-reaching effects of God's mercy are not limited to forgiveness. Consequently, some of Isaiah's most touching images reveal the Savior's ability to succor as well as to save. Through them we come to know a God who nurtures his people throughout life and comforts them in times of distress.

Nurturing Mercy

One of the most ardent symbols of God's nurturing care for his children is taken from the everyday life of Isaiah's people. "He shall feed his flock like a shepherd," declares the prophet (Isaiah 40:11), using a symbol for the Savior which he himself would employ during his mortal ministry (John 10). The comparison loses something for us in the western world, where sheep are little more than herd animals. But in the pastoral fields of the Near East, the image is fraught with meaning.

On a recent trip to the Holy Land, my wife and I encountered a touching scene. The late June afternoon found us in the fields surrounding the ancient city of Bethlehem. There we reflected upon the Savior's birth and sang hymns generally reserved for far colder times. Whether he saw us arrive or was aroused by our off-key singing I'm not sure, but soon a young shepherd boy, clutching a baby goat from his flock, wandered over and sat near us. As we read and testified to each other of the Savior, this shepherd boy played with his charge. He cuddled, stroked, and talked to it soothingly, much the way a parent would a toddler. Occasionally, he set it down from his arms to let it explore, and it would wander near our group. Finally, when the little animal got too close, the boy softly called one word, and the goat went instantly bounding back to the gentle voice and the safe embrace of the boy.

For Isaiah to paint the Lord as our shepherd is a singular declaration of the personal interest he has in the well-being of each of us. A shepherd in the Holy Land does not see his flock as a group but as individuals, each with different personalities and needs. For him, each lamb has a name and is often like a member of his own family. During our visit it was not uncommon to see a single lamb wrapped in its shepherd's arms. Isaiah thus colors the Savior's role in our lives by adding that "he shall gather the lambs with his arm, and carry them in his bosom, and shall gently lead those that are with young" (Isaiah 40:11).

Additionally, Isaiah teaches us that such nurturing care will continue long after we are mature spiritually. To they "which are carried from the womb" (Isaiah 46:3), the Lord declares: "Even to your old age I am he; and even to hoar hairs will I carry you: I have made, and I will bear; even I will carry, and will deliver you" (Isaiah 46:4).

Comforting Mercy

Isaiah further draws images from the land where he gave his message to teach of the Savior's power to comfort his people in times of despair. While Israel is known as a land flowing with milk and honey, there are large portions that are extremely arid and desolate. Most travel undertaken through the Near East region necessitates traversing such barren geography. Using this climate as a backdrop, Isaiah describes the Lord as "an hiding place from the wind, and a covert from the tempest; as rivers of water in a dry place, as the shadow of a great rock in a weary land" (Isaiah 32:2; see also 25:4–5). To the faint traveler, particularly in ancient times, such fortunate discoveries as a cave to shelter from wind and heat or a river of fresh, flowing water were a glorious haven. There one could take a break from the unrelenting elements, be refreshed, and regain strength.

The inherent hardships of mortality are richly symbolized in this journey across Isaiah's homeland, as is the succoring power available to those who seek the Lord's mercy. For "he giveth power to the faint; and to them that have no might he increaseth strength. Even the youths shall faint and be weary, and the young men shall utterly fall" in this difficult journey of life. "But they that wait upon the Lord," the Covert, the River, the Rock, "shall renew their strength; they shall mount up with wings as eagles; they shall run, and not be weary; and they shall walk, and not faint" (Isaiah 40:29–31).

Perhaps the most tender scene in all of Isaiah's writings illustrates best the Lord's desire to comfort the downtrodden. Speaking of the great millennial day, Isaiah exults that "he will swallow up death in victory; and the Lord God will wipe away tears from off all faces" (Isaiah 25:8). Such a promise accentuates the profound love the Savior feels for his people, for the very scene bespeaks the inherent closeness of that relationship. Think of the select few individuals you would allow to wipe tears from your face. Even close friends and lifelong neighbors would not be granted such a personal expression. No, this is a moment reserved for spouses or a parent and child. Or, perhaps most of all, for a merciful Savior, through whom "the voice of weeping shall be no more heard . . . nor the voice of crying" (Isaiah 65:19).

Conclusion

In conclusion I return to Isaiah's allegory of the Great Husbandman, Jehovah, caring for his vineyard. Here, the Lord poses a heartfelt question: "What could have been done more to my vineyard that I have not done in it?" (Isaiah 5:4). In the dual imagery of Isaiah and Jacob 5, the Lord intensifies the query: "Have I slackened mine hand, that I have not nourished it? Nay, I have nourished it, and I have digged about it, and I have pruned it, and I have dunged it; and I have stretched forth mine hand almost all the day long . . . for I have done all. What could I have done more for my vineyard?" (Jacob 5:47, 49). In the imagery of Isaiah, the answer is manifestly clear. Could he have done more than we have seen? Even the most callous and indifferent reader of Isaiah must freely admit that there is nothing more the Lord could have done. He has mercifully given us his patience, teaching, coaxing, forgiveness, nurture, comfort, and, ultimately, his life.

After effectively describing the Lord's perfect mercy, Isaiah ends his work by returning to the theme with which he started: Israel not knowing the Lord. Only now the problem has been rectified. In a glorious prophecy concerning a covenant Israel not to be seen in his lifetime, Isaiah declares: "And when ye see this, your heart shall rejoice, and your bones shall flourish like an herb: and *the hand of the Lord shall be known toward his servants*" (Isaiah 66:14; emphasis added). Those who pay the price to search the imagery of mercy found in Isaiah come to see and know a God of great patience, kindness, and understanding who will do all in his power to bring us back to him.

NOTES

1. Joseph Smith, *Lectures on Faith* (Salt Lake City: Deseret Book, 1985), 38.

2. Isaiah raised his prophetic voice to both sides of the divided kingdom. Although only the northern kingdom was referred to as Israel (the southern being termed the kingdom of Judah), both were the Lord's covenant people. I therefore use the term *Israel* to refer to the combined covenant people and occasionally to God's latter-day covenant people.

3. Further examples include Isaiah 24:1; 13:13; 30:27, 30; 47:3; and 63:3, to name a few.

4. Isaiah 19:1, note *a.*

5. See Doctrine and Covenants 95:1–2 for a modern explanation of this same principle.

6. See Doctrine and Covenants 121:37–38.

7. The New American Standard and New International Version may render Isaiah 28:24 in a clearer light than does the King James Version in this instance.

8. See C. F. Keil and F. Delitzsch, *Commentary on the Old Testament* (Grand Rapids, Mich.: Eerdmans, 1983), 7:2:14–17, as cited in *Old Testament: 1 Kings–Malachi,* student manual, 2d. ed. (Salt Lake City: The Church of Jesus Christ of Latter-day Saints, 1982), 163.

9. See New International Version, Amplified, and New American Standard translations of Isaiah 28:27.

10. The Book of Mormon prophet Zenos draws from both this image and that of the Lord's vineyard: "What could I have done more in my vineyard? Have I slackened mine hand, that I have not nourished it? Nay . . . I have stretched forth mine hand almost all the day long, and the end draweth nigh. And it grieveth me that I should hew down all the trees of my vineyard" (Jacob 5:47).

11. Elder Bruce R. McConkie gives the doctrinal explanation of animal sacrifice, its similitude to the atoning sacrifice, and the redemptive purpose of the ordinance in *The Promised Messiah* (Salt Lake City: Deseret Book, 1978), 248–55.

12. Isaiah penned the image of the exchange between our red-stained souls and the white wool of the ancient messianic symbol, the lamb. Drawing on that image, several prophets in both the Old World and the New World have referred to washing and becoming "white in the blood of the Lamb." See Revelation 7:14; 1 Nephi 12:11; Alma 13:11; 34:36; Mormon 9:6; and Ether 13:10–11.

13. For a further discussion of this concept, see Merrill J. Bateman, *Ensign,* May 1995, 14.

14. New International Version and New American Standard translations of Isaiah 49:16.

15. That the resurrected Christ still bears the marks of the nails in his hands and feet is recorded in Luke 24:38–40 and 3 Nephi 11:13–14. In Doctrine and Covenants 6:37; 45:48–53; 3 Nephi 11:14–15, and John 20:25–27 we learn that these marks signify that he has fulfilled the redemptive mission given him by the Father.

16. Neal A. Maxwell, *Ensign,* May 1985, 74.

14

Researching Isaiah Passages in the Book of Mormon

Jerald F. Simon

Writings of the prophet Isaiah are found in great abundance in the Book of Mormon: Another Testament of Jesus Christ.[1] His name, however, is mentioned only by six individuals, specifically, Nephi (son of Lehi), Jacob, Abinadi, Nephi (son of Helaman), Jesus Christ, and Moroni. In every instance when the charge was given to "search,"[2] "liken,"[3] "understand,"[4] "read,"[5] or "remember"[6] Isaiah's words, a significant covenant-renewing experience had usually just happened or was in process. Likewise, when a Book of Mormon writer commissions us to a greater study of Isaiah, all of the following themes are addressed:

1. Come unto Christ
2. The scattering and gathering of Israel
3. The hope of the latter days/a marvelous work
4. Keep the commandments
5. The future fulfillment of the Abrahamic covenant

Jerald F. Simon teaches at the Ogden Utah Institute of Religion.

Except in the case of Nephi son of Helaman, who briefly mentions Isaiah in passing, and Abinadi, who quoted Isaiah but does not charge us to "search" his writings, the others who refer to Isaiah are determined to teach those in ancient times and particularly us of the latter days that the people of the Book of Mormon were covenant children of Israel. When we witness specific events Isaiah mentioned, which were accentuated by these Book of Mormon authors, we too should take it as a sign "that the work of the Father hath already commenced unto the fulfilling of the covenant which he hath made unto the people who are of the house of Israel" (3 Nephi 21:7).

By studying these key events that preceded or immediately followed the charge to "search" Isaiah's writings, we will come to a greater understanding of these specific invitations.

Laman and Lemuel (1 Nephi 15)

The first instance where Isaiah is cited by name occurred after Nephi's vision, recorded in 1 Nephi 11–14. After Nephi "had received strength," he desired to know the reason for Laman and Lemuel's argument. His brothers indicated a lack of understanding regarding the "olive-tree, and also concerning the Gentiles." After having received a negative response to his query, "Have ye inquired of the Lord?" Nephi charged Laman and Lemuel to soften their hearts, ask in faith, be believing, and "keep the commandments of the Lord" (1 Nephi 15:6–8; see also 15:1–11). Nephi eloquently stated the major parts of the above outlined connection to Isaiah's words when he said: "Behold are we not broken off from the house of Israel, and are we not a branch of the house of Israel? And now, the thing which our father meaneth . . . is, that in the latter days, when our seed shall have dwindled in unbelief . . . then shall the fulness of the gospel of the Messiah come unto the Gentiles, and from the Gentiles unto the remnant of our seed—And at that day shall the remnant of our seed know that they are of the house of Israel, and that they are the covenant people of the Lord; and then shall they know and come to the knowledge of their forefathers, and also to the knowledge of the gospel of their Redeemer. . . . Behold, I say unto you, Yea; they shall be remembered again among the house of Israel; they shall be grafted in, being a natural branch of the olive-tree, into the true olive-tree. And this is what our father meaneth; and he meaneth that it will not come to pass until after they are scattered by the Gentiles; and he meaneth that it shall come by way of the Gentiles, that the Lord may show his power unto the Gentiles, for the very cause that he shall be rejected of the Jews, or of the house of Israel. Wherefore, our father hath not spoken of our seed alone, but also of all the house of Israel, pointing to the covenant which should be fulfilled in the latter days; which covenant the Lord made to our father Abraham, saying: In thy seed shall all the kindreds of the earth be blessed" (1 Nephi 15:12–14, 16–18).

In his attempt to explain Father Lehi's vision to his brothers, Nephi said, "I did rehearse unto them the words of Isaiah, who spake concerning the restoration of the Jews, or of the house of Israel." As a result of these and "many words," "they were pacified and did humble themselves before the Lord" (1 Nephi 15:20).

Liken All Scriptures unto Us (1 Nephi 19–22)

Nephi read to Laman and Lemuel from "the plates of brass, that they might know concerning the doings of the Lord in other lands, among people of old." He said he "read many things unto them which were written in the books of Moses; but that I might more fully persuade them to believe in the Lord their Redeemer I did read unto them that which was written by the prophet Isaiah" (1 Nephi 19:22–23).

Nephi knew how important it was to study the Law of Moses and bore witness many times of the power found in the word of God. Because Lehi's family had had a Mosaic-like experience with a hasty exodus, a wilderness sojourn, a miracle regarding crossing water, and ultimately arriving in a land of promise, the likening possibilities were immense. However, when Nephi really wanted to "persuade them to believe in the Lord their Redeemer," and to awaken them to the knowledge of who they were and how they fit into the larger picture of the plan, he turned to Isaiah's rich messianic messages and assurances that God's promises to his covenant people would be fulfilled in the latter days.

Nephi not only wanted his brethren to see the Savior and come unto Christ, but he wanted them to remember that they were part of the foreseen scattering and gathering of the house of Israel, that they were being led by their prophet-father, and that Nephi, who was soon to succeed Lehi, was also called of God. It is not coincidental that he chose Isaiah to teach these principles to his older brothers. The chapters themselves are types, not only of latter-day events but also of their similar situation. Nephi counseled: "Hear ye the words of the prophet, ye who are a remnant of the house of Israel, a branch who have been broken off; hear ye the words of the prophet, which were written unto all the house of Israel, and liken them unto yourselves, that ye may have hope as well as your brethren from whom ye have been broken off" (1 Nephi 19:24).

Although Nephi clearly understood the futuristic implications of Isaiah 48 and 49, his selection of these Isaiah chapters was most appropriate if Laman and Lemuel were to be persuaded to follow his counsel to "hear ye the words of the prophet" and "liken them unto yourselves." The prophet he wanted them to hear was not only Isaiah but also the prophets Lehi and Nephi. The negative attitudes exhibited by Laman and Lemuel made it unlikely that they were going to listen to Nephi's counsel, but had they truly hearkened and heard, they would have noted that nearly every verse Nephi quoted had great application to them. Additionally, in continuing to reach out to his wayward brethren, Nephi served as a type of Christ to them, even though he knew their return would be through their latter-day posterity.

A few of the phrases that should have caught Laman and Lemuel's attention and reminded them that they were not unlike those of Jerusalem were: "They call themselves of the holy city, but they do not stay themselves upon the God of Israel. . . . Thou art obstinate, and thy neck is an iron sinew, and thy brow brass. . . . Thou hast seen and heard all this; and will ye not declare them? . . .

Yea, and thou heardest not. . . . For my name's sake will I defer mine anger . . . that I cut thee not off. . . . I have refined thee, I have chosen thee in the furnace of affliction" (1 Nephi 20:2, 4, 6, 8, 9, 10).

Perhaps Laman and Lemuel should have "likened" some of the following verses to Nephi: "All ye, assemble yourselves, and hear; who among them hath declared these things unto them? The Lord hath loved him; yea, and he will fulfil his word which he hath declared by them. . . . I the Lord, yea, I have spoken; yea, I have called him to declare, I have brought him, and he shall make his way prosperous" (1 Nephi 20:14–15).

In the events of their journey to this point, Laman and Lemuel might also have recognized their own situation and likened themselves to Isaiah's description of fallen or scattered Israel: "Go ye forth of Babylon. . . . He led them through the deserts. . . . There is no peace, saith the Lord, unto the wicked. . . . Hearken, O ye house of Israel, all ye that are broken off and are driven out because of the wickedness of the pastors of my people; yea, all ye that are broken off, that are scattered abroad, who are of my people, O house of Israel. Listen, O isles, unto me, and hearken ye people from far" (1 Nephi 20:20–22; 21:1).

The main thrust of these verses was not necessarily the immediate "likening" potential for Laman and Lemuel but for their posterity, who would one day realize that Jesus had not forgotten the house of Israel, that he would "lift up" his "hand to the Gentiles, and set up" his "standard to the people" (1 Nephi 21:22), that he would provide the atonement, die, and be resurrected for all mankind. It would be in a future time when people would more fully understand, "Behold, I have graven thee upon the palms of my hands. . . . I will contend with him that contendeth with thee, and I will save thy children . . . and all flesh shall know that I, the Lord, am thy Savior and thy Redeemer, the Mighty One of Jacob" (1 Nephi 21:16, 25–26).

After Nephi had read Isaiah's words to his brethren, they said, "What meaneth these things which ye have read?" (1 Nephi 22:1). They wondered if the message had spiritual implications only. Nephi responded, "Wherefore, the things of which I have read are things pertaining to things both temporal and spiritual; for it appears that the house of Israel, sooner or later, will be scattered upon all the face of the earth, and also among all nations. . . . Yea, the more part of all the tribes have been led away; and they are scattered to and fro upon the isles of the sea" (1 Nephi 22:3–4).

Nephi explained how the Gentiles would nurture and nurse the scattered house of Israel, that "the Lord God will proceed to do a marvelous work among the Gentiles, which shall be of great worth unto our seed" (1 Nephi 22:8; see also 22:6–7). He mentioned the renewal of the Abrahamic covenant, bringing Israel out of captivity, and that "they shall know that the Lord is their Savior and their Redeemer, the Mighty One of Israel" (1 Nephi 22:12; see also 22:9–11). He spoke of the millennium and charged Laman and Lemuel: "If ye shall be obedient to the commandments, and endure to the end, ye shall be saved at the last day"(1 Nephi 22:31).

It is clear that Nephi's charge to "liken" the words of Isaiah was uttered sometime after arriving in the promised land and before the death of Lehi. A closer scrutiny of the passages at the conclusion of 1 Nephi and the beginning of 2 Nephi indicate that these events, although found in two separate books, took place at one time. In other words, 1 Nephi 19 through 2 Nephi 4:12 all happened simultaneously, culminating with the death of Lehi.

Jacob's Charge to Liken Isaiah (2 Nephi 6–10)

Thirty years after leaving Jerusalem, Nephi began keeping his second set of plates, the record from which the Book of Mormon was translated. By the time chapter 6 of 2 Nephi was written, another ten years had passed, and Nephi stated: "We had already had wars and contentions with our brethren" (2 Nephi 5:34). When Jacob delivered his "likening" discourse, he would have likely been between forty-two and forty-eight years old, certainly no more than fifty-five (see 1 Nephi 18:7; Jacob 1:1).

The mature prophet Nephi desired that Jacob read Isaiah's words so that the Nephites might "learn and glorify the name of [their] God" (2 Nephi 6:4). Jacob chose to "liken" Isaiah's words to his people, because they "are of the house of Israel" (2 Nephi 6:5).

Throughout these chapters, Jacob repeatedly teaches the five fundamental Isaiah themes.

Jacob not only reminded his audience of their historic place both then and now, but in true Isaiah-like fashion, focused on teaching of Christ. He prefaced his discourse on the Atonement, Crucifixion, and Resurrection in 2 Nephi 9 by saying he was going to draw upon Isaiah's writings because they were "the words which my brother (Nephi) has desired that I should speak unto you" (2 Nephi 6:4). Some of Isaiah's powerful passages on the Savior which Jacob used in this preface were as follows: "The Mighty God shall deliver his covenant people. . . . Have I put thee away, or have I cast thee off forever? . . . I gave my back to the smiter, and my cheeks to them that plucked off the hair. I hid not my face from shame and spitting. . . . The Lord shall comfort Zion, he will comfort all her waste places. . . . Therefore, the redeemed of the Lord shall return. . . . But I am the Lord thy God, . . . And I have put my words in thy mouth, and have covered thee in the shadow of mine hand. . . . Behold, thou art my people. . . . The Lord and thy God pleadeth the cause of his people" (2 Nephi 6:17; 7:1,6; 8:3, 11, 15–16, 22).

And why did Jacob read these things? "That [they] might know concerning the covenants of the Lord that he has covenanted with all the house of Israel—that he has spoken unto the Jews, by the mouth of his holy prophets, even from the beginning down, from generation to generation, until the time comes that they shall be restored to the true church and fold of God; when they shall be gathered home to the lands of their inheritance, and shall be established in all their lands of promise" (2 Nephi 9:1–2).

In 2 Nephi 9–10, Jacob details the plan of salvation, the necessity of faith, repentance, baptism, keeping commandments and enduring to the end. His teachings on significant doctrines, such as the Atonement, are priceless. Like Isaiah and Nephi, the focus of Jacob's teaching is Jesus Christ. He rejoices in the goodness of the Holy One of Israel, the Creator and Eternal God, who is Christ the King. "For I, the Lord, the king of heaven, will be their king, and I will be a light unto them forever, that hear my words" (2 Nephi 10:14). Jacob concludes his sermon by saying: "And now, my beloved brethren, seeing that our merciful God has given us so great knowledge concerning these things, let us remember him, and lay aside our sins. . . . Wherefore, my beloved brethren, reconcile yourselves to the will of God, and not to the will of the devil and the flesh; and remember . . . that it is only in and through the grace of God that ye are saved. . . . Wherefore, may God raise you from death by the power of the resurrection, and also from everlasting death by the power of the atonement, that ye may be received into the eternal kingdom of God" (2 Nephi 10:20, 24–25).

My Soul Delighteth in Likening Isaiah (2 Nephi 11–30)

Remembering Nephi's intent in keeping this record helps us understand the Isaiah passages. Nephi said, "I desire the room that I may write of the things of God. For the fulness of mine intent is that I may persuade men to come unto the God of Abraham, and the God of Isaac, and the God of Jacob, and be saved" (1 Nephi 6:3–4).

Specifically he tells us that his "soul delighteth in" Isaiah's words, and he would "liken" them to his people and all people because he also "delighteth in proving unto my people the truth of the coming of Christ. . . . And also my soul delighteth in the covenants of the Lord which he hath made to our fathers. . . . And my soul delighteth in proving unto my people that save Christ should come all men must perish" (2 Nephi 11:4–6).

After including Isaiah 2–14 on his plates (2 Nephi 12–24), Nephi tells his people that Isaiah's words are "not plain" to them but would be "plain unto all those that are filled with the spirit of prophecy. . . . For I know that they shall be of great worth unto them in the last days; for in that day shall they understand them; wherefore, for their good have I written them" (2 Nephi 25:4, 8).

No greater witness and invitation than Nephi's to come unto Christ can be found: "Believe in Christ, the Son of God, and the atonement, which is infinite for all mankind. . . . For there is save one Messiah spoken of by the prophets. . . . His name shall be Jesus Christ, the Son of God. . . . For we labor diligently to write, to persuade our children, and also our brethren, to believe in Christ, and to be reconciled to God. . . . And we talk of Christ, we rejoice in Christ, we preach of Christ, we prophesy of Christ, and we write according to our prophecies, that our children may know to what source they may look for a remission of their sins" (2 Nephi 25:16, 18–19, 23, 26).

Nephi chronicles Isaiah's prophecies in 2 Nephi 26–30 as if drawing us a timeline of events that will precede the Lord's "work among all nations, kindreds, tongues, and people, to bring about the restoration of his people upon the earth" (2 Nephi 30:8). In so doing, Nephi again mentions the five outlined themes routinely taught concurrently with Isaiah passages in the Book of Mormon.

Abinadi (Mosiah 11–16)

Although Abinadi does not specifically encourage us to "read," "search," "liken," or "remember" Isaiah's words, his last words before King Noah include references to Isaiah 52 and 53, using the Isaiah passages somewhat the same way as do Nephi, Jacob, Jesus, and Moroni.

Abinadi also hearkens back to Moses' experience in a fashion similar to the ways Nephi, Jacob, and Jesus do when they cite Isaiah. He touches on every major theme relative to the Isaiah verses he shared, just as Nephi and Jacob did before him.

Search Isaiah: Jesus' Covenant Discourse (3 Nephi 20–23)

In his sermon in 3 Nephi 20–23, Jesus twice commands his faithful listeners to "search Isaiah." They had felt the prints in his hands and feet and had thrust their hands into his side. They were the worthy ones who had been "spared because" they "were more righteous than" the others (3 Nephi 9:13). He was the living embodiment of the Abrahamic covenant. Christ was not only the Master but the Master teacher of Isaiah. These disciples truly knew what it meant to "come unto Christ."

Jesus mentions Moses' writing of a future prophet and explains how his coming fulfilled those words. He teaches the Nephites that they are "children of the prophets" and "children of the covenant" (3 Nephi 20:25–26). He also speaks of the time when Isaiah's words will be fulfilled, regarding the scattering, the gathering, the role of the Gentiles, a marvelous work, the Prophet Joseph Smith, the coming forth of the Book of Mormon, and other themes, interspersing in his discourse almost every verse from Isaiah 52 and 54.

As if setting bookends to hold the doctrine in place, Jesus, who quoted Isaiah more than he quoted any other prophet while in his mortal ministry, twice instructs the Nephites to "search Isaiah"—at both the introduction and conclusion of his covenant discourse.[7]

Christ clearly desired there be no misunderstanding regarding his covenant discourse as evidenced by the charge given to Mormon while he was abridging the account of the Savior's visit. At the conclusion of 3 Nephi, Mormon recorded: "I say unto you that when the Lord shall see fit, in his wisdom, that these sayings shall come unto the Gentiles according to his word, then ye may know that the covenant which the Father hath made with the children of Israel, concerning their restoration to the lands of their inheritance, is already beginning to be fulfilled" (3 Nephi 29:1).

Mormon later emphasizes that Jesus had commanded him to restate this theme: "Hearken, O ye Gentiles, and hear the words of Jesus Christ, the Son of the living God, which he hath commanded me that I should speak concerning you . . . that ye may be numbered with my people who are of the house of Israel" (3 Nephi 30:1–2).

Search the Prophecies of Isaiah (Mormon 8:23–Moroni 10)

Moroni does not fully fit the pattern of the model we have been looking at unless one extends his invitation to "search the prophecies of Isaiah" (Mormon 8:23) to be inclusive of chapter 10 of the book of Moroni. He had a comprehensive knowledge of what to include on the plates for people of the latter days. He said: "The Lord hath shown unto me great and marvelous things concerning that which must shortly come, at that day when these things shall come forth among you. . . . Behold, Jesus Christ hath shown you unto me, and I know your doing" (Mormon 8:34–35).

It appears that several times he felt he would not be able to write more on the plates. Hence, the tone of conclusion at the end of Mormon 9, Ether 4, 5, 12, 15 and Moroni 1, in which he chiastically states, "I had supposed not to have written more, but I have not as yet perished. . . . Wherefore, I wander whithersoever I can for the safety of mine own life. Wherefore, I write a few more things, contrary to that which I had supposed; for I had supposed not to have written any more" (Moroni 1:1, 3–4).

Moroni was running out of space on the plates and had no ore to make new plates (Mormon 8:5). He was commanded of the Lord to include the Jaredite record, which he faithfully did. After thirty-five years of wandering as a lonely, hunted exile, he was prudent and judicious as to what he included on the final, few plates.

In his concluding chapter in the book of Moroni, we find the elements of ancient covenant treaties, except in this case, like so many of the Old Testament prophets before him, Moroni's one constant hope was rooted in the latter days.

For years the Church of Jesus Christ of Latter-day Saints has been sending missionaries throughout the world, reading Moroni 10:3–5, and inviting people to join the Church. I know the promise is real and that it works because I put the promise to the test when I was first exposed to the Book of Mormon in 1974; one year later I joined the Church. Yet there is far, far more in chapter 10 than the first few verses that are traditionally taught.

Moroni had been the custodian of the plates for thirty-five years. He knew exactly how much space he had left on the plates and perhaps had been thinking for nearly twenty years about what to include in the room he had available to him. Key elements of priesthood governance are found in chapters 1 through 6, and three powerful discourses from his father take up chapters 7 through 9. He undoubtedly pondered for a long time about what to write in chapter 10.

Moroni 10 is one of the most precise scriptural chapters that has ever been written. It deals with spiritual powers and gifts available to us in mortality. Much of the plan of salvation as it pertains to this life is included. Not only are Moroni's doctrinal declarations and sacred scriptural invitations supreme, however, but he also is sealing the record of the plates. He is not only preparing to place the physical capstone on the sealed stone box but with his writing is symbolically placing the capstone on the covenant concepts taught on the plates from which the Book of Mormon would emanate.

The word *if* appears fifteen times in this chapter and in each usage is coupled with either *you* or *ye*. "If/then," which traditionally has represented covenant language, appears powerfully in verses 32 and 33 near the conclusion of the chapter. The words *you, ye, your* or *yourself* appear fifty-six times, and some mention of one of the names of God appears fifty times, always in connection with you, ye, your, or yourself. The frequency with which these terms are used indicates a sacred covenant sealing taking place.

Where is the Isaiah connection? After nearly completing the covenant-contractual terms, Moroni invites us to "come unto Christ" (Moroni 10:30). He then deftly combines passages from Isaiah 52 and 54 to help us in latter-days see the three-fold mission of the Church, first introduced to us by President Spencer W. Kimball, which is: to proclaim the gospel, perfect the Saints and redeem the dead.[8] Moroni simply uses Isaiah's phrases, "enlarge thy borders forever," "strengthen thy stakes," and "put on thy beautiful garments" (Moroni 10:31) to describe the three aspects of the work of redemption.

Moroni, like Nephi, Jacob, and Jesus before him, was very conscious of what he inscribed on these plates. The difficulty of writing and space limitations forced him to compress concepts and be precise with principles. His doctrine was direct and his message majestic, for this was to be a work of works, a "'marvelous work and a wonder,'" even a "'miraculous miracle'" foreseen by all of the prophets of old.[9]

Joseph Smith said that "the title-page of the Book of Mormon is a literal translation, taken from the very last leaf, on the left hand side of the collection or book of plates."[10] How then did Moroni conclude his covenant discourse? The same way Nephi, Jacob, Abinadi, and Jesus did, with echoes of Isaiah's language:

"Written to the Lamanites, who are a remnant of the house of Israel; and also to Jew and Gentile. . . . Sealed by the hand of Moroni, and hid up unto the Lord, to come forth in due time by way of the Gentile. . . ."

"Which is to show unto the remnant of the House of Israel what great things the Lord hath done for their fathers; and that they may know the covenants of the Lord, that they are not cast off forever—And also to the convincing of the Jew and Gentile that Jesus is the Christ, the Eternal God, manifesting himself unto all nations" (Title Page of The Book of Mormon).

Whenever Isaiah is quoted in the Book of Mormon be prepared for a special "likening" experience. As we further "search," "liken," "understand," "read," or "remember" Isaiah's words in the Book of Mormon, we should look to learn more about the scattering and gathering, how to better keep the commandments and to keep in view the hope to be found during the latter days when the "marvellous work and a wonder" (Isaiah 29:14) rolls on. We must realize as we study Isaiah that his words will "be of great worth" and we will come to "understand" (2 Nephi 25:8) that we are part of the fulfillment of the Abrahamic covenant. Each who longs for the day when "the ends of the earth shall see the salvation of [our] God" (3 Nephi 16:20; Isaiah 52:10) will draw nearer to the Savior than ever before as he or she researches the Isaiah passages that are found in the Book of Mormon.

Notes

1. *Old Testament Resource Manual,* prepared by Church Educational System (Salt Lake City: The Church of Jesus Christ of Latter-day Saints, 1998), 164, which says, in part: "Nineteen of Isaiah's sixty-six chapters are quoted in their entirety in the Book of Mormon, and except for two verses, two other chapters are completely quoted. Of the 1,292 verses in Isaiah, about 430 are quoted in the Book of Mormon, some of them more than once (for a total of nearly 600). If all the quotations from Isaiah in the

Book of Mormon were moved into one place and called the book of Isaiah, it would constitute the fourth largest book in the Book of Mormon."

2. The charge to "search" Isaiah is given three times in the Book of Mormon. Jesus commands us twice to search, as found in 3 Nephi 20:11 and 3 Nephi 23:1. Moroni extends the same invitation in Mormon 8:23. Unless otherwise designated in the text, instead of constantly repeating the words *search, liken, read, understand, write,* or *remember,* for simplicity's sake, the word *search* will represent all six of these words.

3. The challenge to "liken" Isaiah's passages to ourselves is rendered three times. Each challenge comes from Nephi son of Lehi (hereafter cited as Nephi) as found in 1 Nephi 19:23, 2 Nephi 11:2, and 2 Nephi 11:8.

4. The words *Isaiah* and *understand* are found in only two verses, both given by Nephi in 2 Nephi 25:1, 5.

5. *Read* and *Isaiah* are used only by Nephi and Jacob as found in 1 Nephi 19:23 and 2 Nephi 6:4–5.

6. *Remember* and *Isaiah* are combined by Jesus Christ and Moroni in 3 Nephi 20:11 and Mormon 8:23.

7. For a more comprehensive work on this subject, see Victor L. Ludlow, "Jesus' Covenant Teachings in Third Nephi," in *Rediscovering the Book of Mormon,* ed. John L. Sorenson and Melvin J. Thorne (Salt Lake City: Deseret Book, 1991), 177–85.

8. Spencer W. Kimball, Conference Report, April 1981, 3. See also Conference Report, April 1982, 3; *Ensign,* May 1981, 5; and *Ensign,* May 1982, 4.

9. Neal A. Maxwell, *A Wonderful Flood of Light* (Salt Lake City: Bookcraft, 1990), 17.

10. Joseph Smith, *History of The Church of Jesus Christ of Latter-day Saints,* ed. B. H. Roberts, 2d. ed. rev., 7 vols. (Salt Lake City: The Church of Jesus Christ of Latter-day Saints, 1932–51), 71.

15

The Power of Symbol

Charles Swift

While sharing with us his vision through sacred literature called scripture, the Lord also communes with us through the elements that give literature its power, elegance, and goodness. Rather than listing on two or three pages the doctrines of the gospel in a series of concise axioms, the scriptures offer page after page of poetry, imagery, symbolism, dialogue, drama, and narrative that enlightens our minds, uplifts our souls, and edifies our spirits. To approach the scriptures as though they were merely repositories for doctrine would be to remain untouched by the transforming power of the Word.

In his account of Isaiah's teachings, Nephi preserves the imagery of the original writings.[1] As we study Isaiah through the eyes of Nephi, we must be careful to pay close attention to the poetic imagery if we desire not only to understand but to feel what is being said.[2] In particular, Isaiah's use of the imagery of innocence in Isaiah 49, dominated by archetypal symbols, can help us more deeply embrace his message.

Charles Swift is a doctoral candidate in educational leadership at Brigham Young University.

Literary Archetypes: Universal Symbols

The great literary critic Northrop Frye used effective imagery himself to explain the meaning of symbol: "Originally, a symbol was a token or counter, like the stub of a theater ticket which is not the performance, but will take us to where the performance is. It still retains the sense of something that may be of limited interest or value in itself, but points in the direction of something that can be approached directly only with its help."[3] Just as we cannot partake of the performance without the ticket, we cannot directly approach the meaning without the symbol. This does not mean that without the symbol the idea is completely beyond our reach, but the symbol does facilitate our approach in a way that makes the idea more meaningful to us. Since "some of our deepest responses to truth are through feelings,"[4] symbolic language that evokes our feelings can be the ticket to truth that will gain us admittance to a level of understanding not reached through words alone.

One reason symbolic language is so rich is that the similarity of the image to what it represents is revealed by the differences between the two:

"Images based on similarity are the most common in the Bible. In order to describe a person, object, or event, the poet will explicitly or implicitly compare the item with something or someone else that is similar in some way but that is also different. The difference between the two causes the reader to recognize the presence of an image and stimulates him or her to search for the similarity within the difference that the image conceals."[5]

For example, "mountain" can be used as a symbol for the temple. Obviously, the two are quite different: the first is a tall, geological phenomenon, and the second is a comparatively small, man-made edifice. In pondering the differences, the reader may begin to see that the objects are similar because they both bring us closer to heaven.

At the risk of extending Frye's ticket metaphor an inch too far, if a symbol is a ticket, then an archetype is an unusual theater district pass. It is unusual in that, unlike a regular season pass that allows admission to all the plays performed at a given theater, this archetypal pass allows you to see the same play at all the theaters in which it is performed. Even though the play is the same, much is different. The actors portray their characters differently, the director interprets the play differently, the set design looks different, and the lights give a different feel. The performances are different but, since it is the same play, you see common threads of theme and dialogue and characters. This archetypal pass allows its possessor to see not just one play at one theater put on by one company but the richness of what the play offers as it is performed in many theaters by a variety of companies.

Similarly, an archetype is a symbol that recurs throughout literature, bringing meaning to the individual work as it draws strength from its meaning in other works. Simply put, archetypes can be thought of as "universal symbols."[6] This does not mean that an archetype has to be only a symbol; it can certainly correspond to something that exists in the physical world. For example, as we partake of the sacrament we may reflect on what the bread symbolizes. It represents the flesh of the Savior, his sacrifice for us, and his role as the Bread of Life. Yet, it is a real piece of bread we hold in our hands. The fact that it signifies meaning outside of itself does not remove from it the reality of its existence.

Let's consider the archetype of the mountain once again. We can see that mountains play important roles in a number of different scriptural events. Moses sees the burning bush and communes with the Lord on a mountain, he receives the Ten Commandments on a mountain, and he views the Promised Land from a mountain. We read in the New Testament of the Mount of Transfiguration and the mount upon which the Lord gave his life. All of these mountains exist in the physical world, but they also are a universal symbol appearing many times in the scriptures—meaningful and yet growing in meaning as well.

Archetypes are more than just symbols that appear in several places; they are at the very essence of literature:

"We have spoken of the repeating quality in literature, its allusiveness and its almost obsessive respect for tradition. One of the first things I noticed about literature was the stability of its structural units: the fact that certain themes, situations, and character types, in comedy let us say, have persisted with very little change from Aristophanes to our own time. I have used the term 'archetype' to describe these building blocks, as I thought in its traditional sense, not realizing how completely Jung's more idiosyncratic use of the same word had monopolized the field."[7]

Frye refers to Jung's use of the term *archetype* because it frequently brings to mind the psychological theory of the "collective unconscious"—a theory that Frye considers "an unnecessary hypothesis in literary criticism."[8] Other archetypal critics of literature have dropped the theory of the collective unconscious as well.[9] In literature, then, the idea of the "archetype" relies not on Jungian psychology but on the realization that certain symbols are used repeatedly and "are images of things common to all men, and therefore have a communicable power which is potentially unlimited."[10]

While archetypes occur in secular literature, they are prevalent in sacred literature as well, helping to unify the various books into what we call scripture. What Leland Ryken wrote of the Bible can also be said of the Book of Mormon:

"Being sensitive to archetypes is one of the most fruitful literary approaches we can take to the Bible. These master images are an important part of the unity of the Bible. As we read the Bible, we are constantly aware of being in a world of archetypes. Although the Bible appears at first glance to be a heterogeneous collection of fragments, it turns out to be a composite whole and a unified world in our imaginations."[11]

While archetypes help bring together the individual books of the Bible to form a "unified world" and the individual books of the Book of Mormon to form another such world, they also unite the Bible and the Book of Mormon as scriptures with the same gospel message. This unity is readily apparent in such chapters as 1 Nephi 21, in which an American prophet in the Book of Mormon quotes a Jerusalem prophet in the Old Testament. Moreover, when we consider that this Isaiah chapter quoted in the Book of Mormon is addressed to modern Israel,[12] we see that the unifying quality of the archetype is not only among books but also among time periods. "A voice out of Israel's past, Isaiah establishes the grand connection with the house of Israel in the Old World (particularly the Jews), the remnant of Israel in the New World (the Lamanites), and modern-day Israel (especially the blood of Israel intermixed with the Gentiles)."[13]

Archetypes of Innocence

"That Nephi begins his expansive recitations of Isaiah with chapters 48 and 49," Andrew Skinner writes, "and not with other chapters of that prophet's book shows that, as a prophet to his family, to his descendants, and to the Gentiles and Jews of the latter days, Nephi first offers Isaiah's message of hope and redemption in Christ."[14] President Wilford Woodruff said that "the revelations that are in the Bible, the predictions of the Patriarchs and Prophets who saw by vision and revelation the last dispensation and fullness of times, plainly tell us what is to come to pass. The 49th chapter of Isaiah is having its fulfillment."[15] Throughout 1 Nephi 21, what I refer to as "archetypes of innocence"—archetypes that convey the feeling or idea of innocence—support this prevailing message of hope and redemption, a message so relevant to our time.

As we study the archetypes used to convey a feeling of innocence, we should remember that what makes archetypes universal is their correspondence with elements of daily living.

"The values of a symbol may attach themselves to, or grow into by context or repetition, any of the images; instances are the simple archetypes of tree, river, fire, clay, wine, thorns. These are often linked to basic, recurrent and apparently universal symbols, which suggest conscious or subliminal meanings in many literatures. . . .

"The imagery of the Bible is built, in the main, on simple and vivid sense-objects; derived, not from literary sources, but from the everyday life of a people whose problems of living are themselves simple yet profound. They reflect in the Two Testaments the common life of each. For a people at first nomadic and then agricultural, cave, desert, river, well and fountain, storm and rain and drought, tower and wall, have a special immediacy. Images of the plough, the seed and the sower, the vineyard and the shepherd, are more germane to the settled life of the New Testament than the Old."[16]

We are therefore not surprised to see that the archetypes of innocence Isaiah uses are such common elements of life as parents and children, sheep and pasture, fire and water, mountain and pathway, and bride and chastity.

Parents and Children

"In the analogy of innocence the divine or spiritual figures are usually parental," and "[a]mong the human figures children are prominent."[17] The motif of home—of parents and children—weaves throughout the chapter. The chapter portrays modern Israel as children and the Lord as their parent who will gather them home.

"The beautiful imagery in Isaiah 49 provides another reminder of Christ's saving role—that of a protecting, redeeming parent to Zion's children. He comforts his people and shows mercy when they are afflicted very much as any loving father or mother would show toward a child—but, as Isaiah records, the intensity and extent of his care is much greater than that of any other loving father and mother."[18]

While there are images of Israel as parent in this chapter (see, for example, 1 Nephi 21:20, 25), the prevailing parental image is that of the Lord. It is he, not the earthly parents, who will save the children, and it is he who, unlike an earthly parent, will never forget his children. "For can a woman forget her sucking child, that she should not have compassion on the son of her womb? Yea, they may forget, yet will I not forget thee, O house of Israel. Behold, I have graven thee upon the palms of my hands; thy walls are continually before me" (1 Nephi 21:15–16). This is an excellent example of how symbolic language takes us to a meaning that we could not directly approach without it, of how "imagery compensates for the lack of precision by its increase in vividness. Images are frequently clear and memorable. . . . Images also speak directly to the heart. They are emotionally charged and often induce us to action of some sort or another."[19]

Children are prominent throughout this chapter, with the very first verse referring to the youngest stage of a child: "the Lord hath called me from the womb" (1 Nephi 21:1). While being called from the womb certainly suggests foreordination,[20] the phrase also speaks to our hearts about a time of safety when we were protected from the harshness of the world by a loving parent. In addition to being a reminder of a safe time of innocence, the concept of the womb is a component of a much broader vision of the ideal world. Archetypes in literature "fall into a dialectical pattern of opposites," a pattern of the ideal and the "unideal." The womb is an example of one of these archetypes in the ideal world of the Bible, representing the blessed ability and privilege to give birth.[21]

One of the most touching images involving children is found in the Lord's description of the way the children of Israel will be brought home. He says the Gentiles "shall bring thy sons in their arms, and thy daughters shall be carried upon their shoulders" (1 Nephi 21:22). This is not an image of a family at an amusement park, with a small girl being carried on her father's shoulders as she excitedly looks at what ride is coming up next. Rather, this is an image of a "foster-father . . . [who] carries an infant in the bosom of his dress . . . or upon his arms, so that it reclines upon his shoulder."[22] This is an intimate, loving image of parenthood, bringing the child close to the father's heart.

Extending the archetype of the parent and child even further, Isaiah speaks of the roles of those who help bring the children home: "Kings shall be thy nursing fathers, and their queens thy nursing mothers" (1 Nephi 21:23). These kings and queens could represent leaders of nations or members of the Church who are of assistance to a modern-day remnant of Israel.[23] In either case, these kings and queens are depicted through the archetype of parent, enhancing the image of the house of Israel as innocent children who are cared for and loved.

Sheep and Pasture

Another symbol attributed to Israel is a flock of sheep.[24] "They shall feed in the ways, and their pastures shall be in all high places. They shall not hunger nor thirst, neither shall the heat nor the sun smite them; for he that hath mercy on them shall lead them, even by the springs of water shall he guide them" (1 Nephi 21:9–10). Among the archetypes of innocence, "the most obvious [animals] are the pastoral sheep and lambs, . . . in their gentler aspects of fidelity and devotion."[25] Sheep "provide us with the central archetype of pastoral imagery, as well as with such metaphors as 'pastor' and 'flock' in religion."[26] It is significant that Isaiah chooses to use sheep as part of a metaphor for the lost children of Israel. They have been rebellious, turning their back on God and choosing the way of the world, yet Isaiah uses an archetype of innocence, relying on the image of an animal known for following, not rebelling. With the sheep as archetype, a natural corollary follows: their leader is the shepherd, the symbol for the Lord.

The journey home for lost Israel is not made to seem rough. The Lord is not using imagery that conveys the idea that he is displeased with his children or that, while they may return home, it will be a difficult process that will demand much from them. Instead, the image is of sheep with plenty to eat and drink. The interpretation of their pastures being in "all high places" may be as literal as food being readily accessible, even on "barren hillsides," as they make their journey home.[27] Or the image could refer to temples, providing the means by which Israel can return home spiritually.[28] The words may have different symbolic meanings and levels of interpretation, but the archetypal quality of the symbols, their universality, remains constant. The imagery of sheep and pasture creates a feeling of peace, innocence, and well-being.

Fire and Water (and Heaven)

As the children of Israel are being brought home, they are free from the heat and the sun because the Lord—"he that hath mercy on them"—is leading them (1 Nephi 21:10). While on the surface this is an image of a shepherd guiding his sheep through the desert, the image of the sun also acts as an archetype that conveys meaning to the reader. The sun is fire, and in the Biblical, ideal world burning is a positive force that "purifies and refines." In the unideal world, however, burning is a negative force that "destroys and tortures" instead of purifying.[29] Here in the wilderness, part of the unideal world, the sheep are protected from the damage that the sun can do.[30] This helps reinforce the theme of innocence by placing the children of Israel in a setting in which they are protected by their parent, the Lord.

The Shepherd now takes his flock "by the springs of water" (1 Nephi 21:10). In the unideal world, water is often depicted as the sea, full of "sea beasts and water monsters," or as stagnant pools, such as "the Dead Sea and cisterns."[31] In this verse, however, the water is in the form of springs—a pleasant, refreshing image, particularly to those who are on a long journey. These springs are one of the reasons the sheep will not suffer thirst. Water can also act as an archetype symbolizing the Savior, the Living Water, in which case these springs could be offering the nourishment that comes from the Lord.[32] Once again, the image is one of the innocence of childhood, with the Lord treating Israel lovingly as a parent would care for his children.

While being shaded from the sun (fire) and being led by the springs (water) are two separate archetypes that help create the feeling of the innocent being protected and nourished, combined they create a beautiful image of heaven, an archetype itself used throughout sacred literature. Heaven, of course, is part of the Biblical, ideal world,[33] and what is said of Isaiah 49:10 can likewise be said of 1 Nephi 21:10—it is a "picture of heaven according to Rev 7:16–17."[34] "They shall hunger no more, neither thirst any more; neither shall the sun light on them, nor any heat. For the Lamb which is in the midst of the throne shall feed them, and shall lead them unto living fountains of waters: and God shall wipe away all tears from their eyes" (Revelation 7:16–17).

Mountains and Pathways

The Lord proclaims that as he brings his children home, he will "make all [his] mountains a way, and [his] highways shall be exalted" (1 Nephi 21:11). This is a straightforward image of bringing sheep along mountain paths—an image that would probably be familiar to the readers of Isaiah's (and Nephi's) words. On the primary level, the Lord "will facilitate transportation. Roads will appear in mountain passes, and highways will be raised up in valley areas."[35] The mountain in this verse could be more symbolic, however, and represent the temple, marking "an exalted way for the Saints [gathered Israel] to walk."[36] If the idea of the temple is developed even further, the mountain could represent a sacred place of epiphany:

"One important detail in poetic symbolism remains to be considered. This is the symbolic presentation of the point at which the undisplaced apocalyptic world and the cyclical world of nature come into alignment, and which we propose to call the point of epiphany. Its most common settings are the mountain-top, the island, the tower, the lighthouse, and the ladder or staircase. . . .

"In the Bible we have Jacob's ladder, which in *Paradise Lost* is associated with Milton's cosmological diagram of a spherical cosmos hanging from heaven with a hole in the top. There are several mountain-top epiphanies in the Bible, the Transfiguration being the most notable, and the mountain vision of Pisgah, the end of the road through the wilderness from which Moses saw the distant Promised Land, is typologically linked."[37]

While the mountain in 1 Nephi 21:11 may seem far less significant than the mountains that played roles in the dramatic epiphanies mentioned here, it would be a mistake to think it has no significance. In reference to the earlier metaphor of the archetype as a theater district pass, the readers of this verse have seen the mountain "play" in a number of different theaters and would be denying themselves the richness of the image if they were to ignore the explicit and implicit relationships.

Closely related to the image of the mountain is the idea of the Lord providing "a way" or his "highways" for the children's return home. In literature, the "human use of the inorganic world involves the highway or road as well as the city with its streets, and the metaphor of the 'way' is inseparable from all quest-literature, whether explicitly Christian as in *The Pilgrim's Progress* or not."[38] The children of Israel are on a very real quest—the quest to return home. In sacred literature, there is common use of the image of the path or the way, with the Lord leading us in the "paths of righteousness" (Psalm 23:3), guiding us in "wisdom's paths" (Mosiah 2:36), teaching us to "walk in his ways" (Deuteronomy 8:6), and counseling us that "strait is the gate, and narrow is the way" (Matthew 7:14).

The "mountaintop" and the "safe pathway" or "straight road" are archetypes in the Bible that belong in the ideal experience.[39] They contribute to the idea of innocence by providing for the children of Israel a way to go home while preserving their innocence. If the children had to return home through the congested and spiritually polluted streets of Babylon, they would be in danger of becoming too worldly wise. They would no longer be innocent children but street-wise adults. The mountain and path, however, are archetypes of the safe, even near-heavenly, way provided for the children's return home.

Bride and Chastity

One of the most prevalent images of innocence is chastity, "the virtue most closely associated with childhood and the state of innocence" and "which in this structure of imagery usually includes virginity."[40] Isaiah conveys innocence when he speaks of the children of Israel in terms of what brides wear: "Lift up thine eyes round about and behold; all these gather themselves together, and they shall come to thee. And as I live, saith the Lord, thou shalt surely clothe thee with them all, as with an ornament, and bind them on even as a bride" (1 Nephi 21:18). The children who have returned home will be "like the ornamental girdle . . . which a bride fastens round her wedding dress."[41] The image of the bride is a powerful image of innocence—a woman who is not only chaste but a virgin. Even the wedding and wedding clothes contribute to the power of the image, being among the archetypes of the Bible's ideal world.[42]

The Book of Mormon Context of Isaiah 49

To understand how the archetypes of innocence support the message of Nephi as he quotes Isaiah, it is essential to understand why Nephi quoted him to begin with. There are at least three purposes for Nephi's reading of Isaiah. First, "to help all people believe in the Lord as their ultimate Redeemer (see 1 Nephi 19:23); second, to address their personal circumstances (see 1 Nephi 19:24); and third, to provide a profound hope in the future for all the house of Israel, including Nephi's own family (see 1 Nephi 19:24)."[43] Archetypal innocence supports all three of these purposes. First, it helps people believe in the Lord as their Redeemer by portraying him as the merciful Shepherd who guides his flock home, protecting them along the way. Second, it addresses their personal circumstances as it offers the feelings of comfort, safety, and direction that we all desire as we journey home. Third, it provides hope for modern Israel and for Nephi's own family, as it conveys the image of Israel as lost children whose loving parent will ultimately guide them rather than forsake them, nourish them rather than rebuke them, and gather them rather than cast them away.

From an archetypal approach to the chapter, the inclusion of chapters from Isaiah places the action of the Book of Mormon on a "cosmic level. Here the story of the Lehites is linked with Isaiah's prophecies about the scattering and then gathering of the entire house of Israel."[44] This cosmic level strengthens the archetypal nature of the chapter, for these symbols are not limited to the chapter or even the book but span and unite time and place.

After Nephi reads this chapter of Isaiah's writing, his brethren ask him a significant question that strikes at the heart of the archetypal element of Isaiah's words: "What meaneth these things which ye have read? Behold, are they to be understood according to things which are spiritual, which shall come to pass according to the spirit and not the flesh?" (1 Nephi 22:1). Nephi replies that what he has read pertains to both temporal and spiritual—an answer that can be applied to the archetypal approach as well. The images are both temporal (of the physical world) and spiritual (of the symbolic world). For Nephi, as well as for other Book of Mormon prophets, this symbolic approach of "typing or figuring or likening, guided by revelation, is simply the one way to make sense of the universe, time, and all the dimensions of individual and communal human experience."[45]

As we read the words of the Lord in this chapter, the archetypes of innocence speak to our hearts. While the text tells us that Israel has been scattered, and will be gathered, the archetypes help our hearts feel something more: we are all children of the Lord, we are all lost sheep, and we all yearn for the Shepherd to bring us safely home.

NOTES

1. While there will be times when commentaries on Isaiah 49 are incorporated into this essay, most often I will use the text from 1 Nephi 21 rather than that of Isaiah 49. I have made this decision for two reasons. First, because part of the purpose of this essay is to show how the archetypes support Nephi's message to his people, it would be most reasonable to use the words Nephi used. Second, it could be argued that the Nephi text is superior to the Isaiah text. It may be superior, as Monte Nyman argues, because it is based on a more ancient text found on the brass plates. Since the plates of brass were recorded by at least 600 B.C., that would place "the Book of Mormon text of Isaiah within 100 to 150 years of the time of the original writing, making it closer to the time of the original writing than any other Old or New Testament manuscript. Therefore, this text is probably more accurate than any other account of Isaiah, so retentions in the Book of Mormon text should be given prime consideration" (*"Great Are the Words of Isaiah,"* [Salt Lake City: Bookcraft, 1980], 10). As Professor Richard Draper pointed out in a conversation with me, however, it is possible that the changes in the text are for a reason other than reliance upon an older original. Joseph Smith, when he translated 1 Nephi 21, may not have been restoring ancient text so much as depending on revelation to make necessary changes. In either case, whether it be by ancient text or modern revelation, the Book of Mormon version of Isaiah 49 may be considered more reliable.

2. Though, of course, it speaks to the intellect as well, one of the most valued qualities of literature is its ability to help us feel. "Literature engages all our senses; it involves not only thinking but also feeling" (Richard Dilworth Rust, *Feasting on the Word: The Literary Testimony of the Book of Mormon* [Salt Lake City: Deseret Book, 1997], 1).

3. Northrop Frye, *Words with Power: Being a Second Study of "The Bible and Literature"* (New York: Harcourt Brace Jovanovich, 1990), 109.

4. Rust, *Feasting on the Word,* 171.

5. Tremper Longman III, *Literary Approaches to Biblical Interpretation* (Grand Rapids, Mich.: Academie, 1987), 129–30.

6. Wilfred L. Guerin, et al., *A Handbook of Critical Approaches to Literature*, 4th ed. (Oxford: Oxford University Press, 1999), 160.

7. Northrop Frye, *The Great Code: The Bible and Literature* (New York: Harcourt Brace & Company, 1982), 48.

8. Northrop Frye, *Anatomy of Criticism* (Princeton, N.J.: Princeton University Press, 1971), 112. It is interesting to note that Latter-day Saint literary scholar Bruce W. Jorgensen was hesitant to use the term *archetype* in an essay on the Book of Mormon because he did not want to "invoke its Jungian connotations" ("The Dark Way to the Tree: Typological Unity in the Book of Mormon," in *Literature of Belief: Sacred Scripture and Religious Experience*, ed. Neal E. Lambert [Provo, Utah: Brigham Young University Religious Studies Center, 1981], 228).

9. M. H. Abrams, *A Glossary of Literary Terms*, 7th ed. (Fort Worth, Texas: Harcourt Brace College Publishers, 1999), 13.

10. Frye, *Anatomy of Criticism*, 118.

11. Leland Ryken, *Words of Delight: A Literary Introduction to the Bible*, 2d ed. (Grand Rapids, Mich.: Baker Book House, 1992), 28.

12. Victor L. Ludlow, *Isaiah: Prophet, Seer, and Poet* (Salt Lake City: Deseret Book, 1982), 407.

13. Rust, *Feasting on the Word*, 236–37.

14. Andrew C. Skinner, "Nephi's Lessons to His People: The Messiah, the Land, and Isaiah 48–49 in 1 Nephi 19–22," in *Isaiah in the Book of Mormon*, ed. Donald W. Parry and John W. Welch (Provo, Utah: Foundation for Ancient Research and Mormon Studies, 1998), 95.

15. Wilford Woodruff, *Collected Discourses*, comp. Brian H. Stuy, 5 vols. (Woodland Hills, Utah: B.H.S. Publishing, 1992), 5:187.

16. T. R. Henn, *The Bible as Literature* (New York: Oxford University Press, 1970), 63–64.

17. Frye, *Anatomy of Criticism*, 151.

18. Jeffrey R. Holland, " 'More Fully Persuaded': Isaiah's Witness of Christ's Ministry," in *Isaiah in the Book of Mormon*, ed. Donald W. Parry and John W. Welch (Provo, Utah: Foundation for Ancient Research and Mormon Studies, 1998), 10–11.

19. Longman, *Literary Approaches to Biblical Interpretation*, 131–32.

20. Donald W. Parry, Jay A. Parry, and Tina M. Peterson, *Understanding Isaiah* (Salt Lake City: Deseret Book, 1998), 425.

21. Ryken, *Words of Delight,* 26–27.

22. C. F. Keil and F. Delitzsch, *Commentary on the Old Testament,* trans. James Martin, 10 vols. (Grand Rapids, Mich.: Eerdmans, 1983), 7:2:271.

23. Spencer W. Kimball, Conference Report, October 1965, 72.

24. Keil and Delitzsch, *Commentary on the Old Testament,* 7:2:265.

25. Frye, *Anatomy of Criticism,* 152.

26. Ibid., 143.

27. Parry, Parry, and Peterson, *Understanding Isaiah,* 429.

28. Hoyt W. Brewster Jr., *Isaiah Plain and Simple* (Salt Lake City: Deseret Book, 1995), 196.

29. Ryken, *Words of Delight,* 27–28.

30. Keil and Delitzsch translate the Isaiah text as follows: "They shall not hunger nor thirst, and the mirage and sun shall not blind them" (7:2:265). Though these are not the words used in the Book of Mormon account, it is interesting how the different imagery changes the meaning but still retains the power of the archetypes. Instead of the heat and the sun being a potential physical danger, it is now a mirage. The sun can potentially blind the children. Heat is no longer the enemy so much as losing the way through blindness.

31. Ryken, *Words of Delight,* 27.

32. In other verses in Isaiah's writings, water may be interpreted to mean the Savior: Isaiah 35:6–7; 41:17–18; 43:19–20. Parry, Parry, and Peterson, *Understanding Isaiah,* 430.

33. Ryken, *Words of Delight,* 26.

34. Kenneth Barker, ed., *The NIV Study Bible* (Grand Rapids, Mich.: Zondervan, 1995), 1081.

35. Brewster, *Isaiah Plain and Simple,* 197.

36. Parry, Parry, and Peterson, *Understanding Isaiah,* 430.

37. Frye, *Anatomy of Criticism,* 203–4.

38. Ibid., 144.

39. Ryken, *Words of Delight,* 26.

40. Frye, *Anatomy of Criticism,* 151.

41. Keil and Delitzsch, *Commmentary on the Old Testament,* 7:2:270.
42. Ryken, *Words of Delight,* 27.
43. Skinner, "Nephi's Lessons to His People," 99.
44. Rust, *Feasting on the Word,* 54.
45. Jorgensen, "Dark Way to the Tree," 228.

16

Ancient Israelite Psalters

John A. Tvedtnes

A PSALM CAN BE DEFINED AS A RELIGIOUS HYMN, written in poetic style. Most of the biblical hymns are found in the book of Psalms, which attributes many of them to King David. But some of David's psalms are found elsewhere in the Bible. David's poetic lament over the death of Saul and his son Jonathan is recorded in 2 Samuel 1:19–27. One of his most beautiful psalms of praise is found in 2 Samuel 22, of which verses 2–51 were extracted to form Psalm 18:2–50. Segments of Psalms 96 (verses 1–13), 105 (verses 2–15), and 106 (verses 47–48) are found in 1 Chronicles 16:8–36. The "last words" of David found in 2 Samuel 23:1–7 are clearly not his final discourse, which is found in 1 Kings 2:1–9. The "last words," rather, may be David's last poetic composition.

The Book of Psalms

The Old Testament book of Psalms is actually a final redaction that merged several earlier Psalters. A nineteenth century German scholar

John A. Tvedtnes is associate director of research at the Brigham Young University Institute for the Study and Preservation of Ancient Religious Texts.

suggested dividing the book into three parts. The first division, comprising Psalms 1–41, was attributed mostly to King David, who is named as the author at the beginning of many of these psalms. The second Psalter, comprising Psalms 42–89, was attributed to various people, of whom David is one. The third Psalter, comprising Psalms 111–150, consists mostly of the Hallel, or "praise," psalms (111–118) and the "Songs of Degrees," or more properly, "ascents" (120–134).

It is believed that the priests and Levites of the temple later reorganized these three Psalters into five books so that the Psalter would have the same number of divisions as the Torah (the Pentateuch), the five books of Moses. These divisions are found in the Massoretic Hebrew text of the Bible, the early Greek translation known as the Septuagint, and the King James Version of the Bible. Each of the five divisions has a summary statement of praise, or doxology, marking its end.

Book I contains Psalms 1–41, with the doxology at 41:13. Book II contains Psalms 42–72, with the doxology at 72:18–20. Book III contains Psalms 73–89, with the doxology at 89:52. Book IV contains Psalms 90–106, with the doxology at 106:48. Book V contains Psalms 107–50, with Psalm 150 serving as the doxology.

One of the evidences for these five later divisions is the frequency of the use of the divine names Jehovah and Elohim ("Lord" and "God," respectively, in the King James Version) in the Hebrew text. Book I has Elohim 15 times and Jehovah 272 times, while Book II has 164 occurrences of Elohim and 30 of Jehovah. In the first part of Book III (Psalms 73–83), Elohim occurs 36 times and Jehovah 13 times, while the second part (Psalms 84–89) has Elohim 7 times and Jehovah 31 times. Book IV uses only Jehovah and Book V uses mostly Jehovah, with the name Elohim appearing only in Psalm 108, which borrowed from Psalms 57 and 60, and 144.

This suggests to scholars that Book II, as well as the first half of Book III, passed through the hands of a later compiler who changed the name Jehovah to Elohim after the Jews had stopped pronouncing the name Jehovah. This has led to such anomalies as the expression "Jehovah my God" becoming "God my God" in Psalms 43:4, 45:7, and 50:7.[1] That such changes were made is best illustrated by some of the Psalms found in more than one of the five divisions. For example, Psalm 53, which uses Elohim, is the same as Psalm 14, where the name Jehovah is used. Psalm 70 and its parallel in Psalm 40:13–17 interchange the names Elohim and Jehovah. The same phenomenon occurs in Psalm 108, which seems to be a composite of Psalms 57:7–11 and 60:5–12.

While the King James Version and the Hebrew text from which it derives have 150 psalms, the Greek Septuagint reads differently. For example, Psalms 9–10 are a single psalm in the Septuagint, which divides Psalm 147 in two (verses 1–11 and verses 12–20). It also includes Psalm 151, long considered spurious. Scholars have noted that the Psalter in the Peshitta, the centuries-old Bible used by the Syriac Orthodox Church, contained Psalms 151–54 and that Psalm 151 in the Syriac version was the same as Psalm 151 in the Septuagint. With the discovery of the Dead Sea Scrolls, scholars were delighted to see that these additional psalms were included in some of the 36 Psalters found in the caves. Many of the other Dead Sea psalms have not been found elsewhere, but they make it clear that there were other Psalters in use by the Jews two millennia ago.[2]

Some Types of Psalms

The psalms of the Bible are of various types, based on their content. The royal psalms tend to glorify the royal line of David, often by praising the Lord for having established that line. Psalms of national history deal with some of the more important events in the history of Israel, such as the exodus from Egypt and various miraculous events in which the Lord's hand played a role. Other psalms were composed to commemorate events in the life of King David.

Some psalms were used on special occasions. The Septuagint notes in the headers that some psalms, such as Psalms 38, 48, and 94, were for the Sabbath, as was Psalm 92. Psalms 111–118 are known in Hebrew as the *Hallel* ("praise") psalms and were recited during the celebration of the Feast of Tabernacles. Psalms 120–134 are the "Songs of Degrees" (literally, "ascents"), which are thought to have been sung by the Levites standing atop a special choir stairway in the temple. Psalm 102, though a royal psalm, is called in the heading "a prayer of the afflicted."[3]

A few of the Psalms were actually borrowed from other peoples living in the ancient Near East. Psalms 24, 68, and 74, for example, are essentially known to us from the Ugaritic literature of the fourteenth century B.C. The biblical versions replace the name of the Canaanite god Baal with that of Jehovah. Psalm 104 is very similar to the Egyptian "hymn to Aton" (a sun god) from the time of Akhenaton, an eighteenth-dynasty pharaoh. The solar allusions were retained in the biblical psalm. Other psalms have close counterparts in ancient Mesopotamian literature.

Some may be bothered by the fact that the Israelites borrowed psalms from their neighbors and then changed the name of the deity in the Hebrew versions. But we have a parallel in the Latter-day Saint borrowing of hymns from other Christian churches. When Martin Luther wrote "A Mighty Fortress is Our God," he was undoubtedly thinking of the trinitarian idea of the Godhead, which Latter-day Saints reject. Still, we sing the same hymn in our services, while thinking about God as represented in the Bible and as he appeared to the Prophet Joseph Smith.

Authors of the Psalms

Many of the Psalms are credited to King David, and most of these are dedicated to "the chief musician" for use by the Levites, who sang during religious festivals. The Greek Septuagint attributes to David some of the anonymous hymns in the book of Psalms. Indeed, Psalm 72:20 attributes all the preceding psalms in the first two books noted earlier to King David. However, Psalm 72 is said to have been written by David's son Solomon, as was Psalm 127.

The Hebrew version of Psalm 71 says it was written by David, but the Septuagint says it relates to the sons of Jonadab and the first captives who were carried away by the Babylonians. Because Jonadab lived long after David's time (2 Kings 10), and since his descendants were known to the prophet Jeremiah (Jeremiah 35), they evidently were taken captive by the Babylonians about 606 B.C. Other psalms that appear to date from the time of the exile are Psalms 137 and 139. The first of these clearly refers to the captivity of Judah (Psalm 137:1–4), while the marginal and preface notes of the Septuagint manuscripts attribute the second to the same period. The Septuagint assigns authorship of Psalms 137 and 139 to the prophet Zechariah, and it attributes Psalms 146–48 to Zechariah and Haggai. Psalm 106 was also written during the exile, since it asks God (verse 47) to gather the people "from among the heathen."

Headings to Psalms 42–49, 84–85, and 87–88 indicate that they were written by the Levites known as the sons of Korah, while Psalms 50 and 73–74 were written by Asaph, and Psalm 89 was written by Ethan. Moses is said to be the author of Psalm 90, which is not surprising since Deuteronomy 32:2–43 and Exodus 15:1–19 are psalms of Moses. But Moses is not the only one whose psalms are found outside the book of Psalms. Lamentations and Proverbs also include psalms, and Deborah's victory over the Canaanites is celebrated by the psalm recorded in Judges 5:1–53.

The Alphabetic Psalms

Some biblical psalms were written as acrostics, with each new stanza beginning with a different letter of the alphabet in alphabetical order. The length of the stanzas varies from half a verse to as many as eight verses. The absence of one of the letters of the alphabet may be evidence that a stanza has been lost during the centuries of recopying the psalms. In these psalms, the alphabet may have served as a mnemonic device, or memory aid, to help the singers recall each stanza. Alphabetic psalms include the first four chapters of Lamentations, Proverbs 31:10–31, Nahum 1:2–8, and the original Hebrew of Ben-Sirach 51:13–50.[4] Psalm 155 and two other nonbiblical psalms in one of the Dead Sea Scrolls are alphabetic. Here are some examples from the biblical book of Psalms:

- Psalms 9–10 were formerly a single psalm, as in the Septuagint,[5] with two verses per letter, with some corruption in the text.
- Psalm 25 has one verse per letter of the Hebrew alphabet with an extra verse at the end that begins with the same verb as the extra verse added to Psalm 34. Verse 18, which should begin with the letter *qof*, is corrupt, but scholars have been able to restore the first word.
- Psalm 34 has one verse per Hebrew letter, with an extra verse

at the end that begins with the same verb as the extra verse in Psalm 25. The verse with the letter *waw* was lost through corruption.

• Psalm 37 has two verses per letter.

• Psalms 111 and 112 are both alphabetical, with half a verse for each letter of the Hebrew alphabet.

• Psalm 119 is alphabetical, with eight verses for each letter. Each verse within a given section begins with the same Hebrew letter. This means that the first eight verses each begin with the letter *aleph,* the next eight with the letter *beth,* and so on. The King James Version includes the name of the Hebrew letter at the beginning of each section of the psalm, along with the name of the letter transliterated into the Latin alphabet.

• Psalm 145 is alphabetical, with the letter *nun* missing. We are able to restore the lost portion because it is found in one of the Dead Sea Scroll Psalters. Some modern Bible translations add the missing material to the end of verse 13.

The alphabetic nature of some of the biblical psalms has interesting implications for dating some books of the Bible. Bible scholars, believing that the order of the letters of the Hebrew alphabet was established late, have tended to use the acrostics to demonstrate the late composition of these books, some suggesting that they are from post-exilic times, after the Jews returned from the Babylonian captivity.

During the 1970s, however, the discovery of a Hebrew abecedary (a listing of the letters of the alphabet in their alphabetical order) from the seventh century B.C. made it clear that the order had already been established in pre-exilic times, before 587 B.C.[6] Another discovery made at about the same time pushed the dating back by another five centuries. In 1978, an ostracon (inscribed pottery shard) was uncovered at Izbet Sartah, thought by archaeologist Moshe Kochavi of Tel-Aviv University to be the ancient site of Eben-ezer, where the Philistines captured the ark of the covenant (1 Samuel 4:1–11). The text, inscribed in letters dating to the early twelfth century B.C., is a simple abecedary. The order of the letters is virtually the same as in later Hebrew abecedaries, except that the order of the letters *ayin* and *peh* is reversed.[7]

In a more recent article, Harvey Minkoff explained the significance of the ostracon for Bible studies, noting that the early dating suggests that biblical acrostics do not imply a late date for the composition of books of the Old Testament.[8] The *peh-ayin* order of the abecedaries found at Izbet Sartah and Kuntillat Arjud (ninth century B.C.) is used four times in the Bible, including the acrostics that make up Lamentations 2–4,[9] Proverbs 31:10–31, and Psalms 9–10 (10:6–8). Kochavi, Minkoff, and Aaron Demsky all suggest that this unusual letter order may have been a variant used in Israel from about 1200 B.C. to 539 B.C., when Lamentations was written.

This brings us to Psalm 34, which has the usual *ayin-peh* order in verses 15–16 (16–17 in the Hebrew text). The words "the righteous" at the beginning of verse 17 in the King James Version are missing in the Hebrew text,[10] so the verse actually says, "They cry and the Lord heareth." From the present word order, this can only refer to the evildoers of verse 16 and is evidence that the order of verses 16–17 in the King James Version (17–18 in Hebrew) was switched after the psalm was composed in order to follow the later alphabetic order. Thus, the original wording would have been, "The eyes of the Lord are upon the righteous and his ears are open unto their cry" (v. 15). "They cry, and the Lord heareth, and delivereth them out of all their troubles" (v. 17). "The face of the Lord is against them that do evil, to cut off the remembrance of them from the earth" (v. 16).

New Testament Use of the Psalms

The New Testament writers often drew on the Psalms when writing about Christ. Three New Testament verses (Hebrews 5:6; 7:17, 21) cite Psalm 110:4: "The Lord hath sworn, and will not repent, Thou art a priest for ever after the order of Melchizedek." Psalm 2:7 ("I will declare the decree: the Lord hath said unto me, Thou art my Son; this day have I begotten thee") is also cited three times in the New Testament (Acts 13:33; Hebrews 1:5; 5:5). While hanging on the cross, Jesus cited the Aramaic version of a portion of Psalm 22:1: "My God, my God, why hast thou forsaken me?" (Matthew 27:46; Mark 15:34). Matthew 27:35 and John 19:24 also cite verse 18 of the same psalm in reference to Christ's crucifixion: "They part my garments among them, and cast lots upon my vesture."

In addition to quoting Psalm 82:6 (John 10:34), Christ cited Psalm 118:22–23 as prophetic of himself (Matthew 21:42; Mark 12:10–11; Luke 20:17). His chief disciple, Peter, twice cited the same passage in reference to the Savior (Acts 4:11; 1 Peter 2:7–8).

In Acts 2:34–35, Peter quotes Psalm 110:1 as a prophecy of Christ, who had cited the same passage in reference to himself (Matthew 22:43–45; Mark 12:36–37; Luke 20:42–44; see also Hebrews 1:13). Peter also interpreted other portions of the book of Psalms as references to Christ, including Psalm 16:8–11 (Acts 2:25–33), and Psalm 2:1–2 (Acts 4:25–26), and he cited Psalm 69:25 in reference to Judas Iscariot (Acts 1:16–20). Paul followed his example in citing Psalm 16:10 in reference to Christ (Acts 13:35–38). According to John 2:17, Jesus' cleansing of the temple reminded his disciples of the words of Psalm 69:9. John 6:31 may be citing Psalm 105:40, though other Old Testament passages are similar.

Clearly, the book of Psalms played an important role in the lives of the earliest Christians. This alone is sufficient to suggest that they should also be important to us, but there are other reasons as well.

Why Are the Psalms Important to Us?

The psalms of the Bible are among the earliest examples of Hebrew poetry. As such, they have great value as a tool for the study of the Hebrew language and Israelite culture and history that helps us understand other portions of the Bible. Several psalms describe the Lord's assistance to the Israelites during the Egyptian bondage and their wanderings in the wilderness (Psalms 74:12–15; 77:15–20; 78:12–54; 81:5–16; 105:16–45; 106:7–33; 114:1–8; 135:6–12; Psalms 10–22). The psalms also help us understand how the various books of the Bible were put together.

The greatest value of the psalms for the modern Church, however, is what draws most people to them. They provide doctrinal insights and exhortations to do good. Because many of the biblical psalms are hymns of praise to God, they tell us much about God and our relationship to him. From the psalms, we learn that God is a loving, trustworthy, and wise Father to whom we can turn in all circumstances. We learn that even in times of tribulation we can turn to him and receive comfort, support, healing, and forgiveness.

The Psalms are the source of some of our modern hymns. One of the best-known psalm hymns is Psalm 23, "The Lord is My Shepherd." Hymns form part of our worship of God. Through the Prophet Joseph Smith the Lord declared, "For my soul delighteth in the song of the heart; yea, the song of the righteous is a prayer unto me, and it shall be answered with a blessing upon their heads" (D&C 25:12). Reading and pondering the biblical Psalters should be an important part of our scripture study.

Notes

1. Some scholars see this phenomenon as evidence that Jewish exiles returning from Babylon had merged Elohim and Jehovah, originally separate deities, into a single God.

2. A letter written about A.D. 800 by Timotheus I, Nestorian patriarch of Seleucia, Syria, to Sergius, metropolitan of Elam (southern Iran), speaks of the discovery of a collection of books in a cave in the vicinity of Jericho, including more than two hundred psalms of David. This may have been the first cache of Dead Sea Scrolls (then already seven centuries old) ever discovered, but they are unfortunately no longer available to us.

3. Many of the psalms were really poetic prayers, probably set to music. Among the revelations in the Kirtland Revelation Book is an entry that is said to have been a "prayer sung in tongues" and then translated into English. For a discussion of this book, see John A. Tvedtnes, "Historical Perspectives on the Kirtland Revelation Book," in *The Disciple as Witness: Essays on Latter-day Saint History and Doctrine in Honor of Richard Lloyd Anderson,* ed. Stephen D. Ricks, Donald W. Parry, and Andrew H. Hedges (Provo: Foundation for Ancient Research and Mormon Studies, 2000).

4. The Greek version of this book is in the Septuagint, and St. Jerome included it in his Latin Vulgate translation as one of the books of the Apocrypha. It was published in the original (1611) King James Version of

the Bible under the name Ecclesiasticus but was later omitted along with the other eleven books of the Apocrypha. In the mid-twentieth century, the Hebrew version was discovered during archaeological excavations at Masada in Israel.

5. Psalms 42 and 43 are a single psalm in thirty-six Hebrew manuscripts. That they anciently formed a single psalm is evidenced by the repetition found in Psalm 42:5, 11; 43:5, which divides the psalm into three nearly equal parts.

6. Rudolph Cohen, "The Excavations at Kadesh-barnea 1976–78," *Biblical Archaeologist* (Spring 1981): 98–99; Rudolph Cohen, "Did I Excavate Kadesh-Barnea?" *Biblical Archaeology Review* 7, no. 3 (May/June 1981): 25–30.

7. Aaron Demsky and Moshe Kochavi, "An Alphabet from the Days of the Judges," *Biblical Archaeology Review* 4, no. 3 (September/October 1978): 22–30.

8. Harvey Minkoff, "As Simple as ABC: What Acrostics in the Bible Can Demonstrate," *Bible Review* 13, no. 2 (April 1997): 27–31, 46–47.

9. The first chapter of Lamentations is also an acrostic, but it follows the usual *ayin-peh* order.

10. The King James Version marks words not found in the original text by italicizing them. In this case, the KJV translators added the words "the righteous," based on the addition to the Greek version by the translators of the Septuagint.

17

Psalms of the Heart, Prayers unto God

Kim M. Peterson

Psalms are praises. The Hebrew name for the book of Psalms is *Tehillim,* denoting praise or a poem set to music.[1] David's psalm of praise includes these exclamations: "I will extol thee, my God, O king; and I will bless thy name for ever and ever. Great is the Lord, and greatly to be praised; and his greatness is unsearchable" (Psalm 145:1, 3). Referring to the inhabitants of the earth, David continues, "They shall abundantly utter the memory of thy great goodness, and shall sing of thy righteousness" (Psalm 145:7). David concludes, "My mouth shall speak the praise of the Lord: and let all flesh bless his holy name for ever and ever" (Psalm 145:21).

Like David, we are motivated to give praise. The desire to recognize God's greatness and goodness quickly overwhelms our human capacity to utter, sing, or speak praises. This innate tendency to worship God is enhanced, however, by the submissive dedication

Kim M. Peterson is director of the Boulder Colorado Institute of Religion.

of a king attempting to extol deity. Our own capacity to praise is increased when we witness the heartfelt praise of others.

Praise and worship are not inherently commendable. Through the prophet Isaiah, Jehovah chastised Israel for its "multitude of . . . sacrifices" and "vain oblations" (Isaiah 1:11, 13). Similarly, Christ commanded his disciples not to love like the publicans (Matthew 5:46), do alms to be seen of men (Matthew 6:1), pray like the heathens (Matthew 6:7), or fast like the hypocrites (Matthew 6:16). In each example, the Savior condemned an apparently good action because of reprehensible motivations. Works are not the same as good works, and praise is not the same as sincere praise.

Members of the newly restored Church of Jesus Christ in these latter days had to wait only three months for the Lord to reveal the manner in which the new church should praise. The familiar words directed to Emma Smith reveal both the content and intent of the hymns: "And it shall be given thee, also, to make a selection of sacred hymns, as it shall be given thee, which is pleasing unto me, to be had in my church. For my soul delighteth in the song of the heart; yea, the song of the righteous is a prayer unto me, and it shall be answered with a blessing upon their heads. Wherefore, lift up thy heart and rejoice, and cleave unto the covenants which thou hast made" (D&C 25:11–13).

Apparently, the Lord has established a relationship among prayer, singing, and rejoicing. Hymns please him if they are hymns of the heart. Hymns of the heart are hymns sung sincerely.[2] Moroni warns us that prayers can be insincere. In fact, if we pray without real intent, our prayers profit nothing, will be rejected by God, and are "counted evil" (Moroni 7:9). Since hymns can be prayers, the same counsel could apply: Hymns that are not sincere cannot qualify as praise. The validity of hymns and prayers resides in the intent that motivates the praise. Similarly, the validity of the Psalms resides in the intent of the psalmists and the sincerity of the readers. A psalm that is not read from the heart qualifies as bane praise, insincere prayer, vain oblation, or heartless song.

The Psalms and the Heart

The Psalms reveal both the conditions and the capacities of the heart. These parameters for sincere praise guide the student of the Psalms to conclude that heart doctrine includes not only outward, obedient devotion but also inward, sincere desire.

The heart is a receptacle for our attempts to change and an environment for God's interventions. The heart's capacities to change complement our efforts to change and God's interventions to change us. The psalmists distinguish between the things we do to our hearts and the things that God does to our hearts. Consequently, this source distinction differentiates between the assuming posture that we can shape our hearts and the humble reliance upon God to shape our hearts. Consider the following descriptions of self-initiated heart changes:

We can attempt to __ our hearts.

- set aright (Psalm 78:8)
- cleanse (Psalm 73:13)
- have sorrow in (Psalm 13:2)
- harden not (Psalm 95:8)
- hide his word within (Psalm 119:11)
- incline (Psalm 119:112)

Some of these changes are within our capabilities. In the example of cleansing our hearts, however, the psalmist concluded that pain, chastening, and offense accompanied the cleansing until he "went into the sanctuary of God" (Psalm 73:17). This retreat to the sanctuary (possibly symbolic of reliance on God) results in understanding the pain, accepting the chastening, and tolerating the offense. Once reliant upon God, the psalmist made sense of the cleansing.

Complete and total changes of heart rely on God's intervention. Our attempts at heart changes may resemble the predicament of a skilled heart surgeon in need of a bypass. Despite her qualifications, training, expertise, and experience, the surgeon would be foolish to attempt surgery on her own heart. She would never hop on the table, apply a local anesthetic, position a mirror, call for a scalpel, and make her own incision. At some point she would wisely relinquish the scalpel and rely "alone upon the merits" of another surgeon (Moroni 6:4). God's divine intervention to cleanse our hearts illustrates by divine hyperbole our vain attempts to cleanse our hearts. With the psalmist we will likely plead, "Create in me a clean heart, O God; and renew a right spirit within me" (Psalm 51:10).[3]

The Psalms also describe the heart as a receptacle for God's merciful interventions. The heart's capacity to receive God's interventions binds us to him. In these examples, the heart is the forum for the Lord's merciful guidance. Consider this description of God's activities in the environment of our hearts:

God can ___ our hearts.

- unite (Psalm 86:11)
- heal (Psalm 147:3)
- prepare (Psalm 10:17)
- strengthen (Psalm 27:14)
- incline (Psalm 119:36; 141:4)
- bring down (Psalm 107:12)
- fashion (Psalm 33:15)
- cleanse (Psalm 51:10)
- try (Psalm 7:9)

The profound distinction between our human capacity to change our hearts and God's divine capacity to change our hearts emphasizes a kind of covenant relationship. For example, the psalmist's resolve to incline his heart to God's testimonies (Psalm 119:111–12) contrasts with his plea that God incline his heart to those testimonies (Psalm 119:36; 141:4). John A. Widtsoe taught: "A covenant concerns two persons. Both parties must do something to make the covenant effective."[4] Considered in concert, our resolve to incline our hearts and our plea for God to incline our hearts illustrate both a promise on our part and our hope for a promise from God.

The heart can also be the origin of activities. The following descriptions of the heart's capacity center on the proximity of the heart to God's will. The heart has the capacity to align us with, or alienate us from, the desires of our Heavenly Father.

The heart can

- commune (Psalm 77:6).
- observe the law (Psalm 119:34).
- be applied to wisdom (Psalm 90:12).
- err (Psalm 95:10).
- wish (Psalm 73:7).

Heart communion suggests that the heart is the mechanism whereby we understand God, communicate with him, and relate to his instruction. Laws observed by the heart differ from laws simply obeyed. The heart is not only the object of interventions (our own or God's), it is a source of activity.

Heart conditions are also illustrated throughout the Psalms. In contrast to heart capacities, heart conditions describe states of being. Heart conditions are not the same as heart activities; being can be independent of doing. While it is true that heart capacities can affect heart conditions, it is equally true that heart conditions can motivate heart capacities.

The heart can be

- double (Psalm 12:2).
- pure or clean (Psalm 24:4; 73:1).
- fixed or established (Psalm 57:7; 108:1; 112:7–8).
- upright (Psalm 94:15; 97:11).
- perfect (Psalm 101:2).
- froward or proud (Psalm 101:4–5).
- smitten (Psalm 102:4).
- wounded (Psalm 109:22).
- desolate (Psalm 143:4).
- fat (Psalm 119:70).
- contrite or broken (Psalm 51:17; 34:18).

The most common heart condition described by the Psalms is the *whole* heart (Psalm 9:1; 111:1; 119:2, 34, 58, 69, 145; 138:1). With the whole heart, the psalmists praise (Psalm 9:1; 111:1, 138:1), "keep his testimonies" (Psalm 119:2), observe the law (Psalm 119:34), entreat the favor of the Lord (Psalm 119:58), keep the Lord's precepts (Psalm 119:69), and cry (Psalm 119:145). The psalmists seem to invite us to understand that these activities performed with anything less than a whole heart are hypocrisies and heresies before God. Elder Bruce R. McConkie notes that a focus on "religious trifles to the exclusion of eternal principles" is one of the marks of personal apostasy. Elder McConkie continues:

"Abstain from the use of tea, coffee, and tobacco, but indulge in lustful acts or forsake standards of business integrity; refrain from picking an olive or shucking an ear of maize on the Sabbath, but ignore the command to worship the Father in spirit and in truth on his holy day; pay tithing on the leaves and stalks of herbs grown in pots on the windowsill, but give no heed to judgment, mercy, and faith—such are the marks of apostate fanaticism. By such a course it is easy to have a form of godliness and a zeal for religion without doing the basic things that require the whole heart and the whole soul."[5]

Attention to religious trifles and religious forms does not qualify as wholehearted worship or praise. Similarly, halfhearted praise amounts to nothing more than proximal lips with distant hearts (Isaiah 29:13; Joseph Smith–History 1:19). Halfhearted crying is just a sad noise, and observing the law with a partial heart is little more than habitual duty. Praise must be wholehearted in order to be worthy praise.

The Psalm of the Heart

The difference between a psalm and a psalm of the heart depends less on the psalm than on the condition and capacity of the heart. Just as complex sentences, illustrious phrases, and well-timed voice modulations fail to fashion sincerity out of the heathens' repetitious prayers (Matthew 6:7), the mere recognition of a beautiful psalm does not make it a psalm of the heart. We may recognize that the sentence "Thy word is a lamp unto my feet, and a light unto my path" (Psalm 119:105) is intricately phrased and wonderfully symbolic. Until the word of the Lord literally illuminates the direction of our lives, however, the psalm falls short of being a psalm of the heart. Nephi's words to his brothers apply as literally to the Psalms as they do to the words of Isaiah: "I did liken all scriptures unto us, that it might be for our profit and learning" (1 Nephi

19:23). In order for a psalm to become a psalm of the heart, the psalm must become both profitable and a source of learning.

A psalm of the heart is also more than just a psalm about the heart. Instead, a psalm of the heart must be assimilated into the heart of the reader. Assimilation may be a passive discovery that the psalm accurately describes a heart condition, that it is an active attempt to change the heart's capacity, or that it is a submissive admission of God's intervention in our hearts. Psalm 1 stands as an invitation to be righteous. When this Psalm becomes a psalm of the heart the reader hopes to "delight" in the law (v. 2), to bring forth fruit (v. 3), and to be known of the Lord (v. 6). Void of these hopes, the reader can hardly assimilate the instruction or imitate the emotion of praise. Assimilation of the Psalms depends on the condition of the heart. Reflection on the condition of the heart will reveal that hearts that are double, established, or fat will have less of a capacity to assimilate the praise of the psalmists.

A psalm of the heart results in sincere praise. Our modern hymnal instructs worshipers on the role of hymns in praise: "The hymns invite the Spirit of the Lord, create a feeling of reverence, unify us as members, and provide a way for us to offer praises to the Lord."[6]

Each hymn includes an adverb that describes an appropriate way to sing the hymn. Of the forty different adverbs contained in our hymnal, "fervently" is used most frequently.[7] Imagine the hypocrisy of singing some of the titles with a less than fervent intent. "I Need Thee Every Hour" would diminish to "I Need Thee Most Every Hour," "Sweet Is the Work" would become "Palatable Is the Work," and "Love at Home" would regress to "Tolerance at Home."[8] These adverbs frame our hymn praise by shaping the way the hymns are sung.

Familiar Psalms contain adverbs that frame the praise of the psalmists as well as of the readers of the Psalms. Psalm 100 is frequently called the "Thanksgiving Psalm": "Make a joyful noise unto the Lord, all ye lands. Serve the Lord with gladness: come before his presence with singing. Know ye that the Lord he is God: it is he that hath made us, and not we ourselves; we are his people, and the sheep of his pasture. Enter into his gates with thanksgiving, and into his courts with praise: be thankful unto him, and bless his name. For the Lord is good; his mercy is everlasting; and his truth endureth to all generations."

Reading Psalm 100 with less than a joyful noise or gladness may diminish our gratitude to platitudes and our praise to vain oblations. Similarly, Psalm 23 contains the phrase "I will fear no evil" (Psalm 23:4). Reading this Psalm fearfully would erroneously praise the Lord as less than a shepherd. The exultant reaction to a psalm of the heart will naturally inspire sincere praise.

Psalms of the heart are applicable as well as beautiful; they are assimilated as well as recognized; they are sincere as well as reverent. These conditions thrust the reader into the realm of the psalmists. Elder Bruce R. McConkie alluded to our capacity to apply, assimilate, and sincerely consider the beautiful words of scripture.

"In speaking of these wondrous things I shall use my own words, though you may think they are the words of scripture, words spoken by other Apostles and prophets. True it is they were first proclaimed by others, but they are now mine, for the Holy Spirit of God has borne witness to me that they are true, and it is now as though the Lord had revealed them to me in the first instance. I have thereby heard his voice and know his word."[9]

We can share not only meaning but also sentiment with the authors of the Psalms. Their praise can become our praise; our worship can model their exultations, depending on the capacities and conditions of our hearts.

Christ and the Psalms of the Heart

The Savior's ministry is laced with references to the Psalms and illustrates the important doctrine of the heart. Christ regularly emphasized the relationship between the condition of our hearts and the effectiveness of our worship. In the Sermon on the Mount, the Savior delineates the distinction between intent and action. Matthew 7:21–23 emphasizes the importance of doing the will of the Father in addition to casting out devils, prophesying, and doing wonderful works. While it may seem reasonable to assume that wonderful works were unilaterally considered to be the will of the Father, the Savior suggested a distinction. Apparently, our feeble understanding of what is righteous, justifiable, and good does not account for God's ways that are higher than our ways (Isaiah 55:8–9).

To those prophets, workers of wonders, and exorcisers of devils who perform contrary to the will of the Lord, the Savior severely professes, "I never knew you: depart from me, ye that work iniquity" (Matthew 7:23). This reference to Psalm 6:8 includes the realization that the psalmist asks the workers of iniquity to depart because "the Lord hath heard the voice of my weeping." Perhaps the Savior's reference to these words was an invitation to a "wholehearted" commitment to the will of the Lord. The heart can mediate righteousness independent of our actions.

Christ also taught the importance of relying on God to change our hearts. The stone rejected by the builders conjures images of builders who have somehow set their hearts on the kinds of stones that would sensibly add to their building. Perhaps the stones they chose were uncharacteristically beautiful or pleasing. Whatever criteria they used for selecting the stones, the rejected stones probably violated the expectations of the builders. Perhaps the naïve builders thought that some of the stones would marginalize the integrity of their building. Using a rejected stone for the chief cornerstone marks a complete change of attitude and a new set of criteria for the builders. Notice the psalmist's integration of this imagery in Psalm 118:21–24: "I will praise thee: for thou hast heard me, and art become my salvation. The stone which the builders refused is become the head stone of the corner. This is the Lord's doing; it is marvelous in our eyes. This is the day which the Lord hath made; we will rejoice and be glad in it."

Not only did the psalmist recognize that the building codes would change, he rejoiced in the change. This new standard and the resultant structure elicited praise and rejoicing. Surely this change of heart was a glorious experience.

When the chief priests challenged Christ's authority, he asked them by what authority John baptized. The lawyers were stymied by this trap. If they answered that John baptized with heavenly authority, they would be condemned for not following him; if they answered that John baptized by his own authority, the people would stone them (Luke 20:1–7). Reluctantly, perhaps, they answered that they could not tell from whence John's authority was. The standards had changed. Apparently, the people desired something different than the priests, and Christ (and by extension John) was promoted to a position of "head" and "corner."

Christ followed the question of authority with the parable of the husbandmen who killed the heir of the vineyard. The purpose for the parable seems to be summarized in Christ's conclusion: "What therefore shall the lord of the vineyard do unto them? He shall come and destroy these husbandmen, and shall give the vineyard to others" (Luke 20:15–16). The audience replies, "God forbid." Next, the Savior asks the meaning of the Psalm that proclaims, "The stone which the builders rejected, the same is become the head of the corner?" (Matthew 21:42; see also Psalm 118:22). The application of this Psalm illustrates the change of heart that was rejected by the priests but commendable among disciples. This change illuminates the necessity for reliance on the Father as the builder of "many mansions" and his Son as the one who prepares a place (John 14:2). Without heartfelt reliance on God, we risk being the building inspectors who reject the head and corner of our salvation.

Christ also taught the capacities of the heart. His triumphal entry into Jerusalem poised his exuberant followers to fulfill a prophecy found in Psalms. Despite his impending death, rejection by the religionists, and controversial teachings, Christ was greeted by garments spread on the ground, branches waving in the air and shouts of "Hosanna to the Son of David: Blessed is he that cometh in the name of the Lord; Hosanna in the highest" (Matthew 21:9).

"Hosanna," or "save now," was a shout associated with the Feast of the Tabernacles.[10] The feast was also marked by the rite of dwelling in booths, and it celebrated the gathering in of fruits and the sojourning of the children of Israel in the wilderness.[11] Ironically, some devout Jews celebrated the in-gathering but neglected the opportunity to gather (or invite) the Son of God into their hearts. Despite the outward show of booths, lights, and shouts during the triumphal entry, the psalmist's ancient words found little meaning in the hearts of the most devout Jews: "This is the day which the Lord hath made; we will rejoice and be glad in it. Save now, I beseech thee, O Lord: O Lord, I beseech thee, send now prosperity. Blessed be he that cometh in the name of the Lord: we have blessed you out of the house of the Lord" (Psalm 118:24–26).

Tragically, some of the impenetrable hearts of the Jews were confined to palm shanties instead of the mansions prepared by Christ. Their heart capacities were severely limited.

The prevalence of quotations from the Psalms in Christ's ministry illustrates the divine expressions contained in these praises. The Savior seemed to rely on the Psalms to reveal the condition of his disciples' hearts, to enlarge their hearts' capacities, and to increase their reliance on God's interventions.

Prayers unto God

The Psalms inspire wholehearted praise: "I will praise thee, O Lord, with my whole heart; I will shew forth all thy marvellous works. I will be glad and rejoice in thee" (Psalm 9:1–2).

The sincerity with which the Psalms were written can elicit sincere praise from us when we read with real intent. Intent, or the reason for studying the Psalms, can limit or increase our capacity to understand, apply, and assimilate heartfelt praise contained in the Psalms. The final Psalm summarizes both the heart condition and the heart capacity requisite for praise: "Praise ye the Lord. Praise God in his sanctuary. . . . Let every thing that hath breath praise the Lord. Praise ye the Lord" (Psalm 150:1, 6).

As our hearts' conditions align more closely with God's interventions, our hearts' capacities to praise will naturally increase. Then in desire and in deed we can join with the psalmists in heartfelt, sincere, continual praise.

Notes

1. Latter-day Saint edition of the King James Version of the Bible, Bible Dictionary, s.v. "Psalms"; James Strong, *The New Strong's Exhaustive*

Concordance of the Bible (Nashville, Tenn.: Thomas Nelson Publishers, 1984), 64.

2. "God delights in the song of the heart; not in the mere sounds of the lips. Singing from the heart is worship; wherefore Paul says, 'I will sing with the spirit, and I will sing with understanding also' (1 Corinthians 14:15). In such singing God takes delight. No music is as sweet as religious compositions; none is so majestic, so inspiring" (Hyrum M. Smith and James M. Sjodahl, *Doctrine and Covenants Commentary,* 129, as cited in Daniel H. Ludlow, *A Companion to Your Study of the Doctrine and Covenants* [Salt Lake City: Deseret Book, 1978], 1:181). Paul concluded that we can pray with understanding also when we pray by the Spirit (1 Corinthians 14:15). Moroni notes the relationship among prayer, singing, and praise: "Their meetings were conducted by the church after the manner of the workings of the Spirit, and by the power of the Holy Ghost; for as the power of the Holy Ghost led them whether to . . . pray . . . or to sing" (Moroni 6:9).

3. It is interesting to note Ezekiel's description of the Lord's interventions: "A new heart also will I give you, and a new spirit will I put within you: and I will take away the stony heart out of your flesh, and I will give you an heart of flesh" (Ezekiel 36:26). Commenting on this scripture, Elder J. Richard Clarke concluded, "Such complete changes require the power of God" (Conference Report, April 1993, 9).

4. John A. Widtsoe, *Evidences and Reconciliations,* comp. G. Homer Durham (Salt Lake City: Bookcraft, 1960): 253.

5. Bruce R. McConkie, *The Mortal Messiah* (Salt Lake City: Deseret Book, 1980), 3:398.

6. *Hymns of The Church of Jesus Christ of Latter-day Saints* (Salt Lake City: The Church of Jesus Christ of Latter-day Saints, 1985), ix.

7. *Hymns,* nos. 23, 84, 98, 101, 105, 123, 134, 138, 147, 157, 174, 182, 192, 215, 222, 279, 281, 292, 294, 299, 301, 305, 312, 317, 318, 334, 335, 337.

8. *Hymns,* nos. 98, 147, 294.

9. Bruce R. McConkie, Conference Report, April 1985, 9; or *Ensign,* "The Purifying Power of Gethsemane," May 1985, 9.

10. Bible Dictionary, s.v. "Hosanna."

11. Bible Dictionary, s.v. "Feasts."

18

Temple Imagery in the Psalms

Brian M. Hauglid

No longer heard are the strains of biblical songs as they resounded in the ears of those who first penned them under the inspiration of God. Ancient Israelite music has long been buried somewhere in the distant past. There are, however, preserved in the Bible, a collection of 150 songs titled the book of Psalms. The Hebrew term for *psalms* is *tehillim,* which means "praises," but the English word *psalms* "is a transliteration of the Greek" word signifying "songs accompanied by stringed instruments."[1] These songs generally follow a Hebrew parallelistic format with various patterns to emphasize teachings or to add beauty to the performance.[2] About half of the psalms are attributed to David, but other authors produced many psalms as well. Jewish tradition divides the Psalms into five books: (book 1) 1–41; (book 2) 42–72; (book 3) 73–89; (book 4) 90–106; (book 5) 107–150. "The Psalter seems to have been formed very much as modern hymn-books are formed. The earliest collection would be the Davidic, of which a

Brian M. Hauglid is an assistant professor of ancient scripture at Brigham Young University.

large part is preserved in Book 1; later collections would be those of Asaph and the sons of Korah."[3] The psalms were likely compiled and written down over a long period of time, but as to their antiquity there is no question. Only a trained mind well-versed in Hebrew could reconstruct—likely with limited success—what the psalms may have sounded like to the ancient Israelites.[4] But even without the music, the inspired words of the psalms convey meanings and images that transcend time and place, bridging the ancient and modern worlds. This is especially true when looking at the psalms in the context of the temple.

Ancient Jewish sources, such as the Mishnah and Talmud, specify fourteen psalms that were actually sung by the Levites in the temple: Psalms 24, 30, 48, 81, 82, 92–94, 113–118.[5] One scholar, however, estimates that of the 150 psalms, 109, or 84 percent, were likely sung in the temple.[6] A review of selected psalms, with brief historical background added, illustrates how they functioned as part of the processional and enthronement rites in ancient Israelite temple worship. Not surprisingly, the imagery of procession and enthronement were central to the Israelite temple and bear a striking resemblance to Latter-day Saint temple worship. Other allusions to temple worship from the psalms are fruitful for study as well, such as the principles of covenants, obedience, sacrifice, and purity.

As insightful and instructive as these concepts are in their own right, they attain even more significance when viewed with an understanding of the life and mission of the Savior, whose atonement makes temple practices, ancient and modern, meaningful and operative in our lives. In the Psalms, Jesus Christ emerges as the preeminent image and figure, adding needed light to the deeper meanings of the temple.

Ancient Israelite Temple Psalms

In the Old Testament, ancient Israel used psalms at its festivals, feasts, and temple sacrifices.[7] According to the Mishnah (*Tamid* 7:4), at the daily temple sacrifices, the Levites sang Psalm 24 on the first day of the week, Psalm 48 on the second, Psalm 82 on the third, Psalm 94 on the fourth, Psalm 81 on the fifth, Psalm 93 on the sixth, and Psalm 92 on each Sabbath.[8] Psalms 113–118 were sung at several feasts, such as the Feast of Tabernacles, the Feast of Weeks, and the Feast of Dedication.[9] Psalms 113–118 were also sung at the slaying of the Paschal Lamb, and Psalm 100 was sung "at a special sacrifice, the Sacrifice of Thanksgiving."[10]

Central to Israelite temple rites are the processional and enthronement psalms, symbolizing entering into the Lord's presence. Psalm 24 provides a good example of a processional psalm. Levites would perform this psalm as Israelites made their way to the temple "before the gates, and when the procession winds in through the gates."[11] Upon approaching the temple gates, an interview takes place, and the priestly gatekeepers ask the worshippers, "Who shall ascend into the hill of the Lord? or who shall stand in his holy place? He that hath clean hands, and a pure heart; who hath not lifted up his soul unto vanity, nor sworn deceitfully" (vv. 3–4). Another processional psalm (118) attests to the petition of Israelites at the gate to the temple: "Open to me the gates of righteousness: I will go into them, and I will praise the Lord: This gate of the Lord, into which the righteous shall enter" (vv. 19–20).[12] But before one could pass through the gates into the temple area the question "Who shall ascend into the hill of the Lord" must be answered to assure the worthiness of the petitioners. In Psalm 24:6 the answer is given: "This is the generation of them that seek him, that seek thy face." Israelites must be confident of fulfilling the demands of having "clean hands, and a pure heart"[13] before symbolically entering the presence of the Lord.

Later in Psalm 24 the gates of the temple are themselves addressed, "Lift up your heads, O ye gates; and be ye lift up, ye everlasting doors; and the King of glory shall come in" (v. 7; see also v. 9). One author notes that the Hebrew terms for temple gates in Psalm 24:7 can also mean "gates of eternity." This same author suggests that the notion of passing through gates before entering sacred places and the presence of deity is very ancient, predating even the actual physical gates of Solomon's temple.[14] In Psalm 24:3–4, procession toward the ancient temple also symbolized the *ascension* of an individual from a lower to a higher spiritual state prior to entering the Lord's presence.

Psalms that contain images of enthronement envision Jehovah's ascent to the throne to be acclaimed as king. Usually the enthronement psalms, such as Psalms 47, 93, 96–99, were performed at the harvest (Feast of Weeks, Feast of Harvest) and new year festivals (Rosh Hashanah). A characteristic phrase of the enthronement psalms (for example 47:8; 93:1; 96:10; 97:1) is: "[The Lord] has become king."[15] The Psalter's "vision is of something new and important that has just taken place: Yahweh has now become king; hence the new song of joy and praise to be sung."[16] But the declaration that the Lord has become king "is just such a cry of acclamation as 'Absalom has become king!' 'Jehu has become king!' (2 Sam. 15:10; 2 Kgs. 9:13)."[17] Taking this a step further, the acclamation afforded Absalom and Jehu is just as fitting for each worthy individual admitted to the celestial kingdom.

Procession and enthronement rites were performed together as a new kingship in ancient Israel was established. Usually the person would be anointed with oil before the actual enthronement. An excellent example of a procession, anointing, and enthronement, accompanied by music (psalms), is the account of Solomon succeeding David as king of Israel. According to 1 Kings 1:38–40:

"So Zadok the priest, and Nathan the prophet, and Benaiah the son of Jehoiada, and the Cherethites, and the Pelethites, went down, and caused Solomon to ride upon king David's mule, and brought him to Gihon. And Zadok the priest took an horn of oil out of the tabernacle, and anointed Solomon. And they blew the trumpet; and all the people said, God save king Solomon. And all the people came up after him, and the people piped with pipes, and rejoiced with great joy, so that the earth rent with the sound of them."

Some of the psalms (Psalm 21:3; 132:18; 89:39) depict the final act of enthronement in the presence of the Lord, with God himself placing a crown upon the head of the king. To be sure, "The crown signifies the manifestation and completion of the king's election."[18] Psalm 132:11–12 indicates that once a king is enthroned he can then rightfully sit upon his throne, for "it is the throne which makes the king a king; it is his mother."[19] In verse 12 the honor given to a righteous king extends the blessings of kingship to his posterity: "If thy children will keep my covenant and my testimony that I shall teach them, their children shall also sit upon thy throne for evermore."

Psalmic images of procession and enthronement are, in general, similar to teachings from modern prophets on Latter-day Saint temple worship. Two well-known statements give evidence of both procession and enthronement. When President Brigham Young spoke of the temple endowment on 6 April 1853, he referred to it as a procession back into the presence of the Father:

"Let me give you the definition in brief. Your *endowment* is, to receive all those ordinances in the House of the Lord, which are necessary for you, after you have departed this life, to enable you to walk back to the presence of the Father, passing the angels who stand as sentinels, being enabled to give them the key words, the signs and tokens, pertaining to the Holy Priesthood, and gain your eternal exaltation in spite of earth and hell.[20]

On 7 April 1844, Joseph Smith delivered one of his most famous sermons, the King Follet discourse, at the temple. He counseled the Saints: "You have got to learn how to be a god yourself in order to save yourself—to be priests & kings as all Gods has done—by going from a small degree to another—from exaltation to ex[altation]—till they are able to sit in glory as with those who sit enthroned."[21] Just as an ancient Israelite king underwent processional and enthronement rituals, the righteous Latter-day Saint ritually proceeds toward God to become a god, a priest, and a king to "inherit thrones, kingdoms, principalities, and powers, dominions, all heights and depths" (D&C 132:19). In addition to the processional and enthronement images, the psalms contain other allusions that can enhance our understanding and appreciation of temple worship.

Other Temple Allusions in the Psalms

Other imagery in the psalms, although less directly connected to the ancient Israelite temple, calls to mind modern temple principles. Templegoers who see these specific temple principles (or practices) in the psalms will know that the Lord wants these emphasized, because they are in the temple as in well as the scriptures. By paying careful attention to these emphases, one's understanding and application of the principles can be strengthened.

Most Latter-day Saints know that when we go to the temple, we make specific covenants with the Lord to prepare to be brought into his presence. These covenants include promises to obey the Lord, to make sacrifices for the good of the Lord's kingdom, and to remain pure and worthy to continue rendering service. Several verses of the Psalms allude to such temple covenants as sacrifice, obedience, and purity. Psalm 50:5 states, "Gather my saints together unto me; those that have made a covenant with me by sacrifice. And the heavens shall declare his righteousness." Joseph Smith indirectly put this verse in a temple context. He said the purpose of the gathering in all ages is "to build unto the Lord a house to prepare them for the ordinances and endowments, washings and anointings, etc."[22] Verse 5 can also mean that the heavens, or Holy Ghost, will sustain those who, by the principle of sacrifice, keep their temple covenants. This would likely be true whether one is newly endowed or has progressed to a more advanced spiritual state.

Psalm 15:1–5 illustrates the temple principles of being obedient to the Lord, sacrificing our egos, and having a pure love for our neighbor:

"Lord, who shall abide in thy tabernacle? who shall dwell in thy holy hill?

"He that walketh uprightly, and worketh righteousness, and speaketh the truth in his heart [obedient, pure motives].

"He that backbiteth not with his tongue, nor doeth evil to his neighbour, nor taketh up a reproach against his neighbour.

"In whose eyes a vile person is contemned; but he honoureth them that fear the Lord. He that sweareth to his own hurt, and changeth not [sacrifice of ego and purity of love].

"He that putteth not out his money to usury, nor taketh reward against the innocent [purity]. He that doeth these things shall never be moved."

This psalm could be considered as a type of temple recommend interview. There is a question and a response, providing confirmation that the worshiper is obedient and worthy to enter into the holy temple. According to this psalm, one who desires to enter into the holy temples must sacrifice the ego, obey the Lord's commandments, and exemplify purity of heart. One who "walketh uprightly," "worketh righteousness," "speaketh the truth in his heart," and treats his neighbor and money appropriately, "shall never be moved." To be not moved in a temple context is to have one's temple blessings secured so that only through pride and unrighteous behavior could these blessings be lost. Commitment and valor in living the gospel are also aspects of being anchored so that one cannot be moved.

Concerning the principle of sacrifice and temple worship, Elder Robert L. Simpson emphasized: "The temple is a house of commitment and sacrifice, for it is truly stated that there can be no true worship without sacrifice; indeed, as the Saints sing, sacrifice brings forth the blessings of heaven."[23] At a general priesthood meeting in April 1990, Elder Robert D. Hales stated: "We are preparing ourselves to take on higher laws and covenants such as obedience, sacrifice, service, chastity, and consecration of our time and talents. Why do we do this? We should learn this before we go to the temple . . . because afterwards it will help each of us to be valiant."[24] Obedience to the higher laws and covenants of the temple will strengthen us to be "steadfast and immovable, always abounding in good works" (Mosiah 5:15).

Psalm 24:3–5 confirms that in relation to the temple our motives and actions should be pure.

"Who shall ascend into the hill of the Lord? or who shall stand in his holy place.

"He that hath clean hands, and a pure heart; who hath not lifted up his soul unto vanity, nor sworn deceitfully.

"He shall receive the blessing from the Lord, and righteousness from the God of his salvation."[25]

Elder Dallin H. Oaks interprets these verses: "If we do righteous acts and refrain from evil acts, we have clean hands. If we act for the right motives and if we refrain from forbidden desires and attitudes, we have pure hearts."[26] Remaining pure in motive and in deed warrants the higher blessings promised in the temple, which lead to receiving the fullness of salvation from the Lord.

As beautiful and wonderful as the higher principles, laws, and covenants of the temple are in their own right, looking at them within the context of the Savior's life and mission lends more sacredness to them and underscores that the temple is the House of the Lord.

The House of the Lord

In the Latter-day Saint edition of the King James Version of the Bible, eighteen psalms are specifically designated in the chapter headings as Messianic psalms.[27] Although the psalms previously discussed are not included in the eighteen, a careful look at any psalm demonstrates that Jehovah (to the ancient Israelites) or Jesus Christ is the paramount presence. Some messianic psalms make specific reference to a particular aspect of the Savior's earthly ministry. For instance, Psalm 22:1 cites a phrase that the Savior repeats on the cross: "My God, my God, why hast thou forsaken me?" Other messianic psalms portray the Lord as vanquishing the enemy (Psalms 68) or displaying his attributes (Psalms 89). All the psalms could be considered as songs of praise and glorification, directed to the Lord—especially within a temple context.

In the King Follet discourse, Joseph Smith explained that everything in the temple prepares us to receive the Savior:

"The spirit of Elias is first, Elijah second, and Messiah last. Elias is a forerunner to prepare the way, and the spirit and power of Elijah is to come after, holding the keys of power, building the Temple to the capstone, placing the seals of the Melchizedek Priesthood upon the house of Israel, and making all things ready; then Messiah comes to His Temple, which is last of all."[28]

Psalm 132:3–5 says, "Surely I will not come into the tabernacle of my house, nor go up into my bed; I will not give sleep to mine eyes, or slumber to mine eyelids, until I find out a place for the Lord, an habitation for the mighty God of Jacob." Truly, the temple is *The House of the Lord.*

Titles applied to Jesus in the book of John, such as "living water" (John 4:10; see also v. 14; 7:38), the "bread of life" (John 6:48), "the light of the world" (John 8:12; 9:5), "the good shepherd" (John 10:14), and "Comforter" (John 14:16), are found also in the Psalms. As to the living water, the psalmist says the righteous [like Christ] "shall be like a tree planted by the rivers of water, that bringeth forth his fruit in his season" (Psalm 1:3). Jesus as the bread of life is alluded to in Psalm 105:40, "The people asked, and he brought quails, and satisfied them with the bread of heaven [manna]." Just as the water and bread brought physical satisfaction to the ancient Israelites, Latter-day Saints can enjoy a spiritual feast in the temple. Psalm 27:1 reads, "The Lord is my light," while Psalm 23:1 states, "The Lord is my shepherd." Jesus is referred to several times in the psalms as a comforter. Psalm 23:4 says, "Thou [Lord] art with me; thy rod and thy staff they comfort me" and in Psalm 94:19, "In the multitude of my thoughts within me thy comforts delight my soul." In the temple we receive added light through instruction and personal revelation. Just as a shepherd gathers his sheep to his bosom, in the protection of his robe, so the Good Shepherd offers spiritual direction in the house of the Lord where he can lovingly instruct and comfort the worshiper. "It is not surprising that many of these symbolic titles are connected in one way or another with the temple, as it is in the temple that we learn more fully the meaning of Christ and our relationship to him."[29]

Just as the Savior is the central figure who gives meaning to the Psalms, and all other scriptures, so is he also the center of temple worship. Everything in the temple prepares us to be worthy of his presence. All the covenants and ordinances performed in the temple are given efficacy, force, and meaning because of the atonement of Jesus Christ. Elder Victor L. Brown emphasized the centrality of the Savior in our temple worship and promised:

"When we go to the temple because we want to go and not because it is an obligation; when we go with an attitude of worship and a reverence for God and for His son Jesus Christ, and with gratitude for the Savior's sacrifice; when we spend sufficient time to leave the cares of the world outside, wonderful things happen which cannot be described. The Spirit of the Lord distills upon one's soul in these holy houses, truly the most sacred places on earth. A new perception comes into focus of who we are, of what this life is really about, of the opportunities of eternal life, and of our relationship with the Savior."[30]

President Howard W. Hunter also taught: "As we attend the temple, we learn more richly and deeply the purpose of life and the significance of the atoning sacrifice of the Lord Jesus Christ. Let us make the temple, with temple worship and temple covenants and temple marriage, our ultimate earthly goal and the supreme mortal experience."[31]

Temple images and allusions from the psalms, including processional and enthronement rituals, and the principles of sacrifice, obedience, and purity, gain added meaning and clarity when viewed as bringing us back into the presence of the Lord. This was the intent of temple ordinances in ancient Israel and remains the central focus of temple worship today. Even without the music, the Psalms still ring with these powerful and sacred images—pointing to the holy temple and enriching our worship of the Lord. As the poet Shelley once wrote, "Music, when soft voices die/ Vibrates in the memory."[32] Perhaps the sanctity of these sacred teachings is an echo of the beautiful music that once accompanied the psalms.

Notes

1. J. R. Dummelow, ed., *A Commentary on the Holy Bible by Various Writers* (New York: Macmillan, 1936), 321.

2. For a recent discussion of Hebrew parallelism in the book of Psalms, see David Noel Freedman, ed., *The Anchor Bible Dictionary,* 6 vols. (New York: Doubleday, 1992), 5:528–30.

3. Dummelow, *Commentary,* 324.

4. "We do not know on what kind of musical system ancient oriental music was built up; to all appearance it was not at any rate on the octave scales. The 'tunes' to which they would sing were very simple and primitive, probably only covering a single line from the poem and consisting of a couple of notes, perhaps the same note over and over again with a rise

or a fall on the last word or syllable of the line" (Sigmund Mowinckel, *The Psalms in Israel's Worship,* trans. D. R. AP-Thomas, 2 vols. [Nashville, Tenn.: Abingdon, 1962], 2:84).

5. Performance of music was primarily the responsibility of the Levites. They sang the psalms and played the instruments. Cf. Ezra 3:10; Nehemiah 12:24, 27–29, 45; 1 Chronicles 15:16–22, 27; 16:4–5, 41–42; 23:3–5; 25:1–7; 2 Chronicles 5:12–13; 7:6; 29:25; 30:21. For a discussion of the Levites' part in music, see Mowinckel, *Psalms,* 2:79–82; and Joachim Jeremias, *Jerusalem in the Time of Jesus,* trans. F. H. Cave and C. H. Cave (Philadelphia: Fortress Press, 1969), 208–9.

6. John A. Smith, "Which Psalms Were Sung in the Temple?" *Music and Letters* 70 (1990): 181.

7. "There are frequent references in the Psalms to the Temple worship and sacrifices. The Psalmists declare their intention of offering burnt offerings and paying their vows in the presence of all the people (e.g. 66:13–15; 116:14, 17). . . . They know that offerings are insufficient of themselves, and that they are only valuable in so far as they typify the 'living sacrifice' of self, which every true worshipper must offer" (Dummelow, *Commentary,* 325).

Solomon's "Temple in Jerusalem had its own guild of singers and musicians" (Mowinckel, *Psalms,* 1:10). Cf. also 1 Chronicles 15:25.

8. *The Mishnah,* trans. Herbert Danby (Oxford: Oxford University Press, 1989), 589. Orthodox Jews believe the Mishnah was the oral law revealed to Moses on Mount Sinai. It spells out many practices not in the Torah, or the five books of Moses. Rabbi Judah had it written down in the second century after Christ.

9. Mowinckel, *Psalms,* 1:3.

10. Ibid.

11. Ibid., 1:6. "In the First Book of Chronicles (ch. 9) the Levites are divided by families into singers and gate-keepers, and these divisions were carefully preserved during the entire existence of the Temple. The gatekeepers had to close the gates, guard the Temple area at night, and supervise the daytime visitors to the Temple to ensure that none entered in impurity" (*The Herodian Period,* ed. M. Ari Yonah and Z. Baras, vol. 7 of *The World History of the Jewish People,* ed. B. Netanyahu, et al. [New Brunswick: Rutgers University Press, 1975], 294).

12. Mowinckel notes that the Hebrew word for "procession," *hagh,*

means circling or ambulation. "In Pss. 48 and 118 the circling of the city wall or the altar is itself the procession and the dance" (*Psalms,* 1:11).

13. "Before an Israelite entered the Temple court he bathed in water; this was required even if he was clean, and he could do so in one of the many ritual baths to be found in the Temple courts or in front of the gates. It appears to have been the custom to enter the Temple only in white garments, for this was regarded as indicating modesty and piety" (*Herodian Period,* 296).

14. Othmar Keel, *The Symbolism of the Biblical World: Ancient Near Eastern Iconography and the Book of Psalms* (Winona Lake, Ind.: Eisenbrauns, 1997), 172.

15. Mowinckel, *Psalms,* 1:107. The King James Version reads, "The Lord reigneth" (Psalms 93:1; 96:10; 97:1). Mowinckel argues that this is an older translation and is misleading. Ibid.

16. Ibid.

17. Ibid.

18. Keel notes Psalms 5:12; 8:5; 103:4 as connected with the crown manifesting completion of enthronement. Keel, *Symbolism of the Biblical World,* 259.

19. Ibid., 264.

20. Brigham Young, *Journal of Discourses,* 26 vols. (London: Latter-day Saints' Book Depot, 1854–1886), 2:31.

21. *The Words of Joseph Smith,* comp. and ed. Andrew F. Ehat and Lyndon W. Cook (Provo, Utah: Brigham Young University, Religious Studies Center, 1980), 357.

22. Joseph Smith, *Teachings of the Prophet Joseph Smith,* sel. Joseph Fielding Smith (Salt Lake City: Deseret Book, 1976), 308.

23. Robert L. Simpson, Conference Report, October 1980, 11.

24. Robert D. Hales, Conference Report, April 1990, 52.

25. Donald W. Parry translates verse 6, which reads in the King James Version as "This is the generation of them that seek him," as "This is the circle of them that inquire of him." Parry argues that this verse is referring to a temple prayer circle. See "Temple Worship and a Possible Reference to a Prayer Circle in Psalm 24," *BYU Studies* 32, no. 4 (1992): 57–62.

26. Dallin H. Oaks, *Pure in Heart* (Salt Lake City: Bookcraft, 1988), 1. Elder Oaks also said, "It is easier to have clean hands than to have a pure

heart. It is easier to control our acts than to control our thoughts. The requirement that our good acts must be accompanied by good motives is subtle and difficult in practice" (Ibid., 17).

27. Although other chapter headnotes, such as those to Psalms 31 and 34, include the phrase "speaking Messianically."

28. Smith, *Teachings,* 340.

29. Richard Neitzel Holzapfel and David Rolph Seely, *My Father's House: Temple Worship and Symbolism in the New Testament* (Salt Lake City: Bookcraft, 1994), 143.

30. Victor L. Brown, Conference Report, October 1989, 97.

31. Howard W. Hunter, Conference Report, October 1994, 118. Elder Robert L. Simpson also said, "In the temple one gains a superior perspective about his personal relationship with his Maker and with the Savior—yes, special knowledge about God and Jesus Christ, which is essential to the obtaining of life eternal" (Conference Report, October 1980, 10–11).

32. Percy Bysshe Shelley, "To———," in *The Norton Anthology of Poetry,* 3d ed. (New York: W. W. Norton & Company, 1983), 637.

19

Jesus' Use of the Psalms in Matthew

Thomas A. Wayment

One of the most remarkable aspects of Jesus' earthly ministry was his ability to teach the gospel in a way that caused even his most learned followers to reevaluate their thinking. He often taught principles and concepts that were new and exciting and that were difficult to understand and accept without the guidance of the Holy Spirit. In a culture where the Old Testament was accepted as the ultimate source of gospel learning, it is not surprising to find the Master Teacher drawing broadly on this important body of scripture, especially the book of Psalms, to facilitate his message and give credence to his teachings.[1] By looking at the ways Jesus incorporated the Psalter, or book of Psalms, into his teachings, we can gain a more profound understanding of how Jesus taught the gospel, as well as how he chose to explain his earthly ministry to the Jews.

The Sermon on the Mount contains nine relatively short sayings known as beatitudes.[2] This major discourse contains the Savior's

Thomas A. Wayment is an assistant professor of ancient scripture at Brigham Young University.

teachings on the higher law of salvation. It has also been suggested that this sermon was a type of missionary preparation for the disciples.[3] The beatitudes form an introduction to the body of the sermon, and they maintain a certain organizational consistency that helps to reveal their original meaning and function. In our biblical account of the Sermon on the Mount, there is some confusion regarding the Savior's audience. The event, as recorded by Matthew, indicates that the Savior went to the mountain to remove himself from the multitude (Matthew 5:1); yet at the end of the sermon, the multitude is said to be astonished at what the Savior has taught (Matthew 7:28). This confusion is eliminated, however, when we consider the account of the Savior's sermon given at the temple in Bountiful in the Book of Mormon or when we look at the changes made by the Prophet Joseph Smith in his inspired version of the biblical account. The Book of Mormon makes it clear that the sermon to the Nephites was delivered to a believing multitude, whereas some of the Savior's teachings were directed specifically to the Twelve (3 Nephi 12:1; 13:25). We may assume that the sermon delivered in the Holy Land had an audience similar to that in the Nephite setting. The Joseph Smith Translation adds that parts of the Sermon on the Mount were directed to the disciples, thus helping to confirm our comparison (JST Matthew 6:1).[4]

As an introduction to the Sermon on the Mount, the Beatitudes summarize some of its more prevalent themes. The first eight beatitudes represent an independent unit framed by the first beatitude, which promises "the kingdom of heaven" to the poor (Matthew 5:3), and the eighth beatitude, which repeats the promise of the "kingdom of heaven" (Matthew 5:10). The first eight beatitudes (vv. 3–10) are also composed in the third person plural (they), while the ninth and final beatitude (vv. 11–12), with its warning that persecutions may follow, is written in the second person plural (you). The last beatitude also shifts from the indicative "blessed are they" to the imperative "rejoice, and be exceedingly glad" (Matthew 5:11–12). The shift from the indicative to the imperative indicates a shift of emphasis and creates a distinction between the first eight beatitudes and the final beatitude. The "you" of Matthew 5:11 makes the connection explicit between the first eight beatitudes and the ninth one. The newly called disciples should begin to consider that persecution may follow those who seek to obey the commandments and purify their lives. While it may have been comforting to hear in the third person the expectations the Savior has for his people, the disciples have this expectation placed directly on their shoulders when the Savior turns to them and warns them of the perils that will follow the righteous.[5] Jesus strengthens this idea by telling his disciples to expect the same treatment and blessings that the prophets of old received. The Savior's profound reasoning on this issue is persuasive. How could these disciples reject the Savior's call to be like one of the prophets of old, even if it meant enduring suffering and persecution?

A close look at the first three beatitudes and the way the Savior uses them to teach his disciples the higher law demonstrates the characteristics that Jesus expected his disciples to emulate. It also provides an example of the Savior's ability to present new ideas, using the Old Testament as his text. The first three beatitudes, which are structured according to the pattern of Isaiah 61:1–3, incorporate a passage from Psalm 37:11.[6] Isaiah 61 provides the structure and some terminology for Matthew 5:3–5. Isaiah 61 promises good tidings to the poor (KJV "meek") and comfort to those who mourn. The two passages, Matthew 5:3–5 and Isaiah 61:1–2, share a number of verbal similarities. The following will help to demonstrate the verbal relationship between Isaiah 61 and Matthew 5. Matthew 5:3: Blessed are the poor in spirit (*ptochoi*)," Isaiah 61:1: "The Lord hath anointed me to preach good tidings unto the poor (*ptochois;* KJV reads "meek")"; Matthew 5:4: "Blessed are they that mourn (*penthountes*): for they shall be comforted (*parakletheson-thai*)," Isaiah 61:2: "To comfort (*parakalesai*) all that mourn (*penthountas*)"; Matthew 5:5: "Blessed are the meek: for they shall inherit the earth (*klepovomesousin ten gen*)," Isaiah 61:7: "Therefore in their land they shall possess (*kleponomesousin ten gen*) a double portion (KJV reads 'the double')"; Matthew 5:6: "Blessed are they which do hunger and thirst after righteousness (*dikaiosunen*)," Isaiah 61:3, 8, 11 each use the term for righteousness (*dikaiosunes*);

Matthew 5:8: "Blessed are the pure in heart (*katharoi te kardia*)," Isaiah 61:1: "To bind up the brokenhearted (*suntetpimmenos te kardia*)."

One of the reasons the Savior referred to Isaiah 61 may be found in the opening verses of that chapter. Isaiah's prophecy lends authority to the Savior's message, and it forms a remarkable parallel to the power and authority the Savior's teachings would have. Isaiah may well have had the Savior in mind when he said, "The Spirit of the Lord God is upon me; because the Lord hath anointed me to preach good tidings" (Isaiah 61:1).[7] In addition, Isaiah 61 is quoted numerous times in the New Testament with reference to Jesus.[8] Jesus himself, when given a portion of Isaiah 61 to read in the synagogue, interpreted it as a reference to his own ministry. In his Gospel, Luke reported that this reading and interpretation caused such excitement and hostility that some of Jesus' listeners attempted to take his life. They couldn't abide his declaration that this important messianic prophecy pointed to his own ministry—that he was its literal fulfillment.[9] This passage, Isaiah 61:1–3, was interpreted by the rabbis and others as a reference to the end of the world and the redemption associated with the coming of the Messiah at that time.[10] The Qumran sectarians, the authors and compilers of the Dead Sea scrolls, likewise understood this passage messianically and eschatologically, or as a reference to the time when the Messiah would come to redeem his people at the end of the world.[11] It is significant that the Savior used this passage of scripture, one that many Jews of his day believed had reference to the ministry of the Messiah, both at the beginning of his public ministry and as the prelude to one of the greatest sermons ever given.

In using Isaiah 61 as a preface to the Sermon on the Mount, Jesus drew on an image that was highly familiar to those who were looking for the Messiah. Jesus often incorporated the Old Testament into his teachings in a manner that was completely unexpected or contrary to popular opinion.[12] This is the case with the Sermon on the Mount. Many of the Jews were expecting a national hero who would use physical force to liberate them from their Roman captors.[13] The Jews also viewed themselves as the legitimate heirs of the covenant, the only people whom the Messiah would visit and redeem, and a nationalistic pride led many of them to despise other peoples and nations. For some, Isaiah 61 was part of this mindset and rhetoric.[14] In this setting of national fervor and excitement, the Savior did something that would cause many Jews to reflect upon their own assumptions. Instead of playing to the Jews' nationalistic hopes and expectations and the pride they took in being the chosen people, the Savior pointed out that God blesses the meek, the poor, and the persecuted, supporting that doctrine with wording derived from Psalm 37:11: "But the meek shall inherit the earth." This psalm, which the Savior converts into a beatitude, is linked with Isaiah 61 to help the Jews understand Isaiah's true meaning. This reversal of conditions would signify a dramatic shift in thinking for many of Jesus' followers, as evidenced by Matthew's commentary: "The people were astonished at his doctrine" (Matthew 7:28).[15]

Instead of emphasizing the parallel between his own ministry and the messianic ministry described in Isaiah 61, the Lord chose to focus on the plight of the poor and brokenhearted and to indicate that it is they who will receive the kingdom of heaven. In doing so, he directed the attention of the leaders of the Jews to those whom they had typically despised.[16] Both Isaiah 61 and Psalm 37 contain the Hebrew term *'anawim* or "meek." In both passages, the Lord promises a certain blessing to the poor or meek and defines who the poor really are. The term used for poor in both of these passages is the same one used to describe the meekness of Moses (Numbers 12:3). Psalm 37 interprets this to mean those who have been pushed aside by society, criticized by the wicked, and deprived of land ownership by the wealthy (Psalm 37:1–13). The Lord promises that this class of despised servants will be given the necessities they lack, namely the land that has been usurped by the wealthy and powerful. The Savior's use of Psalm 37 in the context of Isaiah 61 helps us see that the poor spoken of in Matthew 5:3 are different from the meek of Matthew 5:5, even though both terms derive from the same Hebrew word.[17] The King James translators attempted to accentuate this difference by translating Matthew 5:5 as "meek" and Matthew

5:3 as "poor." The subtle nuance of comparing the meek of Psalm 37 with the meek of Isaiah 61 helps us to see that the Lord had two different groups in mind.[18]

The term for "meek" in Isaiah 61 connotes slavery, bondage, and oppression by a foreign power. The meek to whom Isaiah referred have their liberty taken away; they are in prison and are brokenhearted because there seems to be no relief (Isaiah 61:1). The meek in this context are those who suffer under the weight of the oppression this world often inflicts on those who seek to live righteously. In a way, they are subject to the demands and punishments of this world, even though they are waiting to hear the good news of the gospel promised by the Lord. In a sense, Isaiah 61 may be speaking to all those who would hear the good tidings despite being taken into bondage by the world. To this group of downtrodden and afflicted, the Savior promises the kingdom of heaven. The promise of the kingdom in Matthew 5:3 is essentially the promise of all the rights, powers, and ordinances necessary for salvation. The prophet Joseph Smith summarizes this promise: "Whenever men can find out the will of God and find an administrator legally authorized from God, there is the kingdom of God; but where these are not, the kingdom of God is not."[19]

In contrast to the meek of Isaiah 61 are the meek of Psalm 37. These are they who, due to their meekness, have been denied privilege, standing, and honor in this world. They are persecuted because they are willing to stand up to the ways of the world and "do good" (Psalm 37:3). In this psalm, the Lord calls on the meek to trust him even though the wicked seem to prevail. The meek are also called on to cease being angry and to let go of wrath (Psalm 37:8). The meek of Psalm 37 are those who are trying to live in the ways of the Lord even though the unrighteous prosper and appear to be blessed. The Lord reiterates his promise that the meek shall ultimately inherit the earth as a result of their humility and patience. The magnitude of that blessing is better understood through latter-day revelation, which teaches that the earth, in its sanctified and immortal state, will become the final resting place of the righteous (D&C 88:17–20, 25).

The Savior's skill in teaching from the scriptures is unparalleled. We find in the Beatitudes a marvelous example of the Savior's ability to teach new concepts using familiar sources. Psalm 37 and Isaiah 61 evoked certain ideas in many of Jesus' followers and antagonists. Many among those who heard the Savior teach were astonished to learn that the very groups that society had learned to despise were those whom the Lord would ultimately bless, while those who were typically thought to be blessed would be left wanting. Using these two Old Testament passages to introduce the Sermon on the Mount, the Lord declares the entrance requirements for the kingdom of heaven. The reformulation of the old law turns its attention to those who suffer, are meek, are poor, and seek after the things of God.

Psalm 118 and Matthew 21

Psalm 118 has a familiar ring to many Latter-day Saints. Phrases such as "The stone which the builders refused is become the head stone of the corner" (v. 22) and "Blessed be he that cometh in the name of the Lord" (v. 26) remind us of the Savior's mortal ministry and his final days on earth. These scriptures, and others like them, confirm that the Savior came in fulfillment of the prophecies spoken of him by David and Old Testament prophets. This scripture in particular was used by the prophet Jacob in the Book of Mormon to explain that the Jews would reject the Messiah, be gathered again after having rejected him, and once again become his covenant people. Jacob quoted from Psalm 118 when he described the Jews' turning away from and eventually returning to the Messiah. One might even say that Psalm 118 forms an introduction to the Allegory of the Olive Tree (Jacob 4:15–17).

What did the Jews at the time of Christ understand this particular scripture to say? Did they, like the Nephites, believe it referred to the mortal ministry of the Messiah and his first coming, or did they expect something entirely different? Another related question Psalm 118 raises is how the Savior used this scripture to refer to his own ministry.

There is little, if any, evidence that the Jews at the time of Christ understood that Psalm 118 referred to the initial coming of the Messiah. On the other hand, there is ample evidence that the earliest Christians regarded Jesus Christ as the literal fulfillment of Psalm 118. One New Testament scholar has remarked that there is no evidence to suggest that the rabbis at the time of Jesus interpreted Psalm 118 as a reference to the Messiah.[20] The earliest evidence that can be adduced to support a messianic understanding of Psalm 118 dates to the late second century after Christ, when the Jews had already lost their homeland.[21] Before this time, it appears that the Jews understood the rejection of the chief cornerstone and its eventual reestablishment as a reference to their own nation and the return of the Davidic dynasty.[22] The structure of Psalm 118 lends itself, on one level, to this interpretation.

Verses 1 through 4 of Psalm 118 are a song of thanksgiving for deliverance; verses 5 through 18, a description of divine rescue; verses 19 and 20, a triumphal entry into the gates of the Lord (i.e., into the temple of the Lord); verses 21 through 28, a celebration of Israel's rescue; verse 29, a final call for thanksgiving.

Psalm 118 reads as though it were written to celebrate the Lord's redeeming Israel following the persecution and suffering she had endured at the hands of her political oppressors. The celebration is centered in the temple (verse 27) and has to do with Israel's miraculous deliverance from those who sought Israel's demise. It is no surprise, then, that many Israelites derived a certain nationalistic hope from Psalm 118. For many, it was the Lord's promise that Israel would finally be vindicated and that the stone, symbolic of Israel herself, would no longer be rejected by the world.[23]

Even though the Jews at the time of Christ may not have interpreted Psalm 118 as a reference to the Messiah, they were deeply aware of its content. According to the Mishnah, one of the earliest Pharisaic oral interpretations of the Old Testament, Psalm 118 was sung as part of the *Hallel* at the Feast of Tabernacles, Hanukkah, and at the Feast of the Passover, where it was recited at the sacrificing of the Paschal Lamb and at the Passover Feast.[24] The context of these recitations of Psalm 118 suggests that this psalm was of significant importance to the Jews at the time of Christ. The fact that this scripture was also a Jewish hymn helps us to gain an appreciation of the extent to which its content would have become ingrained for faithful Jews at the time of Christ. If we are correct in stating that many of the Jews looked at this psalm as an indication of God's promise of deliverance, then the repeated recitation of Psalm 118 makes sense, given the Jews' concern over the loss of their nation's sovereignty. Roman oppression caused many Jews to look to the heavens for deliverance. For many, the continued recitation of Psalm 118 reminded them that God had delivered them in the past and that he would once again establish this rejected stone.

The evidence suggesting that Psalm 118 was understood as a promise of the coming and rejection of the Messiah at the time of Christ has been very weak. Most of the evidence suggests that Jews at the time of Christ were interpreting this psalm as a promise of the reestablishment of their nation. When we turn to the early Christians, however, there is very strong evidence that the early Christians thought the rejected stone and other prophecies of Psalm 118 had reference to the Messiah. Psalm 118 is, in fact, cited or alluded to at least fifteen times in the New Testament, if we do not count the occurrences where different gospel writers have recorded the same event.[25] This evidence suggests that Psalm 118 was one of the most cited Old Testament scriptures and indeed one of the most important statements about the coming of the Messiah from any Old Testament figure. The interpretation of Psalm 118 and its relative importance goes back to the Savior himself as he sought to explain the meaning and importance of his mortal ministry to a people who were for the most part looking for a leader who would liberate them from foreign oppression.[26]

One of the most interesting ways the Savior used Psalm 118 as a reference to his own ministry can be found in Matthew 21. This chapter begins with Jesus' entry into Jerusalem on the back of a donkey, thus fulfilling the prophecy of Zechariah (Zechariah 9:9). According to the Gospel of Matthew, many people immediately recognized the significance of this sign, and they laid out their clothes for the Savior to ride upon. They also prepared a path for him so that he could ride into the city triumphantly. While he entered, they recited the now famous words of Psalm 118:26: "Blessed be he that cometh in the name of the Lord." After his triumphal entry, making his whereabouts public, he immediately entered the temple and cast out the money changers. The following day he again entered the temple. On this occasion his authority to do such things as cleanse the temple was challenged. His response, in part, includes the parable of the vineyard, wherein the Lord of the vineyard prepares all that is necessary for his vineyard to flourish. He then rents it out to those who end up abusing his servants and ultimately taking the life of his son (Matthew 21:33–40). After reciting this parable, the Savior asks his inquirers what action the Lord of the vineyard should take against these wicked servants. Matthew records their response as "He (the Lord) will miserably destroy those wicked men, and will let out his vineyard unto other husbandmen" (Matthew 21:41).

Having backed his accusers into a corner, the Savior summarizes the implications of the parable of the vineyard. He begins by saying that the son of the vineyard is equated with the rejected stone of Psalm 118:22, asking "Did ye never read in the scriptures, The stone which the builders rejected, the same is become the head of the corner: this is the Lord's doing, and it is marvellous in our eyes?" (Matthew 21:42). The Savior then gives them to understand that the Jews represent the hired servants and that the kingdom of God (the vineyard) will be taken from them and given to someone else who is worthy.[27] To appreciate fully the impact of such teachings, one must look back at the Jews' understanding of this passage. Many of them believed that this scripture, Psalm 118:22, promised the return of their nation to a position of prominence, and they believed that the Lord would ultimately deliver them. Instead, the Savior interprets this scripture to mean the very opposite—the Jews become those who have oppressed the Lord's people, and the Lord will punish them as wicked servants. Moreover, the land of their inheritance will be taken from them and given to the worthy followers of Jesus, a man whom many Jews despised. Matthew underscores the impact of this interchange by saying, "When the chief priests and Pharisees had heard his parables, *they perceived that he spake of them. But when they sought to lay hands on him, they feared the multitude"* (Matthew 21:45–46; emphasis added). These Jews became so enraged at the Savior's teachings that they wanted to take his life, but they feared that the multitude would cry out against them.[28]

Summary and Conclusion

It is difficult to overstate the impact the Savior's statement had on his listeners. Many in the exuberant crowd that welcomed Jesus to Jerusalem saw in that event a fulfillment of the prophecy in Psalm 118. Others, however, thought the Savior's interpretation of this passage was self-serving and blasphemous. They could not see that Jesus of Nazareth was the Messiah promised by the prophets. For his critics and enemies, he was simply a man caught up in his own pride who deserved to be put to death. Jesus' use of Psalm 118 cuts to the very core of this division. Will the followers of Jesus be able to accept him as their Redeemer even though their prior understanding of scripture indicates that he is not what they expected? For many, as indicated by Matthew 21:8, the answer is yes.

These two examples give us an insight into the ways the Lord taught from the Old Testament during his mortal ministry. In the first example, the Savior reveals his complete mastery of scripture, though he often uses familiar scriptures in new and different ways. The Lord has revealed in our dispensation that revelation helps us know when we have erred, and that it will guide us on the strait and narrow path (D&C 1:25). For those who were ready and willing, the Savior's message was one of profound enlightenment and intelligence. In the second example, we see the Savior boldly apply to himself the scriptures that speak of the coming of the Messiah. For many people, these scriptures were of national importance, providing hope that when the Lord came, he would redeem his people from the oppression of the world. Instead, the Savior offered a dramatically different interpretation. In both instances, the reaction of the crowd is marked; in the first, his audience is surprised, while in the second, a portion of his audience seeks to take his life as a result of his teachings.

Notes

1. See John 5:39.

2. The term *beatitude* derives from the Latin adjective *beatitudo*, meaning happy or blessed. The Latin *beatitudo* translates the Greek *makarismos*, which indicates a happy and blessed state of existence that was generally achieved only by the gods in Greek-speaking cultures. At times, this state of blessedness could be achieved by mortals after death. Hans D. Betz, *A Commentary on the Sermon on the Mount, including the Sermon on the Plain (Matthew 5:3–7:27 and Luke 6:20–49)*, ed. Adele Yarbro Collins (Minneapolis: Fortress Press, 1995), 92–97.

3. Catherine Thomas, "The Sermon on the Mount: The Sacrifice of the Human Heart," in *The Gospels*, ed. Kent P. Jackson and Robert L. Millet, vol. 5 of the Studies in Scripture series (Salt Lake City: Deseret Book, 1986), 5:237.

4. W. Jeffrey Marsh, "Prophetic Enlightenment on the Sermon on the Mount," *Ensign*, January 1999, 15–16.

5. Several scholars have noted this method of drawing the disciples in and then pointing out that they may expect persecution. See W. J. Dumbrell, "The Logic of the Role of the Law in Matthew V 1–20," *Novum Testamentum* 23 (1981): 2–3; Mark Allan Powell, "Matthew's Beatitudes: Reversals and Rewards of the Kingdom," *Catholic Biblical Quarterly* 58 (1996): 447.

6. This parallel has been consistently noted by biblical scholars for many years. See Robert A. Guelich, "The Matthean Beatitudes: 'Entrance-Requirements' or Eschatological Blessings?" *Journal of Biblical Literature* 95 (1976): 423–26; W. D. Davies and D. C. Allison Jr., *A Critical and Exegetical Commentary on The Gospel According to Saint Matthew*, 3 vols. (Edinburgh: T & T Clark, 1988), 1:436–38; James E. Talmage, *Jesus the Christ* (Salt Lake City: Deseret Book, 1915), 74.

7. The term *gospel*, a term used by the earliest Christians to characterize the teachings of Jesus, may derive from Isaiah 61:1. The Hebrew *basher* is translated in the LXX, or Greek translation of the Old Testament, as *euangellion*. The term can most accurately be translated as "gospel." The parallel to the servant who teaches the gospel in Isaiah 61, and to Jesus who likewise teaches the gospel, is profound. The early Christian usage of the term "gospel" or *euangellion* may indicate that they were intentionally drawing attention to Jesus' fulfillment of Isaiah 61.

8. The 27th edition of Nestle-Aland, *Novum Testamentum Greace,* lists fifteen references or allusions to Isaiah 61: Matthew 5:3, 4; 11:5; Luke 1:47; 4:18; 6:20–21; 7:22; Acts 4:27; 10:38; Hebrews 13:20; Revelation 1:6; 5:10; 19:8; 21:2.

9. See James A. Sanders, "From Isaiah 61 to Luke 4," in *Luke and Scripture,* ed. James Sanders and Craig Evans (Minneapolis: Fortress Press, 1993), 14–25.

10. The Targum Pseudo-Johnathan on Numbers 25:12 indicates a move toward interpreting this passage eschatologically and messianically. James Sanders, "From Isaiah 61 to Luke 4," 48–57, discusses the history of interpretation of this passage.

11. The Qumran text 11Q13 or Melchizedek is a Midrash on Isaiah 61:1–3 and clearly understands it eschatologically and as reference to the redemption of God's covenant people. The difference of interpretation here is that Melchizedek will act as the savior of God's people instead of the Messiah. For a translation of this passage see Michael Wise, Martin Abegg Jr., and Edward Cook, *The Dead Sea Scrolls: A New Translation* (San Francisco: Harper, 1996), 455–57. On the meaning of this passage in general, cf. D. Flusser, "Blessed Are the Poor in Spirit . . . ," in *Israel Exploration Journal* 10 (1960): 1–13; Merrill P. Miller, "The Function of Isaiah 61:1–2 in 11Qmelchizedek," *Journal of Biblical Literature* 88 (1969), 467–69.

12. Robert J. Matthews, *A Bible! A Bible!* (Salt Lake City: Bookcraft, 1990), 221–23.

13. Talmage, *Jesus the Christ,* 74.

14. This can be seen clearly at Qumran, where Isaiah 61 is interpreted as a vindication of God's chosen people. The translation of 11Qmelchizedek (11Q13) adequately demonstrates this idea of separation and vindication: "Therefore Melchizedek will thoroughly prosecute the vengeance required by God's statutes. Also, he will deliver all the captives from the power of Belial, and from the power of all the spirits predestined to him. Allied with him will be all the 'righteous divine beings' (Isa. 61:3)" (Wise, Abegg, Cook, *Dead Sea Scrolls,* col. 2, 456).

15. Powell, "Matthew's Beatitudes," 460. Powell argues that the structure of the beatitudes allows them to be interpreted in two distinct groups. He calls the first four beatitudes a list of reversals while he considers the next four to be a list of rewards. Although I have some reservations in

making such a sharp distinction between the first and last four beatitudes, I believe that the rewards promised by the beatitudes increase in degree, see Matthew 5:8.

16. At the time of Jesus, popular sentiment held that God had blessed the rich and punished the poor. Therefore, according to popular opinion at the time of Jesus, being righteous meant being rich. Davies and Allison, *The Gospel According to Saint Matthew,* 442.

17. Guelich, "The Matthean Beatitudes," 426–27.

18. JST Matthew 5:3 helps to clarify this issue by adding "who come unto me" to qualify the poor who are blessed (see also 3 Nephi 12:3).

19. Joseph Smith, *History of the Church of Jesus Christ of Latter-day Saints* (Salt Lake City: Deseret Book, 1964), 5:259.

20. J. Ross Wagner, "Psalm 118 in Luke-Acts: Tracing a Narrative Thread," in *Early Christian Interpretation of the Scriptures of Israel: Investigations and Proposals,* ed. James Sanders and Craig Evans (England: Sheffield Press, 1997), 157–61. Joachim Jeremias (*The Eucharistic Words of Jesus,* trans. Norman Perrin [Philadelphia: Fortress Press, 1966], 255–62) and Eric Werner ("'Hosanna' in the Gospels," in *Journal of Biblical Literature,* 65 [1946], 97–122) argued against this position in two earlier studies. Their position, however, has been greatly diminished by the discovery and publication of the Dead Sea Scrolls, which confirm the fact that the Jews expected something other than the coming of the Messiah as the fulfillment of Psalm 118. For a discussion of the problem of dating Rabbinic sources, see Craig A. Evans, "Early Rabbinic Sources and Jesus Research," in *Society of Bibilical Literature: Symposium Proceedings,* ed. E. H. Lovering (Atlanta: Scholars Press, 1995), 53–76.

21. R. Jose, *b. Pesher* 118b cited in Wagner, "Psalm 118 in Luke-Acts," 158.

22. Mitchell Dahood, *Psalms,* vol. 16 of the Anchor Bible series (New York: Doubleday, 1970), 154–59.

23. A similar sentiment is expressed by Solomon Freehof when he equates the rejected stone of Psalm 118:22 with the nation of Israel. He cites several Rabbinic sources as evidence of this position, among whom is Ibn Ezra (*The Book of Psalms* [Cincinnati: Union of American Hebrew Congregations, 1938], 338).

24. Wagner, "Psalm 118 in Luke-Acts," 160. The Mishnah was fixed in

writing around the year 200 A.D. under the leadership of Rabbi Judah ha-Nasi.

25. Matthew 11:3; 21: 9,42; 23:39; Mark 8:31; 11:9; 12:10–11; Luke 7:19; 9:22; 13:35; 17:25; 19:38; 20:17; John 12:13; Acts 4:11; Romans 8:31; Hebrews 13:6; 1 Peter 2:4,7.

26. Richard T. Mead, "A Dissenting Opinion About Respect for Context in Old Testament Quotations," in *New Testament Studies* 10 (1963/64): 286–87.

27. J. Ching has suggested that the controversy represented in Matthew 21 is not based on a division between Christians and Jews but is meant to point out the division between Jesus and the Jewish hierarchy. "No Other Name," *Japanese Journal of Religious Studies,* 12 (1985): 259.

28. This idea frames Matthew 21 and forms an inclusion. It begins with a quotation of Psalm 118:26 (Matt 21:9) and ends with a quotation of Psalm 118:22 (Matt 21:42). The belief of the multitude at the beginning of the chapter is summarized as a reason for Jesus' deliverance at the end of the chapter.

20

The Witness for Christ in Psalm 22

Paul Y. Hoskisson

For the faithful Saints of New Testament times, the only written testament of Jesus Christ available to them was the Old Testament. It is not surprising, therefore, that the New Testament, particularly the Gospel of Matthew, quotes frequently from the Old Testament and uses its messages to give weight, meaning, and understanding to its witness of Christ and his work. The Old Testament bears a faithful testimony of the Messiah. Of particular interest is the messianic text of Psalm 22.

While on the cross, sometime about the ninth hour, Jesus cried with a loud voice, saying, "Eli, Eli, lama sabachthani?" which is Aramaic for, "My God, my God, why hast thou forsaken me?" (Matthew 27:46). In addition to previous explanations of what Christ might have intended with these words,[1] I suggest an additional reason: These words constitute the opening words of Psalm 22. A close examination will help us understand why Christ chose these words as one of his last statements in mortality.

Paul Y. Hoskisson is associate dean of Religious Education at Brigham Young University.

In general, Psalm 22 is a messianic prophecy of unparalleled detail in both content and doctrine. Verses 1–21 contain references to the events of the last twenty-four hours of Jesus' mortal life, especially details about the Crucifixion. Verses 22–31 describe in poetic terms the result of Christ's atonement.

After the opening words, "My God, my God, why hast thou forsaken me?" we read, "why art thou so far from helping me, and from the words of my roaring? Oh my God, I cry in the daytime, but thou hearest not; and in the night season, and am not silent" (Psalm 22:1–2). This is an introduction to the "passion" of Jesus Christ, as it is often called among traditional Christians. His extreme suffering, which helped bring about the Atonement and overcome the effects of the fall of Adam and which caused him "even God . . . to tremble because of pain, and to bleed at every pore, and to suffer both body and spirit" (D&C 19:18), does not appear to have been diminished by the intervention of the Father.

The night before the Crucifixion, while suffering in Gethsemane, Jesus "fell on his face, and prayed, saying, O my Father, if it be possible, let this cup pass from me: nevertheless not as I will, but as thou wilt" (Matthew 26:39). In answer, "there appeared an angel unto him from heaven, strengthening him" (Luke 22:43). In the end, however, Jesus drank the "bitter cup" and finished his "preparations unto the children of men" alone (D&C 19:18–19). No wonder, though strengthened by angelic ministrations the night before, he cried from the cross the words of Psalm 22:1: "My God, my God, why hast thou forsaken me?"

None of this suffering was unforeseen; it was all part of the plan of salvation from before the world was created. So even though Christ would cry out in agony, he would also say, "But thou art holy, O thou that inhabitest the praises of Israel" (Psalm 22:3)—a poetic rendition of "Thy will be done." With these words Christ acknowledged that he would partake of the bitter cup and complete his assignment, and that his Father was holy and worthy of the praises of Israel.

Though God did not remove the bitter cup this time, in the past he had provided a way out for his people. Verse 4 of Psalm 22 expresses this concept, along with the idea of trust: "Our fathers trusted in thee: they trusted, and thou didst deliver them. They cried unto thee, and were delivered: they trusted in thee, and were not confounded." This verse refers to, among other incidents recorded in the Old Testament, events of the Exodus. The Israelites in the wilderness cried unto God for deliverance, and he delivered them on several occasions: when they faced the Red Sea, when they were hungry, and when they were thirsty. All who place their trust in God will receive the help and strength they need to weather the challenges and vicissitudes of life.

As another great Old Testament prophet said of the Messiah, "he hath no form nor comeliness; and when we shall see him, there is no beauty that we should desire him. He is despised and rejected of men; a man of sorrows, and acquainted with grief: and we hid as it were our faces from him; he was despised, and we esteemed him not" (Isaiah 53:2–3). The Messiah would not be characterized by any outward signs. No one would be attracted to him because of physical good looks. Psalm 22:6 makes this point in a manner that not only expresses how people would view him but also hints at the fact that despite appearances he was and is the king of Israel: "But I am a worm, and no man; a reproach of men, and despised of the people." With one word, "worm," this verse captures the Isaiah expressions "no beauty," "despised," "rejected," and "esteemed him not."

At the same time, "worm" also hints at the royal heritage of the Messiah. The Hebrew term *tôlaʿat* (verse 7 in the Hebrew Bible) is a variant of the name for a worm that was a source in the ancient world for the color scarlet.[2] Because the color made from this worm was expensive, only the richest of people could afford clothes dyed with scarlet. Therefore, the color was associated with royalty. In the Gospel of Matthew, the soldiers who mocked Christ before his crucifixion placed a scarlet robe upon him, crowned him with thorns, passed him a reed scepter, and mockingly worshiped, "Hail, King of the Jews!" (Matthew 27:30; see also 27:27–29). Matthew's mention of scarlet[3] as a symbol of royalty, along with the scepter and crown, seems intended to draw attention to the irony of "worm" mentioned in Psalm 22. Thus Christ, though not esteemed by his contemporaries, was not only associated with kingship but also was and is the source of the royalty that lasts through the eternities.

The psalmist was also aware of the taunts and teasing Christ would have to endure on the cross. In the language of Hebrew poetry, he prophesied of the Messiah: "All they that see me laugh me to scorn: they shoot out the lip, they shake the head, saying, He trusted on the Lord that he would deliver him: let him deliver him, seeing he delighted in him" (Psalm 22:7–8). The passersby, the thieves who were crucified with Christ, and the chief priests, scribes, and elders all contributed to the fulfillment of this prophecy.

Notice the emphasis Matthew, echoing Psalm 22, put on trusting and delivering, along with sneering scorn: "And they that passed by reviled him, wagging their heads, and saying, Thou that destroyest the temple, and buildest it in three days, save thyself. . . . He saved others; himself he cannot save. If he be the King of Israel, let him now come down from the cross, and we will believe him. He trusted in God; let him deliver him now, if he will have him" (Matthew 27:39–40; 42–43). Luke recorded similar remarks: "He saved others; let him save himself, if he be Christ, the chosen of God" (Luke 23:35). Likewise, Mark recorded the derisive words of those who mocked, "Save thyself, and come down from the cross. . . . He saved others; himself he cannot save." And with even more sarcasm the chief priests mocked, "Let Christ the King of Israel descend now from the cross, that we may see and believe" (Mark 15:30–32).

Despite the pains and derision Christ would suffer on the cross, the psalmist recorded the faith and trust the Messiah would have in his Father's love and support. "But thou art he that took me out of the womb: Thou didst make me hope when I was upon my mother's breasts. I was cast upon thee from the womb: thou art my God from my mother's belly" (Psalm 22:9–10). These words poetically express Heavenly Father's watchful care over Christ. Even before his birth, God was with him in the womb; God helped him come forth out of the womb; and God gave him hope even before he was weaned.

Despite God's tender care for the Messiah, through the psalmist he cries out to his Father in verse 11, "Be not far from me; for trouble is near; for there is none to help." It is possible that this verse refers to the arrest of Christ in the Garden of Gethsemane, where he was deserted by all his apostles and disciples. No mortal remained at his side to help or succor him. Therefore, in his heartfelt cry to his Father, "Be not far from me," we feel the anguish he must have felt.

Of the subsequent trial and crucifixion, the psalmist records the Savior's thoughts: "Many bulls have compassed me: strong bulls of Bashan have beset me round. They gaped upon me with their mouths, as a ravening and a roaring lion" (Psalm 22:12–13). First mentioned in Numbers 21:33, Bashan was one of the territories on the east side of the Jordan River and was called "the land of giants" (Deuteronomy 3:13). This territory was given to half the tribe of Manasseh as its inheritance (Deuteronomy 3:13; Joshua 17:5). The "hill of Bashan" was compared to the "hill of God . . . an high hill" (Psalm 68:15), meaning that Bashan was a beautiful and desirable place. Its oaks were compared with the cedars of Lebanon (Isaiah 2:13). Jeremiah, Ezekiel, and other prophets employed Bashan as a metaphor for the proud and mighty who will be made low (Jeremiah 22:20; 50:19; Ezekiel 27:6). It is likely that the "bulls of Bashan" symbolize all that is worldly and proud about the Israelites (Amos 4:1) and, in the case of Christ, the haughty and arrogant Jewish leaders who would bring Jesus to trial and would, with a quick shift of metaphor, seek his life as would "a ravening and a roaring lion."

After Christ's trial came the Crucifixion. The psalmist describes the physical suffering and agony Christ experienced on the cross in the following words: "I am poured out like water, and all my bones are out of joint: my heart is like wax; it is melted in the midst of my bowels. My strength is dried up like a potsherd; and my tongue cleaveth to my jaws; and thou hast brought me into the dust of death" (Psalm 22:14–15). When the psalmist writes that the Messiah is "poured out like water," he refers to the soldiers, under orders to hasten the death of the three people who were crucified, who pierced Christ's side with a spear "and forthwith came there out blood and water" (John 19:34). The expression "my heart is like wax;

it is melted in the midst of my bowels" is possibly the poet's way of describing the cause for the fluid in Christ's chest cavity being poured out like water. It is also possible that "all my bones are out of joint" refers to the strain and probable joint failure that ensues from crucifixion.

While on the cross Christ said, "I thirst" (John 19:28), no doubt a result of the trauma caused by his crucifixion. There is no better poetic imagery for extreme thirst than a potsherd, a broken piece of pottery. In those days, everyday pottery was not glazed. Therefore, if a drop of water was put on a broken piece of unglazed pottery, the drop would be soaked up almost instantly. Severe dehydration also causes the mouth to become dry and the tongue to swell up so that it "cleaveth" to the jaws.

The psalmist, after mentioning that the Messiah's bones are out of joint, that he is poured out like water, and that he experiences extreme dehydration, reports that the Messiah is brought "into the dust of death," referring to the fact that Christ had been brought to the very gates of death. Yet Christ does not have to die. No man can take his life from him. "I lay down my life, that I might take it again. No man taketh it from me, but I lay it down of myself. I have power to lay it down" (John 10:17–18). Christ freely gave up his life on the cross as a sacrifice for us. It is interesting that the psalmist juxtaposed thirst with "dust of death." That is the precise order in the Gospel of John. Immediately after Christ's expression of thirst and the proffer of vinegar, he proclaimed: "It is finished: and he bowed his head, and gave up the ghost" (John 19:30). At this point Christ, who had been brought to "the dust of death," chose to die.

The psalmist offers many details of the scene at the Crucifixion. For example, verse 16 tells us, "For dogs have compassed me." Dogs in the Old Testament are unclean animals.[4] They are used as a metaphor for something base and are often paralleled with swine, a decidedly non-Israelite animal. Perhaps for this reason, dogs in the New Testament are a metaphor for Gentiles.[5] The "dogs" in Psalm 22:16, therefore, probably refer in general to non-Israelites and base persons, and, more specifically, to Roman soldiers.

In the same verse, the psalmist records of the Messiah: "The assembly of the wicked have inclosed me." This most likely refers to "the chief priests, and elders, and all the council, [who] sought false witness against Jesus, to put him to death" (Matthew 26:59). Last of all in this verse, notice the psalmist's graphic description of Christ being nailed to the cross: "They pierced my hands and feet."[6]

Verse 17 then begins, "I may tell all my bones." "Tell" is an Old English word that means to count, from which the word *teller,* as in bank teller, comes. Therefore, the meaning of the phrase is, "I may count all my bones." This reading of the verse conveys the fact that none of Christ's bones were broken, thus fulfilling the requirements of the law of Moses that the Passover offering (of which Christ was the last such sacrifice) be whole, complete, and unblemished.[7] The second phrase in verse 17, "They look and stare upon me," is an apt description of what bystanders might have been doing.

In verse 18 the psalmist reports that "they part my garments among them, and cast lots upon my vesture." This prophecy is so exact that both Matthew and John mention its fulfillment when they record the event. John's record is more detailed than Matthew's: "Then the soldiers, when they had crucified Jesus, took his garments, and made four parts, to every soldier a part; and also his coat: now the coat was without seam, woven from the top throughout. They said therefore among themselves, Let us not rend it, but cast lots for it, whose it shall be: that the scripture might be fulfilled, which saith, They parted my raiment among them, and for my vesture they did cast lots" (John 19:23–24).

At this point the psalmist refers to the Messiah's death, but it is not of the usual, mortal death. In words that recall the opening of Psalm 22, we read, "But be not thou far from me, O Lord: O my strength, haste thee to help me. Deliver my soul from the sword; my darling from the power of the dog. Save me from the lion's mouth: for thou hast heard me from the horns of the unicorns" (vv. 19–21). This refers to Christ's suffering on the cross and his appeal, like his appeal in the Garden of Gethsemane the evening before, for help from his Father. The New English Bible renders this passage with slightly different wording: "Do not remain so far away O Lord. O my help, hasten to my aid, deliver my very self from the sword, my precious life from the axe. Save me from the lion's mouth and my poor body from the horns of the wild ox." In accordance with the Messiah's plea, Christ's soul and body would not forever remain in the "lion's mouth" or on the "horns of the wild ox." As mentioned above, crucifixion did not kill the Messiah. Rather, he voluntarily gave up his life as a ransom for our sins, thus completing with his suffering and death the Atonement on our behalf.[8] But his voluntary death was not the end of his work. Rather, it was just the end of the mortal phase of his work and the time to move on to the next phase. Therefore, he pled not to be left alone in the jaws of death.

With the Atonement complete, the psalmist seems to switch voices. Previously, through verse 21, he spoke as if he were the Messiah. Indeed, it may be that many of the descriptions up to this point apply both to the mortal life of David, as critics have pointed out, and to the Messiah's sojourn on earth. However, beginning with verse 22 it seems that the psalmist begins to make a transition from first person to second person and third person when speaking of the Messiah. The reason for this change may be that the rest of the Psalm, which contains a poetic description of the postmortal mission of Christ, contains no parallels with the mortal life of King David. Thus, the psalmist must now wax poetic about Christ's visit to the spirit world, the Judgment, and the eternal rewards of the faithful, and he must describe these events as if he were watching them instead of personally experiencing them.

Verses 22–23 introduce the transition of voice through a clever use of the first person narrative to speak of the Messiah in the second person, then shifting again, addressing the audience in the second person and the Messiah in the third person. The psalmist states, "I [the poet] will declare thy [the Messiah's] name unto my brethren: in the midst of the congregation will I praise thee [the Messiah]. Ye [in the congregation] that fear [the Messiah, Jehovah], praise him; all ye the seed of Jacob, glorify [the Messiah]; and fear him, all ye the seed of Israel." Then, in verse 24, he makes the final transition to the third person: "For he [God] hath not despised nor abhorred the affliction of the afflicted [of the Messiah]; neither hath he [God] hid his face from him [the Messiah]; but when he [the

Messiah] cried unto him [God], he [God] heard." God hearkened to the words and works of the Messiah in order to bring about his resurrection and his eternal life, and through the Atonement, the resurrection and eternal life of all mankind.

The "congregation" mentioned in verse 22 could refer to the spirits in the spirit world whom Christ visited, wherein "there were gathered together in one place an innumerable company of the spirits of the just," and to whom Christ "preached . . . the everlasting gospel" (D&C 138:12, 19). All those who would have accepted the gospel, reverenced the Lord, and taken upon themselves the covenants of the gospel and become part of the seed of Jacob had they been given the opportunity in this life will have that opportunity in the spirit world. And when they accept the gospel, they will praise God and will "fear the Lord."

The psalmist moves seamlessly from these verses to the Judgment and eternal life. We are accustomed to making sharp divisions between this mortal life, the spirit world, the Judgment Day, and the eternities. However, seen from an eternal perspective, the seams we create may be more due to our desire to organize and categorize than to any real division. In reality, our existence is one continuum from our premortal existence to our eternal reward without great divisions or seams. Baptism, with the laying down of one life and the immediate taking up of a new life, would appear to symbolize, among other things, the seamlessness of our existence. In this manner the psalmist can continue his poetic description of the Judgment Day and eternal life without drawing the line between spirit world and eternity. Poets have, after all, license to wax more poetic than a strictly factual relating would allow, and in doing so they often capture reality more perfectly than a straightforward telling could accomplish.

Thus, in verses 25–31, we read: "My praise shall be of thee in the great congregation: I will pay my vows before them that fear him. The meek shall eat and be satisfied: they shall praise the Lord that seek him: your heart shall live for ever. All the ends of the world shall remember and turn unto the Lord: and all the kindreds of the nations shall worship before thee. For the kingdom is the Lord's:

and he is the governor among the nations. All they that be fat upon earth shall eat and worship: all they that go down to the dust shall bow before him: and none can keep alive his own soul. A seed shall serve him; it shall be accounted to the Lord for a generation. They shall come, and shall declare his righteousness unto a people that shall be born, that he hath done this."

The psalmist moves effortlessly from praising the Messiah in that great gathering in the spirit world to the inheritance the meek will receive as they "live for ever." In that great day when all will receive the reward they have earned, every knee shall bow and "worship before" Christ. Then, the kingdom will be Christ's because he was and is the ruler "among the nations." All those who have died will eat at the banquet table of the Lord and worship him, not because of their own merit, for no one has the power to save himself, that is, to "keep alive his own soul." Only Christ can save souls from the consequences of the Fall and from the effects of sin.

When we have accepted Christ, bowed the knee and worshiped him, we become his "seed" and are counted as Christ's children or "generation." This is the fulfillment of the prophecy of Isaiah concerning the Messiah that "when thou shalt make [the Messiah's] soul an offering for sin, he [the Messiah] shall see his seed" (Isaiah 53:10). Christ will behold and acknowledge those who, because of the covenant they have made, "shall be called the children of Christ, his sons, and his daughters" (Mosiah 5:7).

In the last verse of Psalm 22, we read that all the children of our Heavenly Father "shall come, and shall declare his [the Messiah] righteousness." Indeed, they will "be constrained to exclaim: Holy, holy are thy judgments, O Lord God Almighty" (2 Nephi 9:46), because Christ "hath spiritually begotten" them (Mosiah 5:7). They have become a new people, "a people that shall be born" into eternal life, for Christ "hath done this" (Psalm 22:31).

Psalm 22 contains one of the most powerful witnesses of the Messiah, of his work on the earth, and of his accomplishments for the eternities. As a treatise on the Atonement, it stands unique in the Old Testament. Yet this Psalm is an example of more than prophecy and doctrine. When Christ quoted the opening lines of

Psalm 22, "My God, my God, why hast thou forsaken me?" he was calling attention to this prophecy of his life, his death, and his work for the salvation of all mankind.

Those who stood at the cross and who knew the Psalm would have recognized in it details unfolding before their very eyes on Golgotha. Thus, Christ's words would have been one more witness, to believer and nonbeliever alike, that the events they were witnessing fulfilled prophecy. Christ, with tender compassion and consummate love, despite terrible suffering, was reaching out one more time to tell the house of Israel who he was and what his death would mean. In the gospel of Matthew, these words on the cross became Christ's last testimony of himself as the mortal Messiah, not only to those who personally witnessed the final act of the Atonement but also to all who would thereafter read Matthew's account. His testimony is powerful and true. The psalmist, in expressing this testimony, has couched his witness of the Messiah in poetic beauty and sublime metaphor.

Notes

1. "That the supreme sacrifice of the Son might be consummated in all its fulness, the Father seems to have withdrawn the support of His immediate Presence, leaving to the Savior of men the glory of complete victory over the forces of sin and death" (James E. Talmage, *Jesus the Christ,* 3d ed. [Salt Lake City: Deseret Book, 1915], 661).

2. See sub חולע and חולעה in *Hebräisches und Aramäisches Lexikon zum Alten Testament,* ed. Ludwig Koehler and Walter Baumgartner, 3d ed. (Leiden: Brill, 1995). The color is variously called scarlet or crimson (carmine), "karmesin" in German. This word in combination with other words stands behind the color "scarlet" in numerous passages in the Old Testament; see in particular Exodus 25:4 and often in the next fourteen chapters.

3. Mark (Mark 15:17) and John (John 19:2) say the color was purple.

4. See, for example, Deuteronomy 23:18; 1 Samuel 17:43; 2 Samuel 3:8; 9:8; 16:9; 2 Kings 8:13; Isaiah 66:3.

5. This is most clearly brought out in the story of the Canaanite woman who asks Christ that her daughter be healed. He replied, "It is not

meet to take the children's bread, and to cast it to dogs" (Matthew 15:26), meaning that he was sent to minister only to the Israelites and not to the Gentiles.

6. This is the wording of the King James Version, taken no doubt from the Greek translation of the Old Testament, the Septuaginta. The Joseph Smith Translation makes no change in this text. The Masoretic text reads literally, "Like a lion my hands and my feet," yrak, which makes little sense in this passage. The pre-Christian Dead Sea Scroll psalm fragment from Nahal Hever reads wrak. See Peter W. Flint, The Dead Sea Psalms Scrolls and the Book of Psalms, vol. 17 of *Studies on the Texts of the Desert of Judah* series (Leiden: Brill, 1997), 83. The root כאר can mean "to hollow out, dig," and "to bind together" (Kohler and Baumgartner, Hebräisches und Aramäisches Lexikon) sub כארי, citing this passage, with references to כרה I and IV respectively). The Septuaginta also must have been translated from a Hebrew text that read כארו, rendering it into Greek as "gouge" or "pierce." Other modern translations have suggested that the passage be amended to read "They bound my hands and my feet," which could also refer to crucifixion.

7. See Exodus 12:5, where it is recorded that the Paschal Lamb must be without blemish.

8. Alma 22:14.

21

Eliza R. Snow, Psalmist of the Latter Days

Karen Lynn Davidson

The Psalms of the Old Testament spoke to Eliza R. Snow as if they had been written yesterday. As closely as they once had echoed the convictions of ancient Israel, the Psalms echoed Eliza's own convictions and experiences: gratitude to the Lord for the privilege of serving as part of his covenant people, acceptance of trials as proof of divine destiny, and, most of all, faith that promises would be fulfilled.

She loved the book of Psalms—so much, in fact, that she wrote thirteen psalms of her own.[1] In her total output of approximately five hundred poems, thirteen may seem a small number. But Eliza's psalms represent a larger truth about her poetry and her life. Her writing reflected the God of the Old Testament, and her thinking was governed by the majesty and personality of God. Her attitudes, favorite phrases, and even the heroes of her poetry can usually be traced not to the New Testament or modern revelation but to the Old Testament.

Karen Lynn Davidson is a former member of the English Department and Honors Program faculty at Brigham Young University.

Eliza was a poet long before she was a Latter-day Saint. As a schoolgirl, she "frequently made attempts at imitations of the different styles of favorite authors."[2] At the beginning of her career as a published poet, it was another land, not ancient Israel, that filled her heart with idealism and her poetry with subject matter. As a young woman of twenty-three, Eliza read a newspaper report of the Turkish attack on the Greek town of Missolonghi. The heroism and sacrifice of the Greek defenders moved her so greatly that she wrote a poem in their honor and sent it to the newspaper in Ravenna, Ohio. This poem, titled "Missolonghi," was her first published work.[3]

The newspaper invited her to write a second poem, this one a memorial to Thomas Jefferson and John Adams on the occasion of their almost simultaneous deaths. To give proper weight and dignity to this tribute, Eliza once again turned to Greece. She invited the deities of the ancient world to join in mourning the two statesmen, assuring the reader that

> *Apollo's touch, the dubious wound shall heal*
> *And stamp their features with immortal youth.*[4]

Eliza's third published poem, titled "Greece," was yet another homage to the courage of Greek nationalist heroes.[5] In the fashion of the day, she concealed her identity, signing all three poems with, of course, a Greek pseudonym: Narcissa. How the young Eliza must have loved Greece! How the gods and heroes, the myths and history, must have fired her poetic imagination.

But during these same years her thoughts turned at least occasionally to another distant civilization, one that would come to eclipse Greece and every other poetic wellspring as her idealized society. A poem from 1828, this one unpublished, gives us a hint—and "hint" is really the right word, because in this poem she is almost playing a game—that Old Testament learning is already part of her poetic storehouse. Titled "The Farmer's Wife," this poem at first glance seems idyllic and almost simpleminded, a town girl's romanticized notion of rural life. But a careful reading shows it to be much more. Consider the implied reference in this stanza:

The wool and flax which he provides
She manufactures and divides
Among her household as they need.
She's blest in blessing—rich indeed!
Well busied at the wheel and loom
Her constant feet abide at home:
Her husband's heart rewards her toil,
Without distrust—no fear of spoil.[6]

These words are an unmistakable echo of the book of Proverbs.[7] By implication, the faithful farmer's wife of the nineteenth century, like her Old Testament sister, is worthy of a price above rubies. Eliza footnotes nothing and makes no direct reference to Proverbs, but this apparently simple, sentimental poem is in fact a skillful and subtle tribute.

Seven years after writing "The Farmer's Wife," Eliza was baptized a member of The Church of Jesus Christ of Latter-day Saints. She viewed her baptism not only as a new spiritual covenant but also as a new poetic covenant. Most of her subsequent poetry would address or involve a gospel topic in some way. In an unpublished poem written in 1843, she speaks of this new poetic commitment almost as a repentance:

When young in years—in all a child—
With thought untrain'd, and fancy wild
'Twas my delight to spend an hour
Beneath the Muse's fav'rite bow'r; . . .

But when from the eternal throne,
The truth of God around me shone;
Its glories my affections drew
And soon I tun'd my harp anew: . . .

It surely is a glorious thing
To mount imagination's wing;
With Inspiration's chart unfurl'd
That bids defiance to the world.[8]

As she "tun'd" her harp anew, the Old Testament, for her, was much more than just a metaphor or a set of poetic parallels. As God's paradigmatic chosen people, the children of ancient Israel were the key to understanding the role of the Saints in the latter days. Why invoke Greece or any other secular people when ancient Israel could offer colorful history, vivid scenes, and compelling allusions, all within the framework of a profound and unique spiritual purpose?

To think of herself as a part of the modern-day chosen people was deeply satisfying to Eliza's soul. She loved Old Testament ideals of physical might and military courage; she loved the symbolism of the journey of the chosen people to the promised land. Her poetry was an opportunity to remind the Saints that obedience, loyalty, and even suffering were to be embraced in the present day because the Saints held promised blessings far exceeding those in store for any other people. Modern Israel needed a psalmist, and her heart and pen were ready.

Other scriptures played their role in her poetry, of course. Certainly her fine sacrament hymn texts bear poetic testimony of the redeeming mission of Jesus Christ as taught in the New Testament.[9] The Book of Mormon also makes its contribution. The early Saints as a whole did not tend to mine the Book of Mormon for its poetic and spiritual riches, as Noel Reynolds and others have shown,[10] but Eliza loved using the metaphor of the "iron rod,"[11] and one poem speaks of the American Indians in terms of their Lamanite history.[12] But even with a broad awareness of other scriptures and other traditions, Eliza chose the Old Testament as the unchanging backdrop before which she thought and wrote.

During her creative process, each time she consulted her mental index under such topics as "strength in times of trial," "the rewards of obedience," or "the inexorable triumph of the kingdom of God," that index was likely to suggest Abraham rather than Paul, a relevant psalm rather than a parable, a prophecy from Daniel rather than from Revelation. Old Testament quotations and epigraphs abound. Thousands of Old Testament references scattered throughout her huge poetic output reminded her fellow Saints of their role in the unfolding of the Lord's plan, teaching them, in a sense, how the Lord's covenant people should behave. The parallels, large and small, gave purpose and meaning to the daily trials of the Saints, emphasizing that tragedy and hardship in the life of an individual chosen *person* were relatively trivial when compared with the glorious mission of the chosen *people.*

Eliza R. Snow's passion for the Old Testament was not lost on her contemporaries. Edward W. Tullidge saw in her the modern embodiment of a daughter of Israel. In his 1877 volume *The Women of Mormondom,* he referred to her as "our Hebraic heroine," a woman possessed of a "Hebraic soul." He goes on to say, "From her personal race indications, as well as from the whole tenor and mission of her life, she would readily be pronounced to be of Hebrew origin. One might very well fancy her to be a descendant of David himself; indeed the Prophet Joseph, in blessing her, pronounced her to be a daughter of Judah's royal house." Tullidge acknowledged not only Eliza's personal Hebraic traits but also the influence of her supposedly Jewish persona upon the Latter-day Saint community: "Her Hebraic faith and life have given something of their peculiar tone to the entire Mormon people."[13]

To realize the key role of the Old Testament in the poetry of Eliza R. Snow, we need only note that in her poems we find the word "Israel" mentioned ninety-eight times, several times as part of the title; she quotes the book of Daniel twenty-one times and Isaiah twenty-five times. No New Testament source even comes close; poetically, even Jeremiah is more useful to her than any gospel or epistle from the New Testament. Her bias toward the Old Testament is particularly evident in an unpublished 1841 poem called "Time and Change,"[14] a massive work of six hundred twenty-four lines that she describes as "A Historical Sketch, commencing with the Creation, and extending to the year 1841." This mini-epic recounts at length the Lord's dealings with Adam, Noah, Abraham, and Moses, but astonishingly, the poem says nothing about the birth or ministry of Jesus Christ; within twenty lines, she jumps from ancient Rome to Martin Luther and the Reformation, and then finishes with a patriotic ode and a millennial vision of the glories of Zion. The Old Testament was where she was most at home.

Eliza believed that just as in ancient times, the latter-day prophets chosen by God were evidence of his greatness. In an 1855 psalm, she wrote this sentence: "He is the God of Abraham, Isaac and Jacob—He is the God of Joseph, Brigham and Heber."[15] To her, the two expressions were perfectly appropriate parallels, each one honoring the three named patriarchs, of course, but more to the point, honoring the God who was so mighty that he could raise up these giants, whether ancient or modern, to lead his people.

In a similar way, her first psalm, published in 1841, compares the prophetic role of Joseph Smith with that of two well-known Old Testament figures. Eliza draws parallels that serve to defend Joseph Smith against enemies who would belittle his humble origins:

"In ancient time [the Lord] call'd his servant David from the sheep-fold to preside over the nation of Israel; yea, from a tender of flocks did he raise him to the sovereignty of his covenant people.

"He call'd Elijah [Elisha] from the occupation of husbandry, even when 'ploughing in the field with twelve yoke of oxen;' to be a prophet in Israel. . . .

"In these last days the Lord hath call'd his servant Joseph—the son of an husbandman; to be a prophet and a teacher: yea, to be a mighty instrument in rolling forward and establishing that kingdom which 'shall fill the whole earth.'"[16]

What was it about the Psalms that attracted Eliza R. Snow? What was it about the psalm format that she aspired to imitate? Freedom from the traditional poetic demands of rhyme and meter probably did not mean much to Eliza. She rhymed quickly; for her, that was the easy part. However, a second freedom was very important: If a poet writes in imitation of the Psalms, that poet is free to express anger. The Hebrew psalmist might be angry with the enemies of the chosen people or even with his personal enemies. He might lament his personal tribulations. He might even express some impatience with the Lord himself. All of us are familiar with this refreshing and distinctive aspect of the Psalms: The writer feels free to complain, sometimes in a really loud voice. Although Eliza's modern-day psalms do not reflect the intricacies of Hebrew poetic devices nor show the figurative imagination of the Old Testament writers, they do adopt this important feature of the Psalms: the license to speak her mind.

In deciding exactly how to complain, however, Eliza was judicious. Many different voices of complaint are found in the Psalms, and she did not allow herself the whole range. It is a mark of her strength of character that she seemed to have posted a personal "No Whining" rule in her mind. No Eliza R. Snow psalm, or in fact any of her poems, is anything like Psalm 13:1: "How long wilt thou forget me, O Lord? for ever? how long wilt thou hide thy face from me?" Whatever heartbreak or disappointment may have gone up in her personal prayers, she accepted her role as a spokeswoman for the Saints; her words were public words. She was not about to make any personal discouragement a matter of public record.

Furthermore—and this is quite remarkable—for all her noting of hardships and misfortune, she does not, anywhere in her poems, ask the Lord for deliverance from suffering. We look in vain for her to say something like "O Lord, come to the aid of thy sorrowing children." In her mind, there was a fine line between petitioning the Lord and instructing the Lord; she wanted to avoid the very appearance of telling the Almighty what to do. To Eliza R. Snow, having faith meant knowing that everything was proceeding according to plan, even if certain events and detours might puzzle mortal understanding. Why question the Lord's timetable? Everything that had happened, and would happen, was by definition part of a divinely established, perfect, unalterable design for modern Israel. To petition the Lord was to imply that some part of the plan was tentative, or that the Lord was tardy or remiss in something he ought to be doing right now.

It was more Eliza's style just to predict, in a confident voice, that justice would be done and righteousness fulfilled. Where the Old Testament psalmist might ask for vengeance upon his enemies—"Break their teeth, O God, in their mouth" (Psalm 58:6)—Eliza would simply have said, "Their teeth shall be broken." She is not really presuming to prophesy; she is just a faithful Saint and therefore sure of what will happen.

Very much like the Old Testament psalmist, she saw the world as divided into two camps: the children of Israel on the one hand, and the enemy arrayed against them on the other. Some lines from her last psalm, published in 1885, show this kind of us/them dichotomy:

"Driven from the land that gave us birth, to the western wilds, for an asylum of peace and religious liberty, which for a season we enjoyed unmolested; 'the accusers of the brethren,' like bloodthirsty hounds, scented our track o'er the pathless desert, and sought out our far-off retreat.

"With wanton eyes and greedy hearts they lusted for the possession of the hard-earned fruits of our untiring industry, and with measures concocted in the pest-house of deceit, supported by falsehood, they have sought to supplant us.

"All this, O Lord, Thou hast suffered, that the wicked may fill their cup, and that the Scriptures may be fulfilled. We know that persecution is a portion of the legacy which the Messiah left to those who would follow Him."[17]

These are harsh words, but she is simply following the scriptural model. As Psalm 139:21 notes: "Do not I hate them, O Lord, that hate thee?"

Eliza describes herself as "born a patriot."[18] She expands on these feelings in an autobiographical sketch: "As I grew up to womanhood, I fondly cherished a pride for the Flag which so proudly waved o'er the graves of my brave and valiant ancestors."[19] But years of persecution filled her heart with disappointment and outrage. How could the country she loved so much have failed to protect the Saints? Tragically, ironically, the government was now part of the enemy. In the Psalms she found a precedent not merely for chastising those who would destroy God's chosen but also for strong language and some very unflattering comparisons. Eliza was more than willing to write a latter-day equivalent of Psalm 109, summarized in its modern prefatory note as "David speaks of the cursings due to the wicked and deceitful." She could suggest a few forceful latter-day cursings of her own, as she did, for example, in this excerpt from "Missouri," an 1843 poem in psalmic form:

"What aileth thee, Oh! Missouri! that thy face should gather blackness, and why are thy features so terribly distorted?

"Rottenness has seized upon thy vitals—corruption is preying upon thy inward parts, and the breath of thy lips is full of destructive contagion. . . .

"Thou hast become an ignominious stain on the escutcheon of a noble, free and independent Republic—thou art a stink in the nostrils of the Goddess of Liberty.

"Thou art fallen—thou art fallen beneath the weight of thine own unhallowed deeds, and thine iniquities are pressing as a heavy load upon thee.

"Thou art already associated with Herod, Nero and the 'bloody Inquisition'—thy name has become synonymous with oppression, cruelty, treachery and murder.

"Thou wilt rank high with the haters of righteousness and the shedders of innocent blood—the hosts of tyrants are waiting beneath to meet thee at thy coming."[20]

This furious rebuke appears in her journal without any note or explanation. Four years had elapsed since the Missouri exodus, and it is interesting to ponder what might have triggered this angry psalm. On the same day, she recorded in her journal a wonderful and reassuring patriarchal blessing she had received from Isaac Morley. Did she ponder one promise given in her blessing—"thou shalt have influence & power over all those who have sought to injure thee"[21]—and decide that she might as well begin by pointing out to Missouri the error of its ways? Whatever Eliza's motive, the psalm format was a convenient, acceptable outlet for her considerable anger.

Her outrage against the government was still in full force more than twenty years later, as shown in this unpublished psalm written in 1860. Once again, she notes no specific incident; perhaps she had had enough of the occupation of Johnston's army, since the target of her anger this time was the federal government:

"What is the matter with thee now, O thou once glorious Republic? . . .

"The effusions of thy councils are no longer the high-ton'd sentiments of noble Statesmen pleading for the honor of their country and the rights of man: No: they come to us as the prating of fools, and as the voices of clamorous children contending about trifles. . . .

"Thou mayest well be compared with Babylon of old—thy capitol, with its infamous court; and him who now stands at thy head, is like unto the trembling Belshazzar with a hand-writing before him which he understood not.

"And among all thy wise men—thy politicians—thy astrologers—thy spirit-mediums—thy office seekers, yea, all of thy political demagogues; thou hast not even one Daniel to whom the Most High revealeth secrets, and maketh known things that will shortly come to pass."[22]

For many who know and love Eliza R. Snow, this angry Eliza may come as a surprise. But she allows us so few personal glimpses into her feelings, so few lines of poetry that seem truly spontaneous, that these lines offer a welcome insight. She got angry; she felt justified in that anger; she was undoubtedly grateful for an Old Testament precedent that allowed her to go public with her outrage.

We cannot help but ask a very basic question: Just why is it that the Old Testament appears to predominate over the New Testament, at least in her poetry? The Old Testament is a broad canvas of peoples and nations, and these narratives would have appealed to the patriot Eliza. The God of the Old Testament was a God of battles, and Eliza was thrilled by stories of physical courage. The Old Testament clearly divides who is good from who is bad, and the moralist in Eliza would have taken great comfort in contemplating the hand of God as a dispenser of justice and reward on behalf of his special children. It is even possible that in contemplating the life and atonement of the Savior, Eliza felt intimidated and simply said to herself, "No words of mine can add to this."

Whatever the explanation, we cannot know all the reasons she was more at home with the Old Testament. In simplest terms, it seems that she accepted once and for all, not as her exclusive mission but certainly as a lifelong commitment, the task of quoting, rephrasing, and echoing the Old Testament as a means of endowing latter-day Israel with Old Testament strength. The force of her personality and her writings would have helped many a grieving parent to see beyond personal tragedy, many a disappointed immigrant to remain with the Saints and carry out his role, and many a discouraged missionary to trust the sacred nature of his assignment. Her message was: Do not weaken; do not doubt; like Israel of old, we will persevere as an obedient people, a tried people, a faithful people, to build up the Lord's promised kingdom upon the earth.

Eliza R. Snow rejoiced in her distinctive role; to serve as the Saints' most significant poetic voice was not only profoundly satisfying to her, but also profoundly suited. It was as if she were suddenly called on to step to a stage and enact a starring role in a drama. This play had no script, and yet her heart cued her perfectly as to each word and gesture. And it turned out not to be a play at all but real life—more intense, more engrossing, and more in tune with her essential character than anything in her past. The Saints watched every scene as she helped them to define their beliefs, their mission, and their emotions to themselves and to the rest of the world.

Notes

1. The thirteen Snow poems titled "Psalm" or written in psalm format are as follows:

1. "Psalm," *Times and Seasons* 2, no. 18 (15 July 1841): 482.

2. "Psalm No. 2," *Times and Seasons* 2, no. 21 (1 September 1841): 523.

3. "A Song for the Latter-day Saints" (original title from the Eliza R. Snow Journal: "Psalm Third"), *Times and Seasons* 5, no. 18 (1 October 1844): 671.

4. "Missouri," *Times and Seasons* 5, no. 3 (1 February 1844): 430–31.

5. "Chant," *Deseret News* (25 April 1855).

6. "Psalm: Written for the Literary and Musical Assembly," Eliza R. Snow Journal (1842–44); dated 1855.

7. "What Aileth Thee?" Eliza R. Snow Papers, LDS Church Archives, July 1860.

8. "Psalm for 1860," *Deseret News* (21 November 1860).

9. "My Country: A Lamentation," *Poems* 2 (Salt Lake City, 1877): 119–22.

10. "Psalm: For the Twenty-Fourth of July, 1877," *Woman's Exponent* 6 (15 August 1877): 41.

11. "O Justice! Whither Hast Thou Fled?" *Deseret News* (18 February 1885).

12. "Psalm," *Woman's Exponent* 14 (15 September 1885): 57.

13. "The Lord Has Delivered His People," *Poems* 1 (Liverpool, 1856): 201.

2. Eliza R. Snow, *The Personal Writings of Eliza Roxcy Snow*, ed. Maureen Ursenbach Beecher (Salt Lake City: University of Utah Press, 1995), 7.

3. *Western Courier* 2 (22 July 1826): 4.

4. "Adams & Jefferson," *Western Courier* 2 (5 August 1826): 4.

5. *Western Courier* 3 (26 January 1828): 1.

6. Eliza R. Snow Journal (1842–44); dated Portage County, Ohio, 1828; lines 9–16.

7. Proverbs 31:11, 13, 15.

8. "Lines Addressed to Mr. Huelett," Eliza R. Snow Journal (1842–44); dated 28 August 1843; lines 33–36, 41–44, 49–52.

9. Three of Eliza R. Snow's sacrament hymn texts are included in the 1985 hymnal: "Again We Meet around the Board" (no. 186), "Behold the Great Redeemer Die" (no. 191), and "How Great the Wisdom and the Love" (no. 195).

10. Noel B. Reynolds, "The Coming Forth of the Book of Mormon in the Twentieth Century," *BYU Studies* 38, no. 2 (1999): 7. See also Grant Underwood, "Book of Mormon Usage in Early LDS Theology," *Dialogue: A Journal of Mormon Thought* 17, no. 3 (1984): 59.

11. For example, in 1842 Eliza wrote in "As I Believe," *Poems* 1 (Liverpool, 1856), 75; lines 9–12:

> *What boots it, though the darkness encompass us round,*
> *With tradition's shrill thunderbolts ringing,*

If we in obedience to Jesus are found,
And are still to the "iron rod" clinging?

12. See especially "The Lamanite," *Deseret News* (20 September 1865). This poem is an expanded version (with Book of Mormon allusions added) of "The Red Man of the West," *The Ohio Star* (31 March 1830).

13. Edward W. Tullidge, *The Women of Mormondom* (New York, 1877; reprint, Salt Lake City, 1965), 31–32.

14. "Time and Change," *Poems* 1 (Liverpool, 1856): 237, 250–53.

15. "Psalm" (subtitle: "Written for the Literary and Musical Assembly," unpublished; Eliza R. Snow Journal (1842–44); dated 1855; line 3.

16. "Psalm," *Times and Seasons* 2, no. 18 (15 July 1841): 482; lines 6, 7, 9.

17. "Psalm," *Woman's Exponent* 14 (15 September 1885): 57; lines 6–8.

18. Beecher, *Personal Writings*, 8.

19. Beecher, *Personal Writings*, 8.

20. "Missouri," *Times and Seasons* 5, no. 3 (1 February 1844): 430–31; lines 1–2, 9–10, 13–14.

21. Beecher, *Personal Writings*, 90.

22. "What Aileth Thee?" Eliza R. Snow Journal (1842–44); dated July 1860; lines 1, 8, 11–12.

Index